CONFLICTED COMMITMENTS

Conflicted Commitments
Race, Privilege, and Power in Transnational Solidarity Activism

GADA MAHROUSE

McGill-Queen's University Press
Montreal & Kingston • London • Ithaca

© McGill-Queen's University Press 2014
ISBN 978-0-7735-4363-8 (cloth)
ISBN 978-0-7735-4364-5 (paper)
ISBN 978-0-7735-9208-7 (ePDF)
ISBN 978-0-7735-9209-4 (ePUB)

Legal deposit second quarter 2014
Bibliothèque nationale du Québec

Printed in Canada on acid-free paper that is 100% ancient forest free (100% post-consumer recycled), processed chlorine free.

This book has been published with the help of a grant from Concordia University's Aid to Research – Related Events (ARRE) Program.

McGill-Queen's University Press acknowledges the support of the Canada Council for the Arts for our publishing program. We also acknowledge the financial support of the Government of Canada through the Canada Book Fund for our publishing activities.

Library and Archives Canada Cataloguing in Publication

Mahrouse, Gada, 1964– author
   Conflicted commitments : race, privilege, and power in transnational solidarity activism / Gada Mahrouse.

Includes bibliographical references and index.
Issued in print and electronic formats.
IISBN 978-0-7735-4363-8 (bound). – ISBN 978-0-7735-4364-5 (pbk.). – ISBN 978-0-7735-9208-7 (ePDF). – ISBN 978-0-7735-9209-4 (ePUB)

   1. Solidarity. 2. Humanitarianism – Political aspects. 3. Social justice – Political aspects. 4. Race – Social aspects. 5. Race relations. 6. Power (Social sciences). I. Title.

HM717.M34 2014   302'.14   C2014-900877-5
                                                                   C2014-900878-3

This book was typeset by True to Type in 10/13 Sabon

For my mother,

and in memory of my father

Contents

Acknowledgments ix

Abbreviations xiii

Introduction: Passport or *Carte Blanche*? On Race, Privilege, and Power in Transnational Solidarity Activism 3

1 Whiteness and the Divergent Responses to Rachel Corrie's Death 25
2 The CPT Kidnapping: Citizenship, Sexuality, and the Racialized "Politics of Life" 45
3 The Compelling Story of the First-World Activist in the War Zone 63
4 Race-conscious Transnational Activists with Cameras: Mediators of Compassion 79
5 Conflicted Commitments: The "Fine Line Between Advocacy and Imperialism" 93
6 "Split Affinities": Gender and Sexual Violence in Solidarity Movements 117
7 Liberal Universalism and Pragmatism: Implications for Decolonizing Solidarity 137

Afterword: Solidarity Tourism and the Depoliticization of Activism 155

Notes 165

Bibliography 199

Index 221

Acknowledgments

The motivation for this study arose from conversations on antiracism education that began at the University of Ottawa. I especially thank Sharon Cook, Awad Ibrahim, and Tim Stanley who modelled a committed pedagogy that has stayed with me over the years, and who drew out the reluctant academic that was lurking inside of me.

I am thankful for the diverse and rich intellectual community of teachers and peers that I found at the Sociology and Equity Studies department of OISE, University of Toronto. I learned a great deal from being a part of this critical mass of scholars determined to create social change. I am indebted to my dissertation committee. My thanks to Kari Dehli, whose insights and guidance helped to sharpen my analysis. I am deeply grateful for her support. I especially want to thank Sherene Razack, whose intellectual curiosity, integrity, and courage inspired this study and continues to shape my work.

In recent years, I have been granted opportunities to work with and be mentored by a remarkable group of scholars for whom I have tremendous admiration and respect. These include Nahla Abdo, Sedef Arat-Koç, Inderpal Grewal, Yasmin Jiwani, Caren Kaplan, Malinda Smith, and Sunera Thobani.

I am very fortunate to work at the Simone de Beauvoir Institute alongside Belinda Bowes, Chantal Maillé, Viviane Namaste, and Gen Rail. Thank you for warmly welcoming me into this unique and dynamic Institute and for helping to make it my academic "home." I am equally grateful for the exceptional and committed students I get to teach and learn from at the Simone de Beauvoir Institute, for constantly challenging me to think about praxis.

I am immensely indebted to the activists who allowed me to interview them for this study and who made a deep and lasting impression on me. I thank them for trusting me enough to share their experiences with me and trusting me to write about them.

My gratitude also goes to Kole Kilibarda, Nahed Mansour, Emily Ekelund, Sarah Fuchs, Sofia Guerrieri, and Indu Vashist who graciously read chapters and offered valuable feedback.

Thanks to Suzanne Lenon who has read every word of this manuscript, more than once, and who has been my best academic friend for over a decade.

I am grateful to the team at McGill-Queen's University Press for their commitment to this book. I owe a particular thanks to Jonathan Crago who believed in this project and who patiently supported me through some unanticipated challenges along the way. I am also grateful to the anonymous readers whose reports helped me to refine my arguments. I also want to thank Malaika Aleba for her professionalism and valuable assistance at the final copyediting stages of preparing this manuscript.

As I bring this project to a close, I find myself surrounded by a generous and thoughtful community of friends and family who nurture and sustain me in more ways than I can describe. I sincerely thank you all for your ongoing support.

Financial support from the Social Sciences and Humanities Research Council of Canada, Concordia University and the Fonds québécois de la recherche sur la société et la culture made this book possible.

Versions of three of the chapters were previously published as academic journal articles.

Chapter Two was published as "Transnational activism/humanitarianism as a racialized 'politics of life': The Christian Peacemaker Team kidnapping in Iraq" in *Citizenship Studies* 13 (4):311–31.

Chapter Three was published as "The compelling story of the white/western activist in the war zone: Examining race, neutrality and exceptionalism in citizen journalism" in the *Canadian Journal of Communications* 34:659–74.

Chapter Four was published as "Race-ethical transnational activists with cameras: Mediators of compassion" in the *International Journal of Cultural Studies* 11 (1):87–105.

I am grateful for Rachel Echenberg's willingness to let me use the 2011 "Blindspots" photo of her artwork (taken by Sebastien Worsnip) for the book cover. Although the image was not used, in my view, it beautifully captures many of the themes covered in this book and I appreciate her collaborative spirit. This photograph can be seen at http://rachelechenberg.net/.

Abbreviations

CPT   Christian Peacemaker Teams
EAPPI   Ecumenical Accompaniment Program in Palestine and Israel
IPT   Iraq Peace Team
ISM   International Solidarity Movement
IWPS   International Women's Peace Service
PA   Project Accompaniment
PBI   Peace Brigades International

CONFLICTED COMMITMENTS

INTRODUCTION

Passport or *Carte Blanche*?[1]
On Race, Privilege, and Power
in Transnational Solidarity Activism

I look forward to increasing numbers of middle-class privileged people like you and me becoming aware of the structures that support our privilege and beginning to support the work of those who aren't privileged to dismantle those structures.

Rachel Corrie[2]

An Internet search for the term "international solidarity" turns up many compelling calls for volunteers by various movements, networks, and organizations in recent years. One is an "urgent" call posted on the website of the International Solidarity Movement (ISM). It is an invitation to "internationals" to come join Palestinian communities for the Olive Harvest Campaign. The presence of these volunteer-activists is needed, the website explains, because "it has proven in the past to help limit and decrease the number and severity of attacks and harassment."[3] Another is the Oaxaca Solidarity Network (OSN) request for an emergency humanitarian delegation to provide "international presence and attention" to help curb the violence, arbitrary detentions, and murders of Oaxacans involved in the struggle for their democratic rights.[4] Similarly, the Montreal-based Project Accompaniment and Solidarity Colombia (PASC) invites delegations of international witnesses to support communities in Columbia whose rights are being violated.[5] The website of Peace Brigades International (PBI) also recruits teams of international volunteers to accompany human rights defenders and communities in areas of conflict because, they explain, their presence "rais[es] the stakes for potential attackers."[6] These are just a few examples of countless similar calls for international volunteers.

The consistent use of the term "international" by these organizations in their calls for volunteers is misleading. It implies that all people from anywhere in the world are being sought out and taking part in these initiatives, when in fact it is people from a handful of powerful First World countries who tend to be drawn towards, and effective in, this type of activism. The OSN call is a good illustration of this. It states: "We invite *any* person or organization to join our delegation, including concerned citizens, activists, journalists, lawyers, professors, students, and others, who, upon return to the US or Canada, will work to put the current abuses into the international spotlight."[7] While the invitation is open to "any," the clear expectation is that they will be citizens of the US or Canada and, judging by the professions they list, economically privileged as well. Likewise, the website of PBI states that they welcome "the services of people from all cultures, languages, religions, beliefs and geographical regions." However, the list of the countries they have offices in and recruit from makes evident the particular countries from which their volunteer base is comprised: Australia, Belgium, Canada, France, Germany, Italy, Netherlands, Norway, Spain, Sweden, Switzerland, UK, US.[8]

What is noticeably absent from these requests is any explicit reference to race. This omission is curious because race, or more precisely "whiteness," is utterly intrinsic to this solidarity activism. In fact, the very basis of this form of transnational solidarity is racialized privilege in the form of an embodied presence. It is a strategy built around the notion that people in positions of power are more likely to take notice of the brutality and injustice going on in various places if white and/or First World citizens become involved and, in some cases, are also put at risk. Those who take part in it – whether they understand themselves to be acting as protective accompaniers, witness-observers, "unarmed bodyguards," or "human shields" – are, in essence, deploying their racialized privilege.[9]

In this book, I hone in on the racialized complexities and contradictions that emerge in this transnational solidarity activism. My objectives are three-fold. First and foremost, I aim to trace and make visible the ways in which race, as a system of power, operates within such solidarity strategies and contexts – that is, to make apparent and open up for contemplation the ways in which racialized systems of power both underpin and complicate these interventions. The second objective is to examine how individual activists manage and negotiate their dominant positioning in these encounters. I am especially concerned with the ways in which Western subject-making practices are enabled through these experiences. The third objective is to reflect more broadly on the ethics and pragmatics of social justice strategies in an increasingly transnational world. In identifying the barriers, contradictions, and concerns that come up in this transnational solidarity activism, the goal, ultimately, is to inform anti-racist and decolonial practices.

The absolute centrality of race in these transnational solidarity contexts is evident in a few existing studies. Writing about PBI for example, Mahony and Eguren challenge the misconception that volunteers come from all parts of the world as the term "international" implies.[10] Although some volunteers have come from South American, Asian, and African countries, and some of African or Caribbean descent have participated, Mahony and Eguren state that these are the few exceptions, and that "most accompaniment volunteers have been Western European or North American and white."[11] In no uncertain terms, they explain that the supposed immunity and protective power of the volunteers is based on skin colour.[12] They explain that the "local" community organizers who call for international solidarity volunteers are highly aware of this reality, and in fact sometimes specifically request white people. For example, they write: "Sri Lankans have repeatedly stated that the protection was dependent on the 'white face' and that a volunteer from another South Asian country would do no good, despite the fact that India is the regional superpower. Likewise, although Mexico wields far more clout in Guatemala than does, for instance, New Zealand, a white New Zealander is symbolically more powerful than a Mexican accompaniment volunteer."[13] In addition, they explain how certain citizenships from Western First World countries can be more valuable than others in certain geopolitical contexts. For example, some Salvadorans insisted that because of US political influence, the protection offered by a US citizen would be greater than that of a European.[14] A specific example they offer is about a PBI volunteer of partial Indian descent in Sri Lanka who was the only "foreigner" to be struck by a policeman during a violent break up of a demonstration.[15]

Examining a 2006 fact-finding mission by Canadian grassroots organizations to the Philippines, Geraldine Pratt explores similar dynamics which she refers to as "the entangled geographies of solidarity." She observes, for instance, that despite repeatedly showing their Canadian passports, the Filipina Canadians on the trip were threatened by military officers and their objectivity as Canadians was thrown into doubt.[16] In her writing on the Witness for Peace (WFP) project of the Central American Peace Movement of the 1980s in which American activists travelled to El Salvador, Nicaragua, and Guatemala to witness US aggression in the region, Clare Weber similarly describes a situation in which a Mexican-American WFP volunteer in Nicaragua was told to sit inside a truck where he would be less visible "lest he be mistaken for a Nicaraguan and shot at."[17] Also focusing on WFP, Becky Thompson points out that being willing to risk arrest for civil disobedience largely depended upon having US citizenship and that people with citizenship from other places "simply could not afford to commit such acts."[18] Writing about the ISM, Mica Pollock gives an example of one activist who, because of her blond hair, was deemed most useful for riding around in ambulances with the internal ambulance light on in order to show that there was a foreign presence.[19] That "international" means white in most of these solidarity contexts is also evident in a delegation that went from Delhi to Gaza in December 2010. Because of its entirely Asian composition, the activists who took part in it were not referred to as "international" and instead were identified as "pan-Asian."[20]

Together, these disparate examples reveal that it is precisely the ways in which certain bodies are classified within a global racial hierarchy that make these interventions effective. Indeed, the symbolic and practical actions they perform, ranging from giving eyewitness accounts to accompanying people through checkpoints, are explicitly organized around the meanings inscribed onto their bodies given their skin colour, and to a lesser extent, their citizenship. In this sense, it is a strategy that clearly relies on what Linda Alcoff has referred to as "the visual registry of race."[21] Yet, the few above-mentioned examples aside, in much of the literature on these transitional solidarity interventions (from here on referred to as accompaniment-observer activism) explicit references to race are either largely absent, merely implied, or glossed over.[22]

Two highly publicized controversial cases involving white and First World activists in recent years make evident some of the multifaceted and thorny ways race operates in this site of activism. The first is the 2003 death of Rachel Corrie, a young, white, American member of the ISM who went to Palestine. Her death illustrated that the privileges of being white and a US citizen do not always carry with them increased immunity from violence, nor do they necessarily result in governmental accountability. As I will argue in Chapter One, many believe that her death did not spark the expected attention and outrage from the public and government officials because she sided too much with Palestinians at a time when patriotic anti-Arab "with us or against us" discourses were at their peak. Additional complexities of the pragmatic and symbolic uses of whiteness also became evident in 2005–06, when members of a group called *Christian Peacemaker Teams* (CPT) who were in Baghdad to oppose the US-led war were kidnapped and subsequently rescued by US and allied forces. This kidnapping revealed that in certain geopolitical contexts the bodies of those from the First World can become commodities in high stakes political negotiations rendering them vulnerable and therefore limited in the type of protection they can offer. Given that the activists were kidnapped by the people they were there to protect (Iraqis) and rescued by the people they were there to oppose (US and allied forces), the case also brought to the surface many compelling questions and heated debates about political allegiances and revealed how nationalism is implicated in these activists' interventions.

It is clear that many committed antiviolence, antiracist, and human rights activists from the First World who are well aware of their privileged race positioning are increasingly drawn to participate in accompaniment types of solidarity projects. Indeed, an idea that circulates in some activist circles is that a concrete way to reduce the racist violence targeting specific communities is to put one's passport (i.e. one's First World citizenship) to good use by travelling to stand by their side. As a PBI volunteer who went to Indonesia is quoted as stating on the organization's website, certain passports can be used "as tools to help protect human rights."[23] Thus, international solidarity calls for volunteers have tremendous appeal because they offer immediate, effective, and practical ways to act in solidarity with racialized Others.[24] One can begin to appreciate, then, why less-contentious, euphemistic terms such as "international" might be preferred and why explicit engagement with questions of race tend to be avoided by these organizations and those writing about them.[25] Indeed, race poses quite a conundrum at this site of activism, and engaging with it would require grappling with a myriad of contradictions and tensions related to whiteness, solidarity, privilege, and power. Once they are there, many who take part in this activism soon realize that the idea of using white and First World privilege to offer protection and support is more complicated than it first appears. In fact, the experiences of some of the activists that will be explored in this book reveal a host of contradictions that emerge for them "on the ground." We learn, for example, that many of them find themselves enacting First World arrogance and dominance despite their ongoing and earnest efforts not to. Indeed, it is through these encounters in foreign countries that many of them become self-conscious about their sense of entitlement, assumed authority, and assumptions about their moral superiority. Some activists also come to the stark recognition that their presence may in fact burden rather than help the people they are there to stand in solidarity with.

This book, then, is a critical examination of this form of activism and the ways that it is a racialized and racializing process. As I will illustrate, the complex and pronounced ways in which race operates in this form of activism make it a very rich site from which to study relations of power.

Much of this book is based on eighteen in-depth interviews with individual First World transnational solidarity activists.[26] Interviews were also conducted with four Palestinian community organizers, based in Palestine, to consider what challenges come up for them when working in solidarity with First World activists.[27] Other parts of the book follow a cultural studies approach and offer more theory-driven analyses of media and texts, including, for example, the two above-mentioned, controversial cases of Rachel Corrie and the kidnapping of activists in Iraq.

While this form of activism itself is not new, it has taken a new shape in the last decade.[28] Since the large majority of the activists whose experiences and perspectives are examined here had travelled to Palestine in recent years and a significant number of others went to Iraq, the practices of solidarity activism in the Middle East post-9/11 is a focal point of this study. Some attention is also devoted to activists who travelled to other countries, including Nicaragua, Guatemala, Mexico, and Indonesia. Despite the broad range of geopolitical sites in which this activism is explored, and the important differences between them, it is only possible to offer basic background information on the political conditions that have shaped the recent crises in these regions, as necessary, for the specific analyses I present in subsequent chapters. I begin here with a brief description of some of the key groups examined and their respective mandates.

ACCOMPANIMENT-OBSERVER SOLIDARITY ORGANIZATIONS

The International Solidarity Movement (ISM) is a Palestinian-led movement. The organization's approach is described as "committed to resisting the Israeli apartheid in Palestine by using nonviolent, direction-action methods and principles."[29] ISM provides two resources to support and strengthen Palestinian popular and nonviolent resistance against the Israeli military occupation force: (1) international solidarity and, (2) an international voice. The ISM's mandate is to work with the global mainstream media; [bear] personal witness and transmit information; as well as "break isolation and offer hope."[30] By supporting Palestinian resistance efforts in their demand for political, social, and economic freedom, the ISM's mission includes "direct action [participating in nonviolent demonstrations, disrupting construction of the illegal apartheid wall, accompanying farmers to their fields, and residing with or near families whose homes are threatened with eviction or demolition]"; and "documentation [documenting and reporting to local and international media about the daily life under apartheid and countless human rights and international law violations by the Israeli military]."[31] The ISM works on behalf of Palestinians in global solidarity with other ISM support groups based in the US, Canada, and Europe.[32]

The Christian Peacemaker Team (CPT) is a North American-based organization. Its approach to activism is "to embody an inclusive, ecumenical and diverse community of God's love."[33] CPT members believe that through "the nonviolent power of God's truth," "partnership with local peacemakers," and "bold action," they will transform war and occupation in their own lives, and in the wider Christian world.[34] The organization's mandate is to support persons committed to faith-based, nonviolent alternatives to war by enlisting "the response of the whole church in conscientious objection to war, developing nonviolent institutions, and skill training for intervention in conflict situations."[35] Explicitly founded on a Christian theology, and rooted in Mennonite, Church of the Brethren, and Quaker teachings and belief systems, the CPT extends its outreach through its ecumenical networks to support "biblically based and spiritually-centered peacemaking, creative public witness, nonviolent direction action, and protection of human rights." Moreover, its mission is described as to "connect intimately with the spiritual lives of constituent congregations."[36] Gifts of prayer, money, and time from these churches undergird CPT's peacemaking ministries.[37] The CPT's approach is articulated in broad-stroke language such as "undoing oppression," "intervention in conflict situations," and in the "protection of human rights." According to CPT's listing of "Areas of Action," 50 per cent of its geopolitical activity occurs in places such as Colombia, Iraq, Palestine, Africa Great Lakes, Haiti, Bosnia, Chechnya, and Chiapas, Mexico.[38] The materials state that the organization also has "at least one violence reduction project" in the US and Canada – for instance, "US borderlands," and "Aboriginal Justice (North America)."[39] Like the ISM, the CPT promotes non-violent methodologies in resisting oppression and outlines specifically that it is resisting Israeli occupation in Palestine.

Also falling under the "international solidarity" rubric is Peace Brigades International (PBI), one of the longest-standing organizations dedicated to protective accompaniment. This non-governmental organization (NGO) operates through four principals in offering its support: (1) nonviolence, (2) international character,

(3) non-partisanship, and (4) a non-hierarchical functioning. Its mandate is "to create space for peace to promote human rights."[40] To this end, it uses an international team of volunteers offering "protective accompaniment, peace education, independent observation and analysis of the conflict situation."[41] It intervenes in places that include: Nicaragua, Guatemala, El Salvador, Sri Lanka, Colombia, Haiti, Former Yugoslavia Region, Mexico, Indonesia, and Nepal. The accompaniment program has, according to PBI, three primary interests: "(1) protection of threatened activist and organization, (2) moral support for individuals and civil society movements, and (3) contributing to the building of a global movement for peace and human rights."[42] In existence since 1981, PBI situates itself as a "global high level and grassroots emergency network," which has the capacity to "remind decision makers in the country where abuses are occurring of commitments they have made internationally to protect their own citizens." Elsewhere, the organization states that "the accompaniment volunteer is the embodiment of international rights concerns, a compelling and visible reminder to those using violence that their actions will have repercussions nationally and internationally."[43]

As a gender-based alternative to engage with the hierarchal challenges in activism, the International Women's Peace Service (IWPS) is the "only all women international peace team working in the Occupied West Bank and the only international peace team working in the Salfit district, close to Nabulus."[44] Their approach is to train and support international accompaniment to Palestinian civilians, to document and nonviolently intervene in human rights abuses and support acts of nonviolent resistance, and to mobilize the independent media and press to advance an equitable distribution of information. Rooted in the local community, the IWPS places an emphasis on the inclusion of Palestinian women in the activism process "as much as possible." This organization also states that it is open and non-discriminatory with respect to ethnicity, religion, age, sexuality, and class.[45] As a NGO, IWPS draws its support through donations and grants, as well as volunteers, from "the global civil society." IWPS's headquarter is in Dier Istiya and centralizes its interventions in Palestine.[46] IWPS relies on its gendered focus to neutralize any potential visible hierarchies as it attempts to establish a type of "global sisterhood," and asserts that "it places an emphasis on the inclusion of Palestinian women in the process as much as possible."[47]

In May of 2002, Kathy Kelly, the founder of Voices in the Wilderness, proposed the formation of the Iraq Peace Team (IPT). The organization's approach "would bring people from the US and other countries together, in Iraq, well in advance of a US attack."[48] Using a nonviolent approach and a focus on training, the participants would arrive in Iraq, take up residence in cities, and "hold vigils, should bombing raids begin, at places where ordinary Iraqi people go ... in the hopes to safeguard travel for civilians."[49] IPT teams would be supplied with vitamins, health supplies, digital medical journals, and small gifts. IPT states that "rather than take sides in a military confrontation, we would aim to make the strong moral statement that ordinary human beings should not be sacrificed for any government's military goals and purposes."[50] According to online sources, "the Iraq Peace Team intend[ed] to remain with the Iraqi people during an attack and provide accurate reports about the effects of the war (both economic and military) on Iraqis." It indicated "the mere fact of our presence – a powerful symbol of solidarity and a statement that Iraqi lives are no less valuable than Canadian and American lives – can potentially help to build the antiwar movement in North America and beyond."[51]

The Ecumenical Accompaniment Program in Palestine and Israel (EAPPI) has been operating since 2002, and "brings internationals to the West Bank to experience life under occupation." An initiative of the World Council of Churches, the program's mission is twofold: (1) "to accompany Palestinians and Israelis in their nonviolent actions;" and (2) "to carry out concerted advocacy efforts to end the occupation."[52] Their aims are to "be visibly present in vulnerable communities, locations or events, actively listen to local people's experiences, and give voice to people's daily suffering under occupation," as well as to "engage in nonviolent ways with perpetrators of human rights abuses."[53] Moreover, participants are expected to become advocates in their home country following their stay in the field.[54]

Project Accompaniment, or Project "A," was formed in the late 1980s as a national network by Canadians to offer a coordinated response for Guatemalan refugees in Mexico who wanted to return.⁵⁵ It emerged out of an ad hoc group called the Guatemala Network Coordinating Committee with funding from Oxfam, CUSO, the Canadian Catholic Organization for Development and Peace, and the United Church of Canada.⁵⁶ Its members provide emergency response; education; lobbying and advocacy; and physical accompaniment.

As will be illustrated further along, racialized power relations manifest very differently according to the geopolitical sites covered by these groups. While taking care to consider the specificities they operate within, my analysis centres on the larger question of how race works similarly *across* different activist situations and groups. That is, I argue that although the activists travel to different places, the racialized experiences they have abroad are integral to how they come to understand their positioning as First World subjects. The goal, then, is to focus precisely on how participation in this form of activism produces racialized First World subjectivities. Indeed, while CPT, ISM, PBI, IWPS, IPT, PA, and EAPPI are organizations upholding mandates to promote justice and circumvent violence, this book seeks to capture some of the limitations of their respective interventions and the contradictions through which they operate. To this end, using the critical race interdisciplinary theoretical framework delineated below – which brings together elements of feminist, critical whiteness, poststructural, and postcolonial theories – this book examines the activists' experiences, perspectives, and the ways in which they are represented and represent themselves.

RACIALIZATION, NEOLIBERALISM, TRANSNATIONALISM: ON THE CHANGING RELEVANCE OF RACE

This inquiry is concerned with how power operates through contemporary forms of racialization.⁵⁷ The concept of racialization employed here is premised on the idea that there are several systems and processes of power such as race, gender, class, and sexuality that operate through one another. I use the term "interlocking" to refer specifically to an analytic that stresses the simultaneity of co-constitutiveness of systems of power.⁵⁸ Furthermore, as will be argued in this book, processes of racialization occur both explicitly and silently insofar as they are often hidden behind concepts such as "nation" and are therefore not necessarily articulated in terms of "race."[59]

It is important to note that in recent years many have begun to question the relevance of race as an analytic in light of the ways in which neoliberal globalization and geopolitical political processes in the post-Cold-War era have greatly complicated and destabilized it. As Deborah Thomas and Kamari Clarke point out, invoking race in increasingly global contexts conjures up essentialisms, generalizations, and seemingly out-dated notions such as white racial supremacy.[60] While they insist on the need to recuperate a race analytic, their work also makes evident the need to think about racial identification and subject formation in ways that are nuanced and relevant for contemporary geopolitics. Similarly, Sedef Arat-Koç writes: "It appears as if racism has lost legitimacy as a state or societal discourse, as mainstream discussions and practices of race become increasingly sophisticated in the West, taking the forms of the self-proclaimed 'non-racism' of liberal 'colour-blindness' and, more recently, neo-liberal multiculturalism portraying a post-racist world of freedom and opportunity."[61] She argues that it is through a combination of critical race and political economy theories that we can best historicize and contextualize the complexities and contradictions of race as they appear in the contemporary period.[62]

Informed largely by these approaches, my analysis throughout this book understands racialized identities as fluid, constructed, and shifting over time and place.[63] In this regard, the exploration conceives of whiteness as a relational positioning which comprises a complex combination of factors including citizenship, religious identity, and political economics. Additionally, building on the ideas put forth by Arat-Koç, and Thomas and Clarke, as well as other theorists who have sought to transcend dogmatic debates around class and race as exclusionary analytics, the approach I take is one that sees race as interlocking (that is, inextricably linked) with class insofar as it recognizes that encounters in foreign spaces continue to be enabled through the economic and cultural privilege that affords mobility, as well as considers how the activists' bodies represent relative wealth as part of their racialized power.[64] As such, the notion of "First World" as it is used here is intended to draw attention to the political economic agenda that shapes social structures within racist global power relations.[65]

RACE, POWER, AND SUBJECTIVITY

This book offers a nuanced exploration of racialized power and uncovers some of its more subtle practices. To achieve this, the approach I take is embedded within a larger analytical framework as outlined by Michel Foucault because it is one that allows for a multi-layered exploration of the ways in which racialized power is produced and operates through discourse, knowledge, and subjectivity.[66] Power, in Foucault's conception, is a network that extends in many directions, leading him to suggest that the most worthwhile questions for studying power are ones formulated in terms of *how* power is exercised, especially when it is purposefully being resisted. Also important for Foucault is that the processes of "conscious self-knowledge," or how people define who we are, emerge through relations of power and domination.[67] For this aspect of power I draw from poststructural theories and approaches that help to show the dialectical or interactive processes of subject-formation and the multiple and often contradictory subject positions that are produced through power relations.[68]

My focus on the racialized and racializing underpinnings of this embodied form of activism is also intrinsically premised on the concept of "biopower," a word that Foucault uses to describe state practices that focus on bodies including the technologies of defining, studying, counting, and controlling populations.[69] According to this theory, it is biopower, and racism as its corollary, that creates the conditions that make military attacks on certain lives justifiable. For this aspect of the study, in addition to Foucault, I rely heavily on Didier Fassin's notion of "a politics of life" which he uses to refer to the stark inequality between Western and non-Western lives that are taken for granted through such interventions.[70] Fassin explains that in its object of saving lives, this activism is formulated upon the "dialectic" between the lives of the victims and lives of those intervening.[71] The idea of "a politics of life" therefore emphasizes how selectively meaning is attributed to human life – a key point that, in his view, the concept of biopolitics does not capture.[72]

COLONIAL LEGACIES AND EMBODIED ENCOUNTERS IN THE TRANSNATIONAL CONTACT ZONE

To understand race as a system of power, one must examine the legacies and continuities of colonialism and imperialism, both in terms of conquest *and* well-meaning interventions. Thus, the poststructural concepts and methods for studying subjectivity that I make use of are interwoven with postcolonial theories that link subject positions to histories and geopolitical locations in order to account for the production of complex identities within transnationalism. To historicize and understand race as a contemporary system of power, I am guided by M. Jacqui Alexander and Chandra Mohanty's notion of "colonial legacies."[73] Similar to Foucault, they insist upon examining "the continuities and discontinuities between contemporary and inherited practices."[74] The specific concepts that shape this inquiry of colonial legacies can be summed up as a convergence of *the encounter, the contact zone, transnationality*, and *embodiment*.

Frantz Fanon's idea of "encounter" is central to the activism I explore because it demands a careful consideration of how the white, First World activists come to know themselves or experience their "being" through the Other.[75] Closely connected to this, Mary Louise Pratt's notion of "the contact zone" is equally relevant insofar as it defines the encounter as a space in which peoples geographically and historically separated come into contact with each other.[76] It is in the contact zone, she writes, "where disparate cultures meet, clash, and grapple with each other, often in highly asymmetrical relations of domination and subordination."[77] By invoking the idea of "contact," Pratt offers a way to think about racialized relations "in terms of co-presence, interaction, interlocking understandings and practices" and "how subjects are constituted in and by their relations to each other."[78]

My understanding and use of the term "transnational" is indebted to the work of Inderpal Grewal and Caren Kaplan who insist that a transnational feminist approach is needed to reveal how subjectivities are formed through mobility and spatiality.[79] My use of the concept of transnationality refers mainly to the physical crossing of borders of nation-states, and connotes what Ella Shohat refers to as "relationality" to capture the ways "histories and communities are mutually complicated and constitutively related."[80] Lastly, Sara Ahmed's work on embodiment is integral to my analysis because it emphasises that within racialized "postcolonial"[81] encounters, physical and visible attributes are central to distinguishing some bodies as familiar and others as strange. She insists that attention be paid to how these bodies are read.[82]

When applied to studies on whiteness, these ideas about contact, history, and transnationality are best delineated through some seminal theorists. For instance, Ruth Frankenberg's work is central to considering colonial legacies not least because of its emphasis on space, or what she refers to as "social geographies."[83] Specifically, she defines whiteness as "a complexly constructed product of local, regional, national, and global relations, past and present," and one that is co-constructed with a range of other racial and cultural categories, such as class and gender.[84] She emphasizes, however, that this co-construction is "fundamentally asymmetrical" because whiteness is always a position of dominance, normativity and privilege.[85] Similarly, Ghassan Hage illustrates that the relationships between self and territory produce imagined communities, and that these imaginings constitute white subjectivity.[86] Focusing his attention specifically on the racialized fantasies that have emerged through white settler societies, he writes: "'Whiteness' is an ever-changing, composite cultural historical construct. It has its roots in the history of European colonization which universalized a cultural form of white identity as a position of cultural power at the same time as the colonized were in the process of being racialized ... In this sense, white has become the ideal of being the bearer of 'Western' civilization."[87] Expanding upon the imaginings that constitute white subjectivity, Barbara Heron has focused on white Canadian women who work in international development. Her lucid approach has been instrumental for demonstrating how whiteness, middle-class identity, as well as notions of morality must be comprehended as working together to produce white subjectivities.[88]

WHITENESS, WESTERN, FIRST WORLD: DEFINING THE TERMS

Those who study whiteness rightly point out that it has always been a contentious category, and that it is one that poses many risks.[89] This study is no exception. One of my concerns with making whiteness a central analytic revolves around its conceptual inadequacy for capturing the multifarious ways in which racialized power operates for dominant groups in contemporary transnational contexts, or what Arat-Koç refers to as "new whitenesses" and the "cracks" along the colour line that develop through them.[90] Indeed, it is difficult to dispute Arat-Koç's contention that wider conceptions of whiteness are needed in order to examine how it has come to be more conditional on class.[91]

As I will show, these "cracks" are not only glaringly apparent in the site of activism examined in this book, they are also most instructive for examining contemporary forms of racialization. In fact, three of the people who were interviewed for this study self-identified as people of colour: one South Asian; one East Asian; and one self-described as "half Arab." Yet, I contend that their First World citizenship and the positioning that it affords them nevertheless racialized them as members of the dominant group, though of course, to varying degrees. Moreover, who gets to be defined as or define themselves as white depends on a number of complex and context specific geographic and social histories whereby groups and individuals marked as white in one context may be differently racialized in another. These definitions depend on multiple factors including diaspora and mixed-race identities and experiences, religion, access to mobility, and language facility, to name a few. Since there is such a strong emphasis on the Middle East as a geopolitical site in this book, it is important to note how the category of whiteness has been variously applied to Arabs in different times and places. In fact, one of the best illustrations of the instability of "whiteness" emerges out of studies on the historical categorization of Arabs in the West since the early 1900s. Arabs in the US were first marked as non-white, eventually became white, and in recent years were reverted back to being considered non-white.[92]

Religion too, certainly complicates whiteness in myriad and significant ways. As we know from the works of Richard Dyer, Daniel Coleman, and others, Christianity plays no small part in constituting whiteness.[93] Although the convergence of Christianity and whiteness will be explored in depth in Chapter Two, it is important here to note its significance to my analysis given that several of the activists who were interviewed for this study had travelled with Christian-faith-based organizations. In addition to Christianity, Jewish identity was also a complicating factor in constituting whiteness. As one activist put it, "I do think of myself as white, although being Jewish sometimes makes me feel not quite white."[94] In fact, three of the four activists in this study self-identified as both white and Jewish. Their narratives revealed that in the context of Palestine, being Jewish was always very much a part of their racial identity not only because their bodies were "read" differently, but also because for some it was the driving force in their decision to take part in this activism. For example, one explained that she decided to go to Palestine specifically "to do [her] best to stop what Israel was doing in her name as a Jew."[95]

Trying to account for the internal heterogeneity of the category of whiteness, with all its "cracks," and the population of activists to which the term is being applied is no easy task. It is for this reason that throughout this book, I oscillate between using the terms "white," "Western," and "First World," and sometimes use them in combination. I use the term "First World" when I want to emphasize the activists' citizenships. One of the reasons I find it to be useful as a term is that it encompasses those who do not identify as white, but whom I nevertheless consider to be racialized as members of the dominant group in certain contexts, given their citizenship. I employ the terms "the West" or "Western" specifically when I want to emphasize the history of colonization, or because I will be referring to specific countries, such as Canada, that are said to be geographically located in the West.[96] My use of the notion of the West is also greatly shaped by Edward Said's work which has shown that through the colonial encounter, the world was ultimately divided into two groups – what we have come to know as East/West – and illustrates how these binary categories function to construct a polarization of distinctions that continue to define racialized groups.[97] Finally, I use the term "white" to capture the more visible and embodied or corporeal processes of racialization that manifest in this activism.

Importantly however, my use of these terms is strategic and to some extent metaphoric. As such, their uses here should not be understood to be relying upon reductive binary oppositions or essentialisms, but rather as categorizations that suggest a *relational* power-based positioning within particular historical conjunctures. Moreover, although I access and employ these conceptual categories, I recognize, as Chandra Mohanty has illustrated, their imprecision and analytical limitations.[98] For example, my apprehensions about using the term "First World" stem from not wanting to invoke and therefore perpetuate the symbolic reduction of its associated term, "Third World." Yet, I have conceded that, as Mohanty puts it, "all we can have access to at given moments is the analytical language that most clearly approximates the features of the world as we understand it."[99]

Together this terminology and the broader interpretive framework in which it is embedded provide the foundational paths for examining the corporeal, material, psychic, and geographic dimensions of racialized power relations as they emerge through various forms of transnational accompaniment-observer solidarity activism.

OUTLINE AND OVERVIEW

This introduction is followed by seven chapters, each addressing a particular aspect pertaining to the production of racialized First World subjectivity in the site of transnational solidarity activism. In Chapter One, I focus on the actions of the International Solidarity Movement and on the representations of Rachel Corrie who has come to epitomize the perils and the heroism of transnational solidarity activism. In tracing the racialized and gendered dimensions of the various responses her death provoked, I argue that whether she was dismissed, vilified, or celebrated, they all hinged on her whiteness. The responses to her death are worthy of critical examination because they reveal some of the shifting ways in which race operates in post-9/11 geopolitics. I also focus on positive representations of Corrie to show that although they are put forth strategically to lend legitimacy to political claims about militarized violence in Palestine, one must also consider how such representations can inadvertently reify whiteness. Specifically, my analysis reveals that public expressions of mourning for Corrie perpetuated hegemonic discourses of white "saviourism" and were therefore far from subversive due to their racializing effects. I argue that a more complex reading of the role of activists like Corrie is needed in order to recognize their significant efforts, while not necessarily portraying them, as (in her case) the face of Palestinian resistance.

My focus in Chapter Two is on the interlock of citizenship, sexuality, and nationalisms and how they impact and are shaped through this activism. Here, I explore the kidnapping and rescue of the Christian Peacemaker Team (CPT) activists in Iraq. Focusing in great depth on how one of these CPT activists, James Loney, was represented in Canadian news media, my primary goal is to think about how transnational solidarity activism is implicated in a racialized nation-making process, and how Orientalist representations of the violent Other constitute First World subjectivities. The particularities around the case of the CPT kidnapping reveal several complex layers relating to race and citizenship. For example, the kidnapping sparked a notable response by members of Muslim communities, as well as from individuals being detained in First World countries like Canada who called or actively campaigned for the release of the four men. Another significant but equally controversial thread running through the accounts of this kidnapping has to do with Loney's sexuality. After the rescue and return of the men, it was revealed that he is gay – a fact that was hidden from the public at large. Furthermore, in exploring how Loney publicly grappled with and attempted to reconcile being grateful for regaining his freedom, while maintaining a critical stance against the military forces that rescued him, I also consider the ways in which Loney and the CPT managed to subvert the dominant us/them discourses that surrounded the kidnapping. As such, this chapter offers insights into effective ways of using white and First World privilege and highlights the meaningful contributions that these activists can make toward social justice.

Chapter Three explores the racialized dimensions of the witnessing, documenting and reporting practices of Canadian activists who have travelled to Iraq to recount the effects of war. It considers how racialized power is (re)produced through their reporting practices and their work with mainstream media. By weaving together postcolonial feminist theory, scholarship on citizenship journalism, and the activists' narratives, it explores several challenges around "voice" that activists encounter in their representational practices. Specifically, I argue that the counter-hegemonic political potential of their documenting and reporting practices are largely constrained insofar as they maintain a hierarchical positioning as experts, truth-tellers, and as the voices of reason in their reporting practices. Focusing on one activist's dilemma around using her racialized position to obtain and publicize information on behalf of Iraqis, I also explore the politics of voice and argue for more situated antiracist representational practices. The chapter ends by asserting the need for an ongoing critique of the taken-for-granted virtues of "alternative" or "independent" media practices by nonprofessional or citizen journalists.

Continuing to explore the activists' witnessing, documenting, and reporting practices, Chapter Four offers an in-depth analysis of one activist's efforts to publicize human suffering through photographs and how he negotiates ethical dilemmas about spectatorship and voyeurism. By exploring a compelling dilemma he faced when he encountered the body of a dead Palestinian man while doing ambulance accompaniment in the Occupied Territories, I draw out the ways in which he weighed the moral implications of photographing the body for educational purposes against his concern about doing further violence by exposing this dead body to a Western gaze. One of the difficult questions reflected upon in this chapter is how appeals for compassion are racialized.

In Chapter Five, I shift my attention to analyzing some of the inner conflicts, doubts, and misgivings of those who take part in this activism. In particular, I focus on how they understand, negotiate, and manage their power and privilege as well as their concerns about the effectiveness of embodying a white presence vis-à-vis their commitments to social responsibility and justice. I also explore what enables these activists to reconcile their apprehensions. I suggest that in many cases, activists were able to mitigate discomforting concerns about their presence by viewing and portraying themselves as wanted, helpful, and well-meaning. By showing how the activists are both conflicted and comforted, my goal is to bring into question the subject-making processes that emerge through the transnational solidarity encounter. This chapter also explores how transnational solidarity activism is considered from the points of view of some of those being "protected" and "observed," and by those who are requesting this assistance. I draw upon interviews conducted with Palestinian community organizers to consider what challenges come up when working in solidarity with Western activists and how they manage the tensions around asymmetrical relations of power that arise for them in these solidarity projects.

In Chapter Six, I examine how race interlocks with gender to paradoxically situate female activists as protectors who are themselves at peril and to show that accompaniment-observer activism is primarily a masculinist space in which women activists are very precariously positioned. The main point of interest here is sexual violence and the difficulties that come up for the women activists who face it. I argue that the women activists cannot deploy privilege in the same way the men activists can, and that they are therefore required to calculate their strategies much differently. Furthermore, I reveal that the convergence of race and gender greatly complicates the deployment of white bodies as a form of protection. By exploring some of the politics of silence around the perils of being a woman in this activism, my analysis reveals that in seeking legitimacy and demonstrating their commitments to antiracist /anti-state violence, women activists are likely to put issues of sexism aside. I suggest that this false separation of gender and race not only impedes, but greatly contradicts the antiracist goals of the activism.

In Chapter Seven, I conclude by offering theoretical, pedagogical, practical, and political implications of the analysis presented throughout the book. Beginning with a discussion of the terms with which the activists describe their roles, I draw attention to how many of them embraced notions of themselves as disembodied. In short, they see themselves as universal liberal subjects. What is most noteworthy about their grip on discourses of universalism is that they were describing contexts in which embodying whiteness was blatant and integral to their function as activists. Drawing on critical race and decolonial theories, one of the points raised in this chapter pertains to the paradoxes of universalism that come up in this site of activism. I end this discussion by reflecting on the pedagogical implications that this racial liberalism has on anti-racist education. Another point explored in this chapter is the tension between ideology and pragmatism. Here I suggest that the discourses that are mobilized in activism are important to notice because so long as the activists' conceptions are embedded within the dominant liberal paradigm, the political potential of accompaniment-observer activism is compromised. The chapter ends with reflections on the broad implications of my analysis. Specifically, I call for a more complicated articulation of "solidarity" in which it is conceived as both a central element for effective political movements *and* as a set of practices that rely on racialized and gendered structures of colonialism and imperialism. I also offer a discussion on questions of social responsibility, pragmatism, and activism in light of urgent political crises in the world.

In the afterword, I offer a brief discussion on two disconcerting trends related to transnational activism and political tourism that extend beyond the scope of this book but that demand critical interrogation in subsequent studies. The first is the proliferation of various programs offering variations of quasi-political tourism. The second, and sometimes overlapping trend is the growing depoliticization and NGOization of social justice projects and the simultaneous cooptation of terms like "activism" and "social justice."

CHAPTER ONE

Whiteness and the Divergent Responses to Rachel Corrie's Death

> Even I, it seems, have developed a callousness to the deaths of Palestinians, because the murder of this white girl from Olympia, Washington has my heart breaking and my blood faint.
>
> Suheir Hammad, "On the Brink of War"[1]

> What if it turns out that compassion and coldness are not opposite at all but are two sides of a bargain that the subjects of modernity have struck with structural inequity?
>
> Lauren Berlant, Compassion[2]

The white girl from Olympia, Washington, to whom Palestinian-American poet Suheir Hammad is referring in the quote above is Rachel Corrie, a twenty-three-year-old who died in Palestine on 16 March 2003.[3] Corrie went there as a member of the International Solidarity Movement (ISM). In an attempt to block an Israeli army bulldozer from demolishing a Palestinian home, Corrie stood squarely in its way, and it subsequently crushed her to death. Hammad's poem, written just days after Corrie's death, and just prior to the impending American invasion of Iraq, wrestles with ways of maintaining hope in the face of militarism and imperialism and reflects the despair felt by many who were opposed to the war. For Hammad, Corrie's commitment to peace and social justice was a hopeful reminder of "how divine human beings can be."[4] In her poem, Hammad also remarks on some hate-filled responses by those who declared Corrie to be a "treasonous bitch" or characterized her death as "good riddance." By invoking these expressions alongside her own sorrow, Hammad's poem captures the radically divergent responses engendered by Corrie's death.

I begin this chapter with an extract from Hammad's poem because of its resonance with the central issues I explore in this chapter: the relationships between whiteness, grief, and social justice. Specifically, I aim to trace the racialized and gendered dimensions of the various emotions that have circulated in representations of Corrie and her death. As I will show, the varied responses her death provoked are worthy of critical examination because they reveal some of the nuanced ways in which race operates in post-9/11 geopolitics. In short, this chapter contends that whether she was dismissed, vilified, or celebrated, the responses to and representations of Corrie's death were deeply racialized insofar as they all hinged on her whiteness.

My objectives are two-fold. First, I describe the rationale behind the ISM's strategy of offering support and protection to Palestinians through "international" presence, and its historical antecedents. As well, I detail some explanations about Corrie's death and why it failed to generate the expected level of political attention and accountability. In so doing, I show how the meanings attached to whiteness shift, and how they depend upon contemporary forms of patriotic nationalism. Indeed, Corrie's case is a compelling example of how whiteness, in Richard Dyer's terms, is "both in and not about the body."[5] Her death presents us with an occasion to see precisely how whiteness is a constructed identity that morphs according to the geopolitical contexts in which it appears. Corrie's death also uncovers some of the complex ways in which race, gender, and emotions interlock to produce certain social responses.

Second, I focus on commemorations of Corrie. Here, my objectives are instructive and cautionary. While recognizing that the invocation of Corrie's commitment to being an ally can be political and symbolically useful for some social justice movements, I argue that it is still necessary to critically consider how such tributes and commemorations – which flourish even a decade after her death – may inadvertently and paradoxically reinforce global, white hegemony.

PUTTING WHITE BODIES ON THE FRONT LINES: FREEDOM SUMMER – 1964

In 1964, black activist leaders of the US civil rights movement announced their "Freedom Summer" campaign which involved active recruitment of white students from prestigious universities in the Northern states. The white students were invited to travel to Mississippi because their presence would help draw attention to and reduce the racist violence to which the black activists were being subjected.[6] This was viewed as necessary because by the time the Freedom Summer campaign was launched, there had been over 150 cases of violence and intimidation against black civil rights workers and local residents who supported them, yet no actions had been taken by the authorities.[7]

The decision to include white student activists in the movement was not taken lightly by the black leadership. Anticipating some problems that could arise with their presence, explicit measures to guide and control their working relationships were put in place to ensure ongoing black leadership and control. As Becky Thompson explains, "White people were constantly held accountable to black people in the way they handled themselves, in the policy they carried out, and in how they framed events, publicity, and the vision of the organization."[8] In addition, although concerted efforts were made to portray white and black activists as united (interracial harmony was both a public relations strategy and a goal), the white activists were encouraged to work primarily with white communities.[9]

As predicted, the involvement of white students profoundly altered the American public's political stakes in the civil rights movement and increased concern about the violent attacks taking place in the Southern US. This was seen most clearly on the very first day of the Freedom Summer campaign, when three civil rights activists were reported missing. Two of them, Mickey Schwerner and Andrew Goodman, were white men from New York. The third man was James Chaney, a twenty-one-year-old black man from McComb, Mississippi.[10] Pictures of the missing men were displayed on the front pages of major American newspapers, and the news of their disappearance provoked public outrage, prompting then US president, Lyndon Johnson, to call for a "massive manhunt" to track down the missing men.[11] Commenting on the government's swift and serious response, Schwerner's wife said, "We all know that this search is because Andrew Goodman and my husband are white. If only Chaney was involved, nothing would've been done."[12] It was eventually discovered that the three men had been attacked and killed by the White Knights, a branch of the Ku Klux Klan. Their bodies were found on 4 August 1964.[13]

Throughout the Freedom Summer campaign, the participation of white activists seemed to have succeeded in gaining publicity and legitimacy for the movement. However, their involvement also presented serious problems and challenges on a day-to-day level, causing some black activists to rethink the cross-racial strategy. For instance, by the end of the summer of 1964, major ideological tensions about the role of white activists and the nonviolence mandate had fractured the movement. While some historians indicate that the white students began to drift out of the organization, others have characterized this as the "white people kicked out" phase.[14] Moreover, some more militant members were demanding racial separatism and violence as self-defence, which resulted in a faction forming the Black Power movement and the Black Panthers.[15] This period of great "internal upheaval" resulted in fewer white people in the movement.[16]

In spite of the initial deaths of the three men and the interracial tensions that subsequently plagued the movement, many historians, social movement scholars, and activists have retrospectively judged the strategy of bringing white Northerners into the civil rights movement as a success. In fact, it is believed that the disappearance of the three men to some extent served to protect the civil rights activists in Mississippi for the rest for the summer since the media spotlight focused on the campaign more intensively from then onwards.

FREEDOM SUMMER 2001 – PALESTINE

In 2001, the ISM named its first campaign in Palestine "Freedom Summer," thus directly invoking the 1964 civil rights movement. It began recruiting volunteers mainly from First World countries."[17]

Extending the rationale used in 1964, the central founding principle of the ISM was the idea that First World bodies, especially those visibly identifiable as non-Palestinian, could be used as "buffers" enabling Palestinians to engage in direct action against the Israeli military.[18] As one of the ISM's founders, Ghassan Andoni, explains, the rationale behind this strategy was premised on the recognition that "our [Palestinian] blood is not valued. American and British blood is."[19]

The specific origins of the ISM have been traced back to an incident that occurred at a demonstration in the period of what has come to be known as the "Al-Aqsa" or "second *Intifada*" uprising in 2000, which prompted anti-occupation activists to explore ways to encourage nonviolent and safe participation in the protests.[20] At this demonstration, an Israeli anti-occupation activist named Neta Golan intervened in a confrontation that broke out between Israeli soldiers and Palestinian villagers who were trying to pass through an Israeli checkpoint. As Golan explains, "Another Israeli and I stood in [the] middle – between the Palestinians and the soldiers – and I believe it's because we were there that the soldiers didn't shoot, and the villagers were able to open the roadblock."[21] Seeing how her Israeli identity enabled her to offer protection to Palestinians, Golan, along with Palestinian-American Huweida Arraf and Palestinian Ghassan Andoni, both of whom had been actively organizing against the Israeli occupation, reasoned that the presence of American and European activists – or "internationals," as they have commonly become known – could serve to hinder routinized Israeli military aggression and provoke a greater sense of global accountability.[22] Arraf, Andoni, and Golan subsequently formed the ISM, a movement they defined as "Palestinian-led and foreign-assisted."[23]

Typically, people from the West who volunteer with the ISM sign up for a month and are expected to pay their own way. According to one of its founders, nearly half of ISM's volunteers come from the United States, and the rest are mainly from the UK and Canada with increasing numbers more recently coming from other countries in Europe and from Japan.[24] While it is difficult to know how many people have participated with the ISM, it is believed that by 2005 more than 4000 had taken part in its activities.[25]

The ISM emerged as a response to Israel's violation of the Fourth Geneva Convention on the Protection of Civilian Persons in Time of War and as a way to respond to some of the routine military operations through which Palestinians' basic civil and human rights are violated – which include, but are not limited to: forcible entry, search and seizure, bombardment, mass curtailment of mobility, limited access to water, and arbitrary arrests at checkpoints.[26] ISM activists are invited to travel to Gaza and the West Bank to offer protection and support to Palestinians and to oppose the various human rights violations of Palestinian people and the militarized violence of the Israeli occupation in general. The ISM list four reasons why international participation is important for their movement: (1) protection; (2) informing the mainstream media; (3) personal witnessing and the transmission of information; and (4) breaking isolation and providing hope.[27] On a day-to-day level, their activities include escorting children to school, demonstrating against the violent conditions of occupation, delivering food and water to families under curfew or house arrest, removing roadblocks, accompanying farmers to their fields, and occasionally physically intervening, as Rachel Corrie did, to try to protect homes and people who are under threat of attack.[28] Most importantly, the presence of these activists is believed to be effective at summoning international pressure and in reducing military violence because it is presumed that the Israeli defence forces would be reluctant to harm these activists for fear of political repercussions.

RACE, GENDER, AND HIERARCHIES OF GRIEF

In an essay that examines Westerners' exposure and responses to global violence in the post-9/11 era, Judith Butler questions why certain expressions of grief eclipse others.[29] Challenging psychoanalytic understandings of grief that generally situate it in the realm of the private, Butler argues that some expressions of public grief are highly instructive within socio-political debates because they reveal a lot about creating and maintaining communities. Using the phrase "a hierarchy of grief," she contends that lives are supported and maintained differently, and that there are radically different ways in which human physical vulnerability is distributed across the globe. Within such a hierarchy, she explains, "Certain lives are protected, and the abrogation of their claims to sanctity will be sufficient to mobilize the forces of war, while other lives will not find such fast and furious support and will not even qualify as grievable."[30]

To illustrate her point, one example that Butler offers is her own response to hearing about the brutal murder of Wall Street journalist Daniel Pearl in Pakistan.[31] She admits to being affected by news of his death because Pearl, as she put it, "could have been her brother."[32] Butler invites her readers to similarly reflect upon how our sense of grief is tied to what we consider to be familiar. Her argument is that although the killing of a white American like Pearl elicits deep mourning and compassion in the US, the countless victims of American and European military violence do not. It is precisely this racial logic, which Butler refers to as "a hierarchy of grief," that lies behind the strategic, political uses of whiteness in the ISM and in the 1964 Freedom Summer campaign. Insightful as it may be, it is important to note that the poignancy of Butler's argument rests in the fact that it is aimed at a white/Western readership. Indeed, as outlined earlier, Palestinian and black activists, and those from many other disenfranchised, racialized communities, have long recognized where their lives rank on the hierarchy of grief.

There is also an important gendered dimension that works in tandem with whiteness in these transnational, militarized conflict zones. Specifically, it is the shared understanding that women are less of a threat and are therefore less likely to be harmed. Feminist activists who have explored the role that gender plays in accompaniment-observer activism in Palestine have noted that women's bodies can be more effective at offering support and protection because the soldiers tend to avoid entering into extreme confrontation with them. Although they concede that they are more tolerated by the soldiers because of gendered understandings of women as harmless, they contend that such notions allow them more access, thereby rendering them more effective than male activists in some circumstances.[33]

Presumably then, when Rachel Corrie refused to move out of the bulldozer's way she was relying on and deploying a historical and global system of power which, on the basis of race and gender, would protect her from harm. In other words, by the logics of white supremacy and heteropatriarchy, Corrie likely believed that she would not be killed. Moreover, given her "familiarity" as a young, white, and middle-class American woman, the fact that she was killed should have had a profound impact on the mainstream American public. Yet, it did not. Corrie's death in Palestine seemed to have an effect opposite to the disappearances of the white activists during the 1964 Freedom Summer. In fact, her death marked a period of more severe attacks on ISM activists.[34] Brian Avery, a twenty-four-year-old American volunteer in Jenin, was shot in the face and seriously wounded by an Israeli sniper on 5 April 2003, within a month of Corrie's death. Less than a week later, a twenty-one-year-old British ISM activist named Tom Hurndall was shot in the head by an Israeli soldier in Gaza and was in a coma on a life-support machine with severe brain damage until he died in January, 2004.[35] Then in 2009, a young American man named Tristan Anderson was critically injured after he was struck in the forehead and almost killed by a high-velocity tear gas grenade in Bi'iln, in the West Bank. These cases have sparked a great deal of controversy, largely fuelled by the conviction amongst the supporters and family members of these activists who assert that at the level of official state responses, there has been little accountability for these deaths and injuries. Many have observed, for example, that when news of Corrie's death first broke in the US, it was all but ignored by the mainstream media.[36]

How, then, does one account for these incongruities? What makes the grievability of certain lives a reliable political strategy in one temporal and geopolitical context and not in another? More specifically, what is it that made Corrie an "unworthy" victim despite her gender, American citizenship, and racial identity?[37]

GEOPOLITICS AND THE SHIFTING MEANING OF WHITENESS

One of the reasons for the failure of legal accountability in the case of Corrie's death, and those of others killed or injured in similar operations, according to political geographer Derek Gregory, is

Israel's self-determined prerogative to suspend its own laws.[38] He believes that these crimes are indicative of the arbitrary and asymmetrical political conditions in the Occupied Territories. As well, he makes the important point that it is not just Israel, but the larger political community that is ignoring and thereby condoning these conditions. Another example that Gregory gives concerning the ongoing and implicitly sanctioned illegal activity in Palestine is the very form of violence that Corrie was trying to stop when she was killed – the demolition of homes. He writes:

> These demolitions contravene the Geneva Conventions, and it is the responsibility of the High Contracting Parties – the signatory states and their representatives – to compel Israel to honor its legally binding obligations ... it is their duty to safeguard the rights – and lives – of those under military occupation: and yet, like the state of Israel, these sovereign powers have elected to suspend the law and to allow Israel to extend the space of exception. For the most part, they have also elected to ignore the continued assault by the Israel Defense Forces on international observers, including journalists, in Gaza and the West Bank.[39]

To explain this further, Gregory cites Palestinian writer Elias Sanbar, who characterizes this international indifference as a "global construction of new empire."[40] As Sanbar explains, Israel does not just continue its common practice of violating international law, but also declares "loudly and clearly" that it is working outside the parameters of the law.[41] This view appears to have been echoed in 2010 when Corrie's parents filed "unlawful killing" charges against the state of Israel. During questioning at the Haifa District Court trial hearings, an Israel Defense Forces training leader declared, "During war, there are no civilians."[42]

Others extend this argument to contend that the lack of official concern for Corrie's death can equally be attributed to the silencing of dissent that took hold in the US after 9/11.[43] For instance, antiracist theorist Paul Gilroy has argued that owing to her pro-Palestinian actions, Corrie was seen to no longer warrant the response that is usually afforded to white, American citizens. As

Gilroy puts it, both Corrie and Hurndall were killed because "colonial authorities revise and extend the category of infrahumanity to encompass anyone who [in their view] is foolish enough to side with the insurgent locals."[44] In other words, by siding with the Palestinians, the two ISM fatalities were stripped of their privileged, racialized positioning and rendered as "infrahuman," that is, they became as insignificant as the people they were supporting. Malini Johar Schueller incisively describes this dynamic as a form of "political miscegenation."[45] She explains that in various media portrayals of Corrie as misguided, immature, and without a constituency, "Manichean structures of dogmatic nationalism and orientalist racism" were employed in ways that served to demonize and/or ridicule her.[46]

Writing about the gendered dimensions of the official responses to Corrie's death, Naomi Klein and Deepa Kumar offer comparisons to the public's reactions to news about a young American woman soldier, Private Jessica Lynch, who was taken into Iraqi custody a week after Corrie was killed. Both Klein and Kumar highlight the drastically different ways that Lynch and Corrie's femininities were portrayed in the media.[47] As Kumar puts it, although both young women were blond and petite, only Lynch was portrayed as "the girl next door," and became "America's hero/sweetheart" because unlike Corrie, she was on the right side of US foreign policy.[48] Indeed, it is important to recall here that some of the gendered comments about Corrie's death that circulated widely on the internet were not only unsympathetic but were also hateful – for instance, referring to her as a "treasonous bitch."

The crux of these arguments is that by overtly aligning herself with Palestinian rights, Corrie forfeited some of the privileges that would otherwise have provoked compassion for her and greater concern and accountability for her death. In other words, being a young, white, American citizen is not always sufficient to garner support and sympathy; one must also be regarded to be advocating for politics that are accepted by the mainstream. Indeed, there is ample data that clearly reveals how Corrie's moral and political commitments were thrown into question. While it is hardly surprising that these portrayals would appear in conservative rightwing media, it is important to note that they could also be found in left-leaning and alternative media, revealing what Ella Shohat has referred to as a "submerged nationalism" that can take over so-called progressive political circles.[49] One striking example is an article that appeared in *Mother Jones*, a self-described independent magazine that promotes dissent and radical political views and "whose roots lie in a commitment to social justice."[50] Published about six months after Corrie's death, the article was a lengthy exposé sub-titled: "Martyr, idiot, dedicated, deluded. Why did this American college student crushed by an Israeli bulldozer put her life on the line? And did it matter?"[51] Although the tone of the article is somewhat sympathetic, its author, Joshua Hammer, manages to belittle Corrie's political commitments and efforts: "She should be an iconic figure – to foolish idealism, to bravery against impossible odds, to the bittersweet conviction of youth – and to a handful of people she may be, but so far the larger message of her life appears to be one of futility."[52] Hammer's point is that the public was put off by Corrie's naïveté, and he implies that she is at fault for the lack of empathy that her death provoked. Reading Hammer's report, one also sees that his patronizing comments about her "bittersweet" conviction are embedded within a gendered discourse about Corrie being emotionally, rather than intellectually or politically, driven.

The article goes on to subtly but effectively cast doubt on Corrie's political motivations by describing the ISM as a "group [that] has courted controversy from the start, embracing Palestinian militants, even suicide bombers, as freedom fighters."[53] The photographs that are presented alongside Hammer's essay are also significant. On one page there is a small photograph of Corrie as an endearing, blond, wispy-haired child in her home town of Olympia, and on another page, a much larger photo (the largest of all of them) is a close-up of a wild-eyed, open-mouthed Corrie with her head covered in what appears to be a *hijab*.[54] In it, Corrie is burning a replica of an American flag before smiling schoolchildren in Gaza, an act that Western audiences are accustomed to seeing Arabs performing on the news.[55] These representations clearly support the argument that the lack of empathy and accountability garnered by her death can be attributed to what was perceived to be her acts of treason, not only by siding with the enemy, but by becoming one herself.

Taken during a rally in the southern Gaza Strip town of Rafah, 15 February 2003. This photo has also circulated widely on the internet. Another photo that is frequently circulated shows Corrie wearing a checked white-and-black scarf or *kaffiyeh*, a symbol which has largely come to be associated with Palestinian resistance. (Reprinted by permission from the Associated Press, license no: LIC-00057002)

The lack of accountability and compassion for Corrie also illustrate the ways in which whiteness is a shifting and relational positioning, and furthermore suggest that it is only *certain* performances of whiteness that can maintain their rankings within contemporary racialized hierarchies of grief. In order to prompt public support and empathy, it seems, one must avoid being seen as having become the racial and ideological Other.[56]

WHITENESS AND COMMEMORATIONS OF CORRIE

As I have shown, while many have been rightly concerned with how Corrie was either ignored or vilified by the media, few (if any) have critically considered the implications of the on-going commemorations of her as a hero. It is important to note that although her death did not receive the expected official political response, at the civil society level it has provoked a tremendous amount of outrage and sympathy. For example, according to Craig Corrie, Rachel's father, he and his wife received 10,000 emails of condolences within a week of their daughter's death.[57] Furthermore, in the public realm, various tributes continue to be paid to her. Indeed, in the years since her death, Corrie continues to be celebrated and mourned. Essays, poems, and songs have been written about her. Scholarships and foundations have also been set up to honour her legacy.[58] In 2005, a play about her entitled *My Name Is Rachel Corrie* was produced. In 2008, a book of her personal writings was published. In 2009, a documentary film entitled *Rachel* made its debut. In May 2010, a 1,200-ton humanitarian cargo ship carrying reconstruction material, medical equipment, and school supplies into Gaza was named after her.[59] In October of the same year, a new restaurant in Ramallah bore her name.[60]

What does one make of these ongoing tributes to Corrie? Certainly, she has become a valuable symbol for Palestinian solidarity movements insofar as keeping her memory alive helps to illustrate the brutality that is demonstrated against those who dare to stand up to the Israeli occupation.[61] In fact, the strategic uses of paying tribute to Corrie became evident soon after her death. For example, in June 2001, prominent postcolonial scholar Edward Said published an essay entitled "The Meaning of Rachel Corrie" in which he made public his admiration of the young woman and her actions.[62] Said's genuine esteem for Corrie notwithstanding, what is remarkable about his tribute is how he emphasizes her non-Palestinian identity. He wrote: "Born and brought up in Olympia, a small city sixty miles south of Seattle, she had joined the International Solidarity Movement and gone to Gaza to stand with suffering human beings with whom she had never had any contact before."[63] Thus, unlike the conflations of Corrie with Palestinians examined earlier, what Said employs is a reverse strategy of separating her from them. By focussing on Corrie's whiteness, he can more convincingly make the case about the ongoing injustice in the occupation of Palestine. Bearing in mind Said's longstanding commitment to ending the occupation of Palestine, one can imagine that his own political efforts were often constrained by his own subject-positioning as an Arab-American. By drawing attention to

Corrie's commitment and not his own, he was therefore able to advance and legitimize political views that might otherwise be seen as biased.[64] In other words, as a white American, Corrie represents a neutrality and innocence to which Said could never lay claim.[65]

More recently, the play *My Name Is Rachel Corrie* has been used as a vehicle for opening up dialogue around the Israeli occupation of Palestine. Corrie's name has also been effectively mobilized to support campaigns seeking an end to US support for the Israeli occupation. One recent example is an open letter urging President Obama to halt US deliveries of D9 Caterpillar bulldozers – the kind that killed Corrie – to the Israeli military, and to investigate Israel's violations of US laws using this equipment.[66] Clearly, these and numerous other examples show how the figure of Corrie secures a concrete platform from which to resist US imperialism and Israeli occupation.

But what might be some of the hidden costs of this political strategy? What are the effects of hailing this white American woman as a symbol of Palestinian resistance? How might these representations reproduce white supremacist hierarchies of grief? The unspoken consensus within social justice activist and advocacy circles seems to be that the symbolic uses of Corrie's image as a witness to and victim of the violence facing Palestinians overrides such concerns. But does it? To raise these questions is not to suggest that the admiration for Corrie is disingenuous or that it is merely strategic. Certainly the poem by Suheir Hammad and the essay by Edward Said are but two examples that reveal just how many people were genuinely affected by the news of her death. Rather, it is to examine some of the complex ways in which whiteness operates as a system of power. Specifically, I want to consider the inadvertent and insidious ways in which the racial imagery of Rachel Corrie continues to operate, contemplate the implications of her entry into the collective imaginary, and question the effect this has on racialized systems of power.[67]

THE CULTURAL PRODUCTION OF A HERO

The convergence of several interrelated personal and societal factors can help to explain why Corrie has become such an iconic figure in social justice circles. One is the absence of resolution. All the judicial investigations until now have revealed two discrepant versions of what led to Corrie's death. According to Israeli government inquiries, the driver of the bulldozer could not see Corrie, and thus her death was an accident. Yet, many eyewitness reports and photographic evidence assert that she was clearly within his view, wearing a light-reflecting fluorescent vest and using a megaphone, and that her death was therefore a deliberate attack.[68]

The unusual and heinous nature of her death, being crushed by a bulldozer, and the shock value that surrounds it also likely contribute to the charged emotions that her case has incited as compared to some of the other injuries and deaths of solidarity activists that ensued. In addition to this, the fact that some of her personal letters and journal entries were published on the internet within days of her death greatly facilitated her construction as a symbol of social justice. These writings are compelling first-person accounts that offer a glimpse into her youthful bafflement at the injustice in the world, and her committed resolve to do her part to end that injustice.[69] Given that we are frequently reminded of her exceptional bravery and courage in ways that imply a transgression of gendered norms, one can also argue that her being the only First World woman-activist casualty to date has also contributed to singling her out as a hero.[70] This becomes even more apparent when one considers how pronounced her femininity would appear against the backdrop of what Hagar Kotef and Merav Amir consider to be the heightened masculinity in the militarism of Israeli society.[71]

At a broader level, certain temporal and political dynamics surrounding social justice activism at the time of Corrie's trip to Palestine and her death in 2003 can help to further explain why she became a celebrity of sorts. Indeed, it has been observed that globalization, militarism, and war at the turn of the twenty-first century profoundly changed social justice activism and resulted in growing enthusiasm for direct action as a way of denoting that "activism can no longer be about registering symbolic dissent," and rather that it must respond with immediacy to the urgency of the conditions people are living under.[72] Corrie's political coming of age was undeniably shaped by this larger trend. In one journal entry written before she made the decision to join the ISM, Corrie questions the point of participating in antiwar demonstrations in her hometown in light of the need for more radical interventions in war zones like Palestine. She writes: "People [are] offering themselves as human shields in Palestine and I [am] spending all of my time making dove costumes and giant puppets."[73] Indeed, in making the trip to Palestine, and subsequently dying there while boldly refusing to let a bulldozer destroy a family's home, Corrie came to epitomise the principles of using privilege to subvert oppression, as well as the potential sacrifices that come with being a committed social justice activist. It is for these reasons, that for many Palestinians, Corrie came to be seen as a martyr – a victim of their *Intifada* who stood up to the Israeli army in their name.

But what are some of the racializing effects of these representations of Corrie? To explore this question, it helps to notice some articulations of discomfort or self-consciousness that often accompany tributes to Corrie. One example can be seen in the previously mentioned 2005 theatre production of Corrie's letters and journals. Co-produced first by Alan Rickman and Katherine Viner at London's Royal Court Theatre in England, it has been staged in many cities in North America, Europe, and more recently in Nazareth, Ramallah, Jaffa, and Jerusalem.[74] In the afterword of the print version of the play, its producers acknowledge an uncomfortable and self-conscious awareness of their decision to use "Rachel's words rather than those of the thousands of Palestinians or Israeli victims."[75] They go on to explain that the main reason for their decision came down to the quality and accessibility of her writing.[76] While this seems to be well-founded – Corrie's journal entries certainly do provide compelling dramatic text for a theatre production – the implications of their choice are not addressed any further.[77]

A similar articulation was evident during some community discussion panels which accompanied the 2007 run of the play in Montreal. The panels were comprised of various activists, academics, and artists who were asked to comment on topics ranging from the play's artistic and technical production, to the Palestine/Israel conflict, as well as their views on Corrie's activism with the ISM.[78] While, for the most part, the play was highly praised and Corrie was hailed as a symbol of global peace and justice – with some referring to her as a "superhero" and comparing her to Martin Luther King, Gandhi, and Anne Frank – the discussions were also sprinkled with the occasional expression of some ambivalence about using the death of a white American woman to talk about the plight of Palestinians.[79] For example, at the panel that took place on 15 December 2007, one of the speakers said:

> With all due respect to her and her family, I am critical of the kind of public image that gets built around her. I mean, she did do a really amazing thing, and she put her life on the line for ideals that she believed in. I think that has to be respected, but I also think that it's also important to situate that in the context of a struggle … There are a lot of different people, not only in Palestine, but in Israel and all around the world, who are involved in this struggle for the liberation of the people of Palestine.

In another instance, Rachel Corrie's mother Cindy, who, along with her husband Craig, was a panellist at one of the discussions, said, "There are thousands who have suffered similar losses and they're not remembered in the same ways."[80]

A more recent, but remarkably similar articulation of the discomfort around the focus on Corrie can be found in the film *Rachel*, a 2009 documentary by Simone Bitton. Described as a "cinematic autopsy," the film begins in a sentimental tone with various ISM activists reading excerpts from Corrie's letters, and then goes on to reconstruct (in a crime-drama style) an account of what happened on 16 March 2003, the day that Corrie was killed. The bulk of the film is comprised of interviews with a variety of people who were somehow linked to Corrie's death. These include the pathologist who examined Corrie's body, Palestinian activists, Corrie's parents, as well as Israeli soldiers and military spokespersons.

Like Rickman and Viner, Bitton is uneasy about focussing on Corrie's death in light of all the Palestinian deaths which go by virtually unnoticed. This is most evident in one meaningful scene of the film, where an ISM activist named Alice Coy is being interviewed by Bitton, who is hidden from view. Coy explains that she was with Corrie when she was run over by the bulldozer, that she accompanied Corrie to the hospital, and that she was in the room when Corrie's body was examined by the official who is responsible for investigating deaths. At this point Coy recalls that the body of a Palestinian civilian causality named Salim Najjar was also brought into the examiner's room, prompting Bitton to ask, "Do you know the story of this man?" to which Coy replies, "He'd gone outside to have a cigarette outside his house ... and a sniper had shot him. And there was no media about the Palestinian man that was shot. The fact that there was never any news, there's no photos of Salim Najjar on the Internet, there's no story about this man, what he was like." Bitton answers, "Nobody would make a film about him." Coy affirms, "Nobody would make a film about Salim Najjar."[81] As Jimmy Johnson points out in his review of the film, this brief exchange between Coy and Bitton "is revealing."[82] While this dialogue clearly indicates that both Coy and Bitton were cognizant and uneasy about the inadvertent effect of eclipsing the deaths of Palestinian civilians with Corrie's, the poignant scene quickly ends and the film resumes its focus on Corrie.[83]

There are two important points that must be considered about these expressions of unease. The first is that they articulate an anxiety about whiteness. In her investigation of various speech acts like these, Sara Ahmed points out that such expressions are performative and serve to show evidence of anti-racist commitment.[84] Yet, she contends, such utterances in fact reproduce whiteness because they do little more than provide some comfort and redemption for those who articulate them. In this instance, Ahmed's argument would suggest that confessing their discomfort about focusing on Corrie merely conveys to the readers/viewers that they feel bad about doing so. Indeed, what is striking about these moments of acknowledgment is that although they reveal an uneasiness with focussing on Corrie, their focus on her nevertheless persists. Ahmed asks us to consider what the enunciation of such anxieties is doing and contemplates whether such enunciations install a new form of whiteness, what she refers to as an anxious whiteness. She writes: "Is a whiteness that is anxious about itself – its narcissism, its egoism, its privilege, its self-centeredness – better?"

The second and perhaps more significant point about such articulations of anxiety and ambivalence is that they reveal a much larger paradox. That is, they clearly point to an uneasy recognition of what the spotlight on Corrie manages to render invisible. In other words, these commemorations serve to remind us again and again exactly whose lives matter and whose lives do not. This is especially ironic when one considers that the basis behind the solidarity activism that Corrie took part in is specifically geared towards drawing attention to the injuries to the lives that largely go overlooked. Yet, in a remarkable twist, the focus on Corrie effectively serves to distract from what is happening in Palestine rather than bring attention to it, as was her intention.

EMOTIONS IN SOCIAL MOVEMENTS: IMPLICATIONS FOR CRITICAL ANTI-RACISM PEDAGOGIES

Those of us who are interested in questions of antiracist practice need to be troubled by the ways in which Corrie has been constructed as a hero and how her memory has been mobilized. The complexities and implications of using whiteness in these ways must be carefully weighed given that the privileging of white subjectivity so easily runs the risk of reinforcing the very racist systems that it seeks to disrupt. I have shown that the range of responses to Corrie's death – from contemptuous dismissals to deep sorrow and grief – were all strengthened by her being a white woman. Those who sought to belittle and blame her for her death did so by effectively racializing her as the Other. By the same token, representations of Corrie's death that were used to draw sympathy and outrage emphasized that she stood racially apart yet in solidarity with Palestinians. Some would argue that drawing attention and sympathy to Corrie's death in this way is necessary to convey to the general public that this kind of injustice is a daily reality for many Palestinians. I disagree. Despite its attention-grabbing potential, I contend that positing Corrie's death as a critical event in the social justice movement for Palestinian rights is troubling and undermines its fundamental anti-racist claims. In other words, while the ritualized anniversary ceremonies and commemorations of Corrie's death may help to build solidarity for Palestinian struggles, activists and organizers need to be wary of centering her in this movement.

A difficult question that this discussion raises, then, is how might one mourn Corrie's death and employ it for summoning justice while not simultaneously overshadowing the lives of the countless Palestinians whose deaths go unnoticed? The answer to this question lies, in part, in scholarship on the sociology of emotions. In fact, the question raised by Lauren Berlant at the beginning of this chapter is a useful starting point for this dilemma. She asks, "What if compassion and coldness (or withholding) are not opposite at all but are two sides of a bargain that the subjects of modernity have struck with structural inequality?" In her early ground-breaking work, Arlie Hochschild raised similar concerns and coined the term "emotional labour" to consider the roles that certain conscious performances or displays of emotions can serve in specific contexts. For instance, she asked, "What happens when the emotional display that one person owes another reflects a certain inherent inequality?"[85] Some innovative scholarship in recent years has begun to examine the ways in which emotions are mobilized in social movements, showing that emotions not only influence various phases of a movement, they are also the very stakes of a struggle.[86] Drawing from these theories, one can see that Rachel Corrie's death exemplifies the proposition that compassion and coldness are indeed two sides of the same coin of emotional labour that is performed with specific political aims. Most certainly, Corrie's death is a clear instance of an emotional event. As Goubin Yang writes, "Both movement activists and their opponents perform emotion work in order to shape the outcomes."[87]

What is missing from this important body of writing, however, is attention to the racialized dimensions of emotional expressions.[88] The analysis presented in this chapter illustrates the significance of the ways in which systems of racialized knowledge/power shade (if not determine) the possibilities for the public expression of emotions. To resist falling into these trappings, whereby Corrie can be seen as either hero or villain, it is more instructive to notice and draw attention to the racialized logics that equally structure both types of responses. That is, the challenge is to resist taking "a side" in the emotional responses garnered by her death and to instead notice how these responses are structured by race.

CHAPTER TWO

The CPT Kidnapping: Citizenship, Sexuality, and the Racialized "Politics of Life"

In late 2005, four men with a group called Christian Peacemaker Teams (CPT) were kidnapped in Baghdad. Two of the men, James Loney and Harmeet Singh Sooden, were identified as Canadian citizens, Tom Fox as American, and Norman Kember as British. Soon after the kidnapping was reported on international news, the public learned that CPT is a long-established organization whose members are driven by the Christian faith and the principle of nonviolence and that the organization had an ongoing presence in Iraq since October 2002, prior to the last US military invasion.[1] Their motto is "getting in the way" which is meant to convey "multiple meanings including the practice of stepping between aggressors and victims."[2] By sending delegations into war zones, CPT members believe that they are "able to pass on some safety through their presence, with limited risk to themselves."[3] The presence of these First World activists also signifies surveillance to the extent that they document and disseminate reports on the injustices they witness with the aim of summoning international pressure.[4]

Following the news of the kidnapping, an insurgent Iraqi group calling itself "The Swords of Righteousness Brigade" released a videotape on 29 November 2005 indicating that the hostages would be killed unless all prisoners in American and Iraqi detention centres were released within a week. Subsequently, the deadline was extended by other broadcasted, videotaped messages. The fate of the four men remained unknown until 27 January 2006 when a new video was released stating that the US-led forces had one "last chance" to release Iraqi prisoners, or the hostages would be killed. On 10 March 2006, Tom Fox's body was found in Baghdad; he had been killed by gunfire. Later that month, after nearly four months in captivity, the remaining three hostages were rescued during a military operation involving British, American, Canadian, and Iraqi forces in which no shots were fired. On 26 March 2006, the three surviving men returned to their countries of residence.[5]

This kidnapping challenges the assumption that the presence of First World bodies provides safety or protection. Instead, it demonstrates that since the international community is invested in the well-being of First World activists, their bodies can become potential negotiating tools for insurgent forces precisely because of the value placed on white/Western bodies, as discussed in the previous chapter. In fact, the targeting of foreigners was clear in the case of the CPT kidnapping because when the four men were abducted, their driver and translator, both Iraqis, were released.[6] Furthermore, by the time of the kidnapping, it had become common knowledge that in addition to Iraqis, foreigners in Iraq were also at high risk for abductions. The international news media were reporting regularly on kidnappings that had been orchestrated by various groups. According to some of these news reports, more than 200 foreigners had been kidnapped in Iraq in the previous eighteen months.[7] Moreover, several of these publicized kidnappings ended with the hostages being killed. The CPT kidnapping therefore made evident a contradiction in the assumption that whiteness can necessarily be strategically used to increase safety and protection. Instead, this kidnapping revealed that in certain geopolitical contexts, it is the activists' classification as white within a global racial hierarchy that also makes them vulnerable.

In many ways, this kidnapping exemplifies the effectiveness of the strategy of accompaniment-observer transnational solidarity activism. Soon after the news of the kidnapping of the four men spread, political leaders from their countries of residence declared this situation to be of urgent priority and committed substantive resources to attain their safe return.[8] As discussed with respect to the Freedom Summer campaigns in Chapter One, this is the expected response and the reason why the publicized presence of these activists is used.[9] Indeed, the kidnapping did provoke the kinds of official responses that one would expect when First World activists end up in dangerous situations abroad.

My interest in this kidnapping extends beyond pointing to its general outcome. Rather, as I will show, it is the particularities around the case of the CPT kidnapping that are worthy of close examination because of some of the complex and contradictory responses it generated. For example, it is noteworthy and unprecedented that the news of this kidnapping sparked public responses by members of controversial organizations such as Hamas and Hezbollah, as well as from individuals being detained in First World countries like Canada who called or actively campaigned for the release of the four men. An important aspect of the responses to this kidnapping was related to the sexuality of one of the kidnapped men who, after the rescue, publicly revealed that he is gay.

In this chapter I want to examine these particularities to further consider the ways in which citizenship and race operate through these interventions. More specifically, by examining the media representations of the kidnapping of four men, and the subsequent rescue of three of them, this chapter explores how racialization and sexuality work together to construct First World citizen subjectivity and how national identity is integral to this construction.

CITIZENSHIP, FIRST WORLD ACTIVISTS, AND WHITENESS: AN INTERPRETIVE FRAMEWORK

The concept of citizenship will be employed in several overlapping ways. It will be used in the commonplace sense to refer to a legal status put in place through systems of categorizations based on gender, class, ethnicity, and sexuality.[10] The analysis that follows will be especially informed by those who have studied the ways in which questions of race and sexuality are inextricably linked to citizenship.[11] Following the work of David Goldberg, citizenship is understood here as a subject-making practice in which citizen-subjects "interiorize" state discourses.[12] Lastly, citizenship will be conceived as an "act" that is performed.[13]

Since the CPT's strategies of witnessing and/or "getting in the way" centre on a politics of a visible embodied presence, the idea of a marked *whiteness* in this case study pertains to certain national identities and their incumbent notions of civility.[14] This conception of whiteness can be best explained by considering the racialized identity of Harmeet Singh Sooden, one of the two Canadian men who were kidnapped. As a man of colour born into a Sikh family and raised in Zambia, and with legal status in two white-settler states (Canada and New Zealand), Sooden's subject position reveals the shifting, context-specific, and fluid ways in which whiteness operates. In other words, as a First World citizen and member of a Christian organization, Sooden represented what Dyer refers to as a "gradation of whiteness"[15] as compared to Loney's unambiguously white-Anglo-Christian, Canadian identity.[16] That is, it is important to consider how different Canadian nationalist understandings were inscribed onto the two "Canadian" men's bodies.[17]

TRANSNATIONAL ACTIVISM AND THE "POLITICS OF LIFE"

Didier Fassin's study of the medical humanitarian aid project of Médecins Sans Frontières (MSF) in Iraq greatly resonates with the analysis presented here, in part because it too explores a kidnapping.[18] Fassin describes a situation in which two members of the MSF team in Baghdad were abducted by agents of the Iraqi intelligence service within days of the invasion of Iraq in 2003 and released nine days later. After the kidnapping, the MSF subsequently deemed this mission too risky and suspended its activities, and their departure, ironically, coincided with the start of the war. As Fassin points out, they left at the exact moment when their assistance was needed.[19] For Fassin, this response "highlighted the contradictions inherent in a declared politics of risking lives" because as he puts it, the politics "did not hold up in the face of real danger."[20] Although the MSF's reaction to the kidnapping is not unusual, Fassin contends that it nevertheless points to the fact that when faced with danger, these organizations are completely diverted from their initial goals and instead "concentrate on a single aim – saving the abducted companion."[21]

Fassin's incisive analysis also draws attention to the fact that at a tangible level of offering medical care, the handful of First World MSF doctors in Iraq would have very little impact when compared to the hundreds of Iraqi medical professionals working in the thirty-five hospitals in Baghdad.[22] This situation, Fassin argues, demonstrates that it is the First World citizenship and not the medical training *per se* of the MSF doctors that renders them valuable and, therefore, that their effectiveness is clearly underpinned by the "sacredness" attached to their lives as compared to the sacrificial lives of the local civilians.[23] Importantly, Fassin notes that the MSF makes an internal distinction between the lives of "expatriates" who come almost exclusively from First World countries, and "nationals" who are local agents considered as mere paid employees – a distinction that involves not only huge differences in salary and health insurance coverage, but also has consequences regarding social and political protection when violence erupts. For example, whereas attempts are made to spare expatriates from violence, nationals are not given similar institutional protection.[24] Fassin thereby contends that such interventions belie a "radical inequality" in the ways that human lives are imbued with value and meaning.[25]

Although the humanitarian efforts of the CPT and the MSF clearly have different mandates, they share some important commonalities. For one, they both had projects in the geopolitical context of Iraq during the war.[26] A second commonality is that the memberships of both groups are largely comprised of citizens of First World nations who can usually travel to conflict zones around the world without question. Finally, although neither of the groups explicitly frame their interventions in terms of race, their actions are clearly racialized in that they trade on the privilege of First World citizenship. Fassin's work is most pertinent for my purposes not only because his examination of the MSF kidnapping has direct parallels with the CPT kidnapping, but mainly because he is one of the few writers who have theorized this otherwise overlooked or taken for granted core issue of the differential valuing of human life, an issue he captures with the phrase "a politics of life."[27] Although this idea builds upon the more commonly known concept of biopolitics put forth by Michel Foucault, Fassin explains that it differs analytically. Whereas biopolitics mainly relates to the regulation and governance of populations and technologies of power (i.e. defining, studying, counting, and controlling populations), Fassin's "a politics of life" has less to do with the way populations are governed, and more to do with "the evaluation of human beings and the meaning of their existence."²⁸ In other words, while Fassin concedes that humanitarian intervention is biopolitical in the Foucauldian sense because it involves the management and regulation of populations, spaces, knowledge, and authority, he insists that humanitarian intervention is also a "politics of life" because it involves selectively attributing meaning to human lives during the processes of determining which lives are to be saved.²⁹

With this, and how it relates to the racialized hierarchy of grief discussed in the previous chapter, I now turn to several specific representational features of the CPT kidnapping with a particular focus on James Loney, to examine how it exposes a politics of life as well as to consider how it lent itself to subject-making practices and various forms of citizenships.

ORIENTALISM IN THE NEWS

As soon as news of the CPT kidnapping spread in the media, the story became a clear example of what Aamir Mufti and Ella Shohat refer to as a "great drama of origins, loyalty, belonging and betrayal."³⁰ Media reports varied greatly in their portrayal of the CPT activists. In a tone of sympathetic condescension, similar to that used in the case of Rachel Corrie, some reports presented the activists as simpletons lacking in "common sense," too blinded by their spiritual visions to understand the politically charged environment in which they were operating.³¹ Others were much harsher, even hostile, in their criticism, describing the activists as "ridiculous people" who "elected to place their lives at risk," and who therefore got what they deserved.³² By invoking the familiar "either you are with us or against us" refrain heard in the American press coverage of the Iraq war, some reports alleged that the activists' "real though unadmitted motives are hatred of Western democracy and admiration for totalitarianism."³³ The three surviving rescued men were especially condemned for what was seen as the half-hearted thanks they gave the soldiers who freed them and for the statement they issued declaring that they forgave their abductors.³⁴

The controversy surrounding these men continued when in 2007, James Loney was widely criticized for declaring that he would not testify against his abductors; and in 2008, Norman Kember made the British Broadcasting Corporation (BBC) news' headlines for helping to fund the bail of an Islamic preacher who was an alleged aide to Bin Laden. Given the profound limits set by the "good and evil" and "threats to democracy and freedom" discourses used to revive imperialist patriotism after 9/11, it seems predictable that the CPT activists would be negatively characterized as either naive simpletons or as traitors.[35]

On the other end of the spectrum, and in a pattern that closely resembles the extreme responses provoked by Rachel Corrie's death (explored in Chapter One), a few, but no less noteworthy, positive representations of the rescue appeared in the media. Perhaps the most striking was an editorial written days after the rescue by Tony Burman, the News Editor in Chief of the Canadian Broadcasting Corporation (CBC), who publicly reproached his fellow Canadian journalists for their disparaging reports about the kidnapped men.[36] In his view, while criticisms of the activists were to be expected from British and American newspapers, such "outbursts of hostility" in Canada were "somewhat perplexing." He explains:

> Most of us not only felt genuine relief and happiness about the rescue but, more profoundly, saw in these "peacemakers" something that was quite admirable, courageous – and classically Canadian. A desire to get involved. To help out. To make a difference even if it involves real personal risk. That's what Canadians do, in very real terms. I think many of us saw in the actions of this group – at least with the two Canadians – something that was part of a history of peaceful Canadian involvement in the world. Not military conflict or conquests, but peacemaking and peacekeeping. Perfect? Of course not. But constructive and honourable? Yes.[37]

From Burman's perspective, the actions of the CPT activists were not disloyal. Rather, they were exemplary of Canadian identity. Despite the CPT's explicit position of being against many of the foreign policies that Canada supports, Burman represents them as quintessentially Canadian in their values. In other words, the actions of the CPT and specifically those of James Loney came to be seen as symbolic of a peaceful Canadian national identity.

In contemplating such a representation, one must bear in mind that within countries like Canada, news is manufactured through a process that involves fact selection and story construction (using exacting language arranged in a particular sequence) that supports dominant corporate media interests and the force of the state.[38] Furthermore, as will be discussed in Chapter Three, the CBC is a Crown Corporation initially created in 1936 as a public broadcasting service with the explicit mandate of resisting US cultural domination of the Canadian media, and it continues to play an instrumental role in the production of Canadian culture and to instil pride in Canadian national identity.[39] Thus, what is significant in Burman's account of the kidnapped men is the citizen-making processes through which the activists are brought back into the nationalist fold and inscribed with the "Canadian" traits of innocence and benevolence.

More specifically, it is a particularly salient example of how Canadians imagine and represent themselves as *not* implicated in war, despite the concrete evidence indicating the contrary.[40] The message clearly conveyed through Burman's kind portrayal of the Canadian CPT activists is that unlike the direct combat involvement of the US and Britain in the Iraq war, Canadians are humanitarians in this arena. This widespread perception conveniently denies the fact that since the end of the Cold War in 1990–91, Canada's military forces have intervened six times in capacities that exceeded unarmed support or assistance, including participating in three of the four major wars of the period – the Gulf War and wars in Kosovo and Afghanistan. It also denies that Canada is one of world's largest supplier of military goods.[41] In fact, when news of the kidnapping spread, many Canadians were surprised to learn that the Canadian military was in Iraq, prompting Prime Minister Stephen Harper to explain that since the beginning of the war, some troops had been sent there as part of a long-standing exchange program with US, British, and other NATO forces.[42]

Some of the more insidious ways that hegemonic discourses were reproduced in the representations of this kidnapping can be seen in an in-depth interview with James Loney on 6 June 2006 on a popular current events radio show, *The Current*, which is also broadcast by the CBC. Several times during this interview, attributes of violence and peace were differentially assigned to Muslims and Christians, respectively. Indeed, the host's tone of questioning was powerfully suggestive as she continuously marveled at Loney's ability to hold on to the principle of nonviolence while confronting such depravity. For example, in one excerpt, the host focused on Loney's "internal struggle" about using violence to escape from his kidnappers. She stated: "But you were struggling with this as if you would think that you would be a bad person to do something to them to get out even though they had put you in that position ... Your [captors] did not have those qualms."[43] The way violence is naturalized onto particular bodies is evident in the host's confident assertion that the kidnappers did not have the same moral qualms about violence that Loney did. That she assumes to "know" the inner moral workings of the kidnappers is an indication of what postcolonial theorists identify as modes of recognition within systems of power.[44] Another example of an insidious way that hegemonic discourse is portrayed in the representations of the CPT kidnapping occurred in the form of an anecdote that Loney told about the kidnappers questioning him about his belief in nonviolence: "[O]ne of the captors ... he would say, 'You know, if the United States invaded Canada, what would you do? Wouldn't you fight back? Wouldn't you *Mujahideen?*' I said, 'No. I am *Isa Salaam*.' Jesus of peace, that was how we tried to describe ourselves."[45] In considering how the West/Oriental binary is constructed through such assertions, the body of work that has theorized the relationship among whiteness, Christianity, nationalism, and imperialism is useful.[46] These theories would suggest that as a white, male, Anglophone, Christian Canadian, James Loney came to represent a long-established "figure" of civility and democratic values, especially when juxtaposed against the figure(s) of the dangerous Muslim Other(s). Thomas Ross posits that such contemporary representations of the clash of civilizations are underpinned by a racialized notion of "our God versus their God."[47] Indeed, one can see how within this binary Loney is the White Christian warrior – a figure who comes into being against an opposite figure of an archenemy, the radical Muslim terrorist.

While at face value, these depictions of the kidnappers as violent and those kidnapped as peaceful appear to be simply fact-based –

certainly, there is no disputing the fact that the kidnapping was an instance of a violent abduction of peaceful Christians by a group of Muslims – here, it is important to notice the parameters of how this story of the kidnapping *could* be told and how those parameters are already set by existing racialized understandings of the Western self and the Other.[48] The extent to which the story of the CPT kidnapping was always already embedded in a much larger, older, and familiar codified narrative can be best seen in the ways that Loney attempts to offer an account that complicates the good Christian/ bad Muslim dichotomy. Indeed, throughout this interview, Loney repeatedly tries to contextualize the violence in Iraq as a consequence of the militarism and exploitation of imperialism, and in so doing, he depicts the kidnappers as desperate people being pushed to use this kind of violence. In one instance, Loney emphasizes that the captors did not hurt or mistreat them, clearly stating that he and his team-mates were never beaten or subjected to any kind of psychological mind games or terror. He even went so far as to state that "there were many acts of care" shown to them by their captors, for example buying them a cake for Christmas. He also recounted what he referred to as "moments of kindness" that were shared between the kidnapped activists and their kidnappers.[49] In so doing, Loney is clearly attempting to offer less of a one-dimensional and, instead, a more nuanced view of the captors.

Similarly, in Loney's discussion about the soldiers who rescued him, he states that he believes it is important to honour the soldiers' noble spirits and intentions of being willing to risk their lives, to make clear that it is not the individual soldiers he is against, but the larger military system of which they are a part. However, Loney's efforts to offer contextual information about the system he refers to as the "military machine" are obscured by the host, who is more interested in knowing how he reconciles the fact that in the end, he was rescued by the same soldiers whose presence he was in Iraq to protest – a point that virtually all the media reports emphasized.

I propose that the media's emphasis on the fact that the anti-war activists had to be saved by the military functioned as the moral of the story of the kidnapping. A cursory look at postcolonial critiques of the genre of captivity narratives in which white people are captured by the racial Other helps to illustrate this point. This was a theme in publications ranging from mid-nineteenth-century

Canadian newspapers, novels about "invasion," and travel narratives appearing in journals and periodicals. The new media technology of illustrations provided the visual spectacle alongside the texts to reach wider audiences while it cemented the stereotyped matrix of the Other as a national enemy.[50] Mary Louise Pratt explains that in the period of early colonialism and the slave trade, captivity narratives were essentially about the boundary crossing and reintegration that shaped the white settler imaginary.[51] Moreover, captivity narratives were used as a rationale for acquiring land and as warnings during times of war to reinforce the values of Christianity and civilization.[52] The appeal of such stories, according to Pratt, was the vicarious adventure and excitement they provided.[53] Through Pratt's work, one can begin to see that the media depictions of Loney's kidnapping and rescue follow many of the same plot devices as the earlier stories, in which the "crossing" may be voluntary at first but often transforms into violence and force. And as was often the case in early colonial captivity narratives, James Loney, the contemporary protagonist, survived and returned. Thus, the media representations of Loney's kidnapping presented Canadians with a "close encounter" that both satisfied our Orientalist curiosity and confirmed widespread beliefs about the violent Other.[54]

Loney's failed attempts to disrupt the dominant paradigm in the CBC interview also make evident the depth of investments in, and the tenacious hold of, the racialized and Orientalist underpinnings of these representations. As mentioned earlier, at the time that this interview aired, many Canadians were ambivalent about Canada's military involvement, especially the government's decision to extend Canada's "peacekeeping" mission in Afghanistan. Therefore, one must also wonder how the media representations of Loney's kidnapping may have helped the Canadian public justify the occupations and wars in which the country was implicated.

NATIONAL BELONGING AND LONEY'S SEXUALITY

The racialized "us-peaceful/them-violent" dichotomy also emerges through various media representations regarding Loney's sexuality. After his return to Canada, the Canadian public learned that Loney is gay, in a long-term partnership with a man named Dan Hunt, and that the CPT had made a decision to keep Loney's sexuality hidden from his captors (and therefore from the public at large) until he returned because of the fear that it might further endanger him. Certain details about the lives of the other kidnapped men that possibly could have further jeopardized their safety were also kept hidden, including the fact that Fox had previously served in the US Marine Corps, and that Sooden had once worked for a New Zealand defence contractor.[55] Given the already life-threatening situation in which the men found themselves, one can easily understand why Loney's supporters erred on the side of caution by not disclosing any facts that may even have had the remote possibility of exacerbating the risks to the kidnapped men. It should also be noted that Hunt's need to remain invisible throughout this ordeal, at a time when the family members of the other three men were seen and heard from regularly on the news, understandably caused him great distress.[56]

With an appreciation for both the protective instincts that motivated the CPT's decision, and the emotional anguish that Hunt's erasure entailed, the response that not revealing Loney's sexuality provoked from some gay and lesbian media in Canada is worthy of further interrogation, particularly because of the ways in which it was mobilized. For example, referring to the CPT's decision not to reveal Loney's homosexuality while under captivity, an article that appeared in *Capital Xtra*, a free-weekly newspaper for the lesbian, gay, bisexual, and transgender (LGBT) communities, suggested that Loney and Hunt "*were forced to* hide their relationship in the face of intense media scrutiny for fear that the wrong word or a misplaced gesture would cause the kidnappers to kill Loney for being queer."[57] Thus, the difficult struggle of the CPT around this weighty decision in the face of many unknowns was reduced to the idea that Loney's partner was "forced to" hide from the public and framed as evidence of the "backwardness" and lack of freedom of the geopolitical region of the Middle East – a variation on a long-established colonial discourse.[58]

In contrast, Canada, as part of the West, is represented as an exceptionally tolerant space for gays and lesbians.[59]

Indeed, in some of the media representations, Loney and Hunt's relationship is depicted as the epitome of Canadian liberalism and tolerance. We are told they met at summer camp at age 16 and now live "out" in a tolerant community in Toronto.⁶⁰ Yet, the author of the *Capital Xtra* article suggests that this touching love story is interrupted by Muslim Others whose intolerance swept them back into the closet. Perhaps the most salient example of this tolerance positioning came in a statement made by Gilles Marchildon, former executive director of EGALE – a pan-national Canadian lesbian, gay, bisexual, and transgender lobby and advocacy group. In reference to the decision to keep Loney's sexuality hidden, Marchildon declared Canada a "beacon of light in a world still too often darkened by ignorance and intolerance."⁶¹ This demonstrates the depths of investment in this racialized national mythology insofar as Canadian tolerance of homosexuality is being publicly exalted by a man whose job is to draw attention to the injustices that gays and lesbians face in Canada. Bearing in mind that same-sex marriage legislation was passed by the Canadian Parliament within a year of the CPT kidnapping, Marchildon's statement can also be seen as a continuation of a discourse that sets Canada as an international leader on gay rights. Furthermore, this tolerance positioning obscures the fact that many gay and lesbian people in Canada do make the choice to keep their sexual identity hidden to minimize the homophobic threats of job loss, shunning, and physical violence that continues.

The nationalist aspects of the representations of Loney's sexuality are also significant vis-à-vis notions of "multi-layered" citizenship and "the politics of belonging."⁶² Although these concepts are usually applied to illustrate how people of colour who are citizens cannot truly belong, I use them to show that the reverse is true. That is, the national belonging of those racialized as white endures. Indeed, the story of the CPT kidnapping demonstrates how Loney's sexuality comes to reinforce his citizenship as Canadian. What seems to be operating in these depictions can be best understood through what Jasbir Puar describes as "the intersections, confluences, and divergences between homosexuality and nationalism."⁶³ In linking the discourses of nation with discourses of sexuality, Puar persuasively argues that the "gay rights" project buttresses national mythology to produce a form of "homonormative nationalism," which emerges through the Orientalist figure of the terrorist.⁶⁴ Puar points out that the collusion between homosexuality and Western nationalisms is particularly compelling because in allowing for certain sexual others, nationalist imaginings serve to reproduce a racialized other, all the while reiterating heterosexuality as the norm.[65]

Ironically, there *were* repercussions to Loney's public "coming out" in Canada. For example, he and his supporters allege that the publicity around his sexuality prompted an Ontario Catholic camp he once worked at to close.[66] A year later, when Loney was scheduled to speak at a Roman Catholic conference, the invitation was withdrawn because of the church's position against homosexuality.[67] In such instances, the CPT and Loney himself continuously attempt to challenge the racist idea that homophobia only exists "over there." Indeed, Loney has publicly stated that some of the experiences he has faced in Canada "parallel" what made him keep his sexual orientation a secret during the kidnapping, and that some of the silencing attitudes he faces here "feel very similar to those [he] faced in Iraq."[68] More recently, while compiling various accounts of the kidnapping for a book entitled *118 Days: Christian Peacemaker Teams Held Hostage in Iraq*, the CPT ran up against the homophobic attitudes of publishers who demanded that they revise or cut out some of the chapter that Hunt contributed, which discusses his relationship with Loney.[69] The preface of the CPT book explains that after two church presses agreed that there would not be any censorship, they withdrew from the project just before going to print because the CPT refused to make the cuts.[70] One of the publishers said they had received negative feedback from church leaders, one of whom characterized Hunt's chapter as "a pro-gay apologetic."[71] The CPT explains this editing requirement as emerging from the same system of homophobia that led them to the decision to hide Loney's sexuality in the first place. The CPT refused to make the edits and chose instead to self-publish the book.

SUBVERTING THE SCRIPTS:
SOLIDARITY AS RECIPROCITY
AND LONEY'S "ACTS OF CITIZENSHIP"

This kidnapping also gave rise to multiple displays of solidarity from members of Muslim communities worldwide who appealed through petitions and demonstrations for the release of the four

CPT men.[72] For example, in addition to internationally respected Muslim scholars and clerics, militant groups such as Hamas, Hezbollah, and the Muslim Brotherhood all called for the release.[73] In Canada, a strikingly unexpected appeal came from a group of non-Canadian-citizen Muslim men being held indefinitely on "Security Certificates" without charge on the basis of secret evidence. These men, Mahmoud Jaballah, Mohammad Mahjoub, and Hassan Almrei, publicly called on the kidnappers to release the hostages in an open letter released to the Canadian media on 3 December 2005.[74] Addressing the kidnappers, it stated: "If you love Allah, if you have goodness in your heart, please deal with this matter as righteous Muslims and do not let these kind, caring, compassionate and innocent people suffer ... We hope and pray to see these captives freed as much as we hope and pray for our own freedom here in Canada, a freedom for which James Loney has worked so hard."[75] Similar efforts were made by detainees held as suspected terrorists under secret evidence in the UK who also attempted to influence the actions of the kidnappers through televised appeals for "mercy" and open letters expressing their solidarity with the CPT captives.[76]

The extraordinary aspect of these responses is that they represent a rare occasion in solidarity and humanitarianism activism in which the typically one-way relationships between the givers and receivers are challenged.[77] Indeed, such displays of solidarity usually involve people from the First World speaking out on behalf of Others. Yet, in this instance the tables were turned, and as a result a more mutual form of solidarity was sparked. Furthermore, just as First World activists use their influence to pressure their states, these Muslim groups and individuals mobilized and organized to use whatever persuasion they had to sway the kidnappers. In other words, each group strategically used their clout with their respective communities.

In analyzing these events in terms of mutual reciprocity, Peter Nyers points out that the interventions of the men being held on security certificates blurred the separation between hostages/kidnappers.[78] Additionally, he points out that although as detainees they were at the bottom of the social hierarchy ladder of power, these men nevertheless spoke out *as if* they were members of the community of equals," and in so doing disturbed the status quo.[79] However, according to Nyers, "the Canadian media only made passing reference to the detainees' letter, usually in the context of stories about the CPT kidnapping that discussed more 'legitimate' interlocutors, such as family members, civil society groups, and so on."[80] Nevertheless, the surviving kidnapped men and other members of the CPT have since stated that they believe that the interventions by the men held in Canada under security certificates and other Muslim groups helped to keep them alive.[81]

Reciprocity was generated yet again when, after the rescue, Loney resumed campaigning for the release of those held under security certificates and for Iraqis held in detention. After having been held in captivity himself, he was now better equipped to sensitize the public to the horrors and injustices of living in such conditions. In fact, immediately upon his arrival back to Canada, Loney issued a brief statement in which he mentioned prisoners around the world who are being held without charge, and how they need the kind of solidarity that he was shown. At that same time, Loney also put forward a plea for privacy: "I'm eager to tell the story of my captivity and rescue, but I need a little time first."[82] It was nearly two months later that Loney did the in-depth interview on *The Current* discussed earlier in this chapter. That was just one of several appearances that Loney made that week on Canadian news programs to talk about his ordeal – not coincidentally the same week that he was participating in the *Campaign to Stop Secret Trials in Canada*, a protest against the ongoing detainment of the men being held on Security Certificates (some of whom had written the letter appealing to the kidnappers to release the CPT hostages).[83] As a media-savvy activist, his efforts were no doubt, carefully timed. With the knowledge that he had become popular, Loney thus effectively diverted some of the attention about his captivity in Iraq to the captivity of the five men in Canada. Repeatedly, he likened his experience in Iraq to the injustices faced by the men being held on Security Certificates. For example, drawing on his own experience, Loney would say that he came to realize that freedom is a very precious thing, always adding that this realization helped him to imagine how awful it must be for the men held on Security Certificates, and how unjust it was to detain them indefinitely without charge.[84]

Similarly, effective diversion strategies can also be seen in the ways that the CPT handled the media responses to Loney's rescue and in its decisive efforts to use this as an opportunity to make a connection to the ongoing suffering of the Iraqi people. Although the CPT was proactive in their anti-militarism-media work long before the kidnapping, afterwards they could make their case more persuasively.[85] This is best reflected in the first official statement the CPT issued after Loney and the other hostages were released in which they blamed US and British aggression in Iraq, and not the Iraqis themselves, for the capture of their members. The statement expressed outrage that four pacifists were being made to suffer for a war they vehemently opposed: "We are angry because what has happened to our teammates is the result of the actions of the US and UK governments due to the illegal attack on Iraq and the continuing occupation and oppression of its people."[86] In addition, they wrote: "During these past months, we have tasted of the pain that has been the daily bread of hundreds of thousands of Iraqis. Why have our loved ones been taken? Where are they being held? Under what conditions? How are they? Will they be released? When?"[87] By drawing a parallel between what Loney's family and friends went through and the experiences of others living in similar conditions, the CPT sought to rouse the Canadian public into a higher comprehension of the profound injustices of war.

To better understand these interventions by Loney and the CPT, it helps to draw on Engin Isin's analytical approach towards studying how subjects enact themselves as citizens.[88] Isin argues for the need to investigate acts of citizenship as related to but distinct from the more commonly examined notions of citizenship as status or habitus.[89] He believes that the investigation of "acts of citizenship" is especially fruitful in light of the increasing movements and flows brought about by globalization, which have "generated new affinities, identifications, loyalties, animosities and hostilities across borders," making it no longer sufficient to merely examine citizenship as a legal status.[90] This understanding of citizenship shows that the interventions by Loney and the CPT are examples of a demonstration of affinity across borders. Indeed, by all counts, Loney's interventions can be considered as constituting Isin's definition of acts of citizenship in that they are temporally specific and creative examples in which he was subverting the dominant scripts.[91] In so doing,

Loney is not simply transforming himself into a citizen or claimant; rather, he is re-enacting the privilege attached to his legal citizenship and acting as a claimant on behalf of others.

SUMMARY

The rather sensational and dangerous situation that unfolded with the CPT kidnapping makes it an especially rich and somewhat exaggerated site for noticing the potential, contradictions, and imperialistic underpinnings of transnational activist/humanitarian efforts. By highlighting the moments when the dominant racialized script was subverted, this analysis has tried to show that such interventions can trigger meaningful disruptions to the existing systems of power, and can offer ways to contemplate how different acts of citizenship are productive for resistance strategies. Moreover, as Engin Isin explains, when investigating such "forms and modes of being political" we can also begin to identify how subjects become actors who might find their way out of the constraints that exist within the usual.[92]

CHAPTER THREE

The Compelling Story of the First World Activist in the War Zone

In addition to the protection they can offer by being physically present in war zones, many First World solidarity activists who travel to conflict zones also gather and disseminate reports on the conditions of violence and repression that they observe with the idea that they can raise awareness as well as summon political pressure because they relay information that is not readily available in mainstream Western media. Being physically present at the geopolitical site of conflict enables the activists to offer eyewitness testimonials and report on the conditions first-hand. Typically, the information they disseminate are moving accounts of the horrors they witness daily and the experiences of the local people they encounter. Many of them post reports through independent and alternative media while simultaneously working with mainstream media.

The focus of this chapter is the witnessing, documenting, and reporting practices of such activists, hereafter referred to as "citizen journalism."[1] Drawing from interviews with Canadians who travelled to Iraq and Palestine, my discussion is presented in two parts. The first describes four key themes that emerged from the activists' narratives regarding their racialized roles as citizen journalists: (1) a tendency among media to focus on the activists and the danger they face; (2) the ways in which the activists are presumed by others or by themselves to have an aptitude for objectivity and neutrality; (3) a presumption of independence and innocence; and (4) the dilemmas of "voice" faced by some of the activists.

In the second half of this chapter, I present an analytical discussion of these themes. Drawing from select studies on citizen journalism and war correspondence, as well as theoretical perspectives on representational practices, I consider how whiteness is negotiated and/or reproduced in this type of transnational citizen journalism.[2] I also consider the implications of circulating the activists' perspectives within existing mainstream media.

PART ONE: REPORTING FROM THE CONTACT ZONE

(1) A Focus on the Activists and the Danger They Face

A common reporting strategy employed by some of the activists was to set up media contacts in advance of their travel – for example, arranging to be interviewed by local news reporters in their hometowns. One activist who went to Palestine explained that he had programmed the phone number of the producers of a Canadian news radio program into his cellphone so that he could contact them immediately when violence erupted. The effectiveness of this pre-arranged contact with Canadian media was proven, in his view, when it allowed him to instantly report an incident where shots were being fired at civilian protestors. He said that the sound of live gunfire gave further credibility to his report, which was taped and aired on the radio.

The significance of the background sound of artillery was echoed by another activist who said that he "became famous" when, for a few days, his family could not reach him in Palestine: "My daughter got panicky and called [a Canadian newspaper] and said, 'my dad is lost in Palestine. Last time we heard from him he was in Ramallah in Arafat's compound.' Well this sounded like a human interest story so this reporter got a hold of me in Balata and interviewed me ... She called a couple of times, and the tank firing could be heard in the background of the house we were staying in. When I got back there was a photographer and reporter to interview me about the trip." The subtext of this news story, and several other similar ones, is that an extraordinary Canadian left a family and a comfortable, privileged life to help others, even at the risk of coming face-to-face with great danger.

Recognizing how they could use the attention on them to promote their social justice goals, many of the activists tried to use their positioning strategically. One activist referred to this as playing up the "local boy does good" angle. Despite this self-conscious, pragmatic approach, some activists were uneasy with the fact that certain incidents were only reported on because they were there. One example of such an activist is Alex, who explained that although he had only a peripheral role as someone who went to Central America to support a local activist who had long been "on the front lines" of organizing efforts, he was the one the media took most interest in. In other words, his efforts to publicize the oppressive conditions faced by some people in that region were overshadowed by the story of a Canadian activist who went there to help. Alex said this was most evident when, upon returning to Canada, he was met at the airport by what he described as "a circus" of cameras and reporters, all wanting to interview him about his experience. In contrast, when one of his Central American colleagues returned to Canada (where she had been living), she received very little media attention. Alex attributed this to "the importance of the passport and the white skin" and conceded that it was "the only way to get coverage on some of these issues."

(2) Objectivity, Neutrality, and the Capacity for Discerning Truths

In general, the activists said that they were perceived by Western media to be more knowing or trustworthy than the local people and were frequently asked by media to comment on the politics of situations that, in many cases, they knew little about. For example, after being in Palestine for only a few days, some were approached by journalists who wanted to interview them about their views on the political situation there. Many of the activists spoke about the difficult negotiations around their positioning as spokespeople or authorities. This was further complicated by the impression that the media would approach Western activists instead of local people because, as one activist put it, "we were white like them." Where possible, a few activists adopted a guiding principle whereby, rather than making statements to the press, they would try to refer journalists to a local person.

Others, however, took on the role of spokespeople uncritically and in fact seemed to share the view that they are non-partisan, objective observers who can give more accurate and less-biased accounts than locals can. This became evident when some activists described the frustration of feeling manipulated by people on various sides of a conflict and having to do "guesswork" to determine what was true. Judith explains: "One event happens and we would get as many stories about what happened as people that were there, depending on what they wanted you to know." Another activist believed, given her outsider positioning, that she and the other First World activists could better discern and speak "truths." Moreover, she believed that, given their commitment to working towards ending violence, activists are "truth-tellers ... in a world where that kind of truth doesn't always want to be heard."

In their enthusiastic attempts to get at the truth, some activists naively asked inappropriate questions or questions that could put people at risk. One activist named Dan described a particularly volatile time in Palestine when people suspected of being terrorists were being arrested, and gave an example of how tactlessly and inappropriately some activists attempted to gather information: "People were on edge and they were particularly distrustful of any new people around. And some activists would stick cameras in their faces and ask them things like, 'are you a freedom fighter?'" Dan explained that, at the time, this type of behaviour had escalated tensions to the point where Palestinian people in the community wanted those activists to leave. Furthermore, the trouble with such crude reporting practices, according to him, was that they hindered other members of his group who had approached the community sensitively and made efforts to build their trust.

Anticipating another trend in news coverage, several activists who had gone to Iraq in 2003, at the start of the war, tried to collect personal stories from "ordinary" Iraqis.[3] Listening to what ordinary people were saying and observing what effects the war was having on the everyday lives of Iraqis was believed to be valuable in the service of, as one activist put it, "exposing the official lies and spin that rely on distance and doubt to obscure the bloody realities of war."

To this end, one group of activists went to Iraq with the goal of interviewing as many Iraqis as possible. After a few days of trying to arrange interviews, however, they quickly realized that people were nervous about talking to them and reluctant to answer certain questions about the political situation in Iraq. Therefore, in an effort to document less-guarded perspectives, they approached their work more informally, opting not to use a microphone, and instead jotting down notes while socializing, for example, in a coffee shop or over a game of chess. This helped them to gain access to the insights of Iraqis more easily.

(3) The Presumed Independence and Innocence of Anti-war "Guerrilla" Journalism

This section focuses on the narrative of one Canadian activist, whom I will call Jerry, who went to Iraq as part of The Iraq Peace Team. The website of the Iraq Peace Team (IPT) explicitly states that American-dominated, Western media impede the truth from reaching North Americans. According to the website, that is the reason why IPT members "see their role partly as *guerrilla* journalists, disseminating their grounds-eye view of the war to an ever-expanding network of e-mail contacts and alternative press outlets."[4] Jerry joined the Iraq Peace Team because he was drawn to the idea of documenting and disseminating information, a role he had previously undertaken in various other efforts of citizen journalism.

Like some of the activists mentioned earlier, Jerry set up a relationship with the Canadian Broadcasting Corporation (CBC) Radio, a mainstream media outlet, before he went. He explained that CBC Radio was one of the first organizations he and his teammates approached because he had done some freelance work with them before and therefore had some connections there. Jerry and his colleagues believed that this would enable them to reach a much wider audience than they could by only using alternative media. By setting it up in advance, they reasoned that the CBC would know who they were and why they were there and would be prepared to interview them on short notice.

Jerry said that although at first he and his teammates were apprehensive about how the CBC producers would react to their ideas, they were pleasantly surprised with how open and receptive they were and felt very supported and encouraged by them. In practical terms, the support they received from the CBC included the use of recording equipment and space on the CBC website for posting diary entries. In their preliminary meetings with the CBC, Jerry and his teammates were told to report personal stories about ordinary Iraqis trying to survive and function in Iraq. The rationale was that since, under the circumstances, the Iraqis could not communicate their stories themselves, the activists could share those stories for them.

Two significant points emerge from Jerry's narrative. The first relates to his belief that, as an activist, he has increased independence and freedom from censure. Indeed, Jerry imagined himself to be an independent reporter functioning outside of the knowledge production structures of mainstream media. That he was not paid or otherwise compensated (Jerry and his teammates raised funds for their trip and took time off from their jobs to travel to Iraq) strengthened his belief in his independence, despite the fact that he had CBC's "unofficial" sponsorship. The second salient feature of Jerry's narrative is that it reveals that he saw himself not only as more free, but also more righteously motivated than professional journalists. For instance, he explained that he arrived in Iraq a month and a half before the bombing started and saw hundreds of journalists from around the world "waiting and hoping that a war would start." He said, "They were just aching to send anything back home that was newsworthy. And I would say [to myself], my goodness, is this what it comes to? You hope for a tragedy, a crisis like this?" What enabled Jerry to differentiate himself from other journalists were his anti-war political views, his activist intentions, and his mandate to report on the lives of ordinary Iraqis. In other words, he believed that because his position was explicitly anti-war, he would be able to transcend sensationalism and be more attuned to the day-to-day effects of the impending crisis.

The distinction he made between collecting stories as an activist and collecting stories as a journalist was unclear to me, so I asked him to clarify. He replied: "Journalists were not coming in as anti-war activists ... They came in without a preconceived idea of why they were there, most of them. Or they came in with mixed opinions, mixed perspectives ... We had an agenda coming in. We had a prescriptive idea of why we were there, what function we would serve, what kinds of messages we were looking at." Conceding that "everybody has a bias" and explicitly rejecting the notion of neutrality in journalism, he emphasized that what set him and his teammates apart was that their bias was at least "upfront." Another major difference for him was his authorial intention of being "for peace" or "anti-war" which, in his view, distinguished his actions as virtuous.

(4) The Dilemma of Speaking for the Other

The fourth theme pertains to the questions of voice that come up for First World solidarity activists who engage in various media work. This theme was exemplified best in the narrative of "Sarah," a Canadian activist who travelled to Iraq with the Christian Peacemaker Team (CPT). Compared to other human rights and solidarity groups in Iraq at the time of the war, the CPT had a long-established presence in Baghdad and was well respected by Iraqis. It was therefore especially well-positioned to attract media attention in order to publicize these issues. In fact, the CPT has been credited with a leading role in documenting and publicizing the detention of an estimated 14,000 Iraqis held without due process.[5] Furthermore, in January 2004, the CPT held a press conference on its findings regarding abuse in Iraqi prisons, four months before the Abu Ghraib prison scandal broke out in mainstream media.[6] Sarah explained that one of the central roles she and her teammates played in Iraq was to document the arrests and detention of Iraqis by US military forces and the effects this had on the detainees' families. As well, she and her team members acted as intermediaries between Iraqis and the occupying US forces.

What makes Sarah's experience and perspective interesting for this discussion relates to her previous CPT activism with Aboriginal people in New Brunswick, Canada, where she had already faced a dilemma concerning representation and voice. She explained that in an attempt to minimize racialized power relations, the official position of the CPT in its work with indigenous communities in Canada was to avoid making any statements to the media. Instead, CPT activists were encouraged to respond to media by referring reporters to an Aboriginal person because, she said, "colonialism removes the voice of the subject people [because] for years Aboriginal people have been spoken for." Yet, in Iraq, she said she found herself in a context which called for a different approach: "But I have to say, I wouldn't want to generalize this notion of 'speaking for' to all of our work, because with the Aboriginal groups, it is absolutely imperative not to speak for them. But for Iraq, it was different." She explained that, at the time, many Iraqis were desperate to get information about missing family members. However, since American soldiers stationed in Iraq often refused to speak directly to Iraqis, the activists would use their white and First World privilege to try and obtain information on their behalf. Sarah said that she believed using her racialized positioning as a white woman for "getting the ear" of the American soldiers was the right thing to do. She also explained that she and her teammates tried to minimize their concerns about speaking on behalf of Iraqis by constantly consulting with their Iraqi partners.

Although Sarah described her role in these contexts as "fraught," she said there was no other way that Iraqis and American soldiers would come together. With some reservations, Sarah and her teammates believed that if they proceeded cautiously, they could turn their privileged positioning into a meaningful and effective gesture of solidarity.

PART TWO:
NEGOTIATING REPRESENTATIONAL PRACTICES AND
FIRST WORLD POSITIONING

It goes without saying that the intentions behind the type of citizen journalism explored here are admirable. These activists put to use their relative mobility, resources, and authority to raise attention and compassion for people targeted by military violence. It is difficult to dispute that such efforts are especially needed in light of the dominant discourses that have surrounded the Middle East in recent years. As many scholars have shown, the racialized media depictions of Arab and Muslim communities since 2001 are more blatant and dangerous than ever, resulting in little room for the expression of non-binaristic thinking about current global conflicts.[7] My critical examination of these narratives is not meant to eclipse the worthy intentions of these activists. Indeed, I am especially interested in their representational practices because they are intended to be (and are largely perceived as) a form of resistance. In the spirit of advancing the goals of social justice activism, then, the critical race analysis that follows seeks to reveal some of the less obvious ways in which racialized power can pervade such representational practices.

Foregrounding this discussion is the writing of Edward Said who made evident the connections between practices of representation and the relations of racialized power and knowledge that they produce.[8] Following this, the practices that I examine in this chapter are not only understood as being embedded in power relations, but constitutive of them. In other words, my claim is not simply that such representational practices fail to challenge existing power relations, but that racialized power is in fact reproduced through them.[9]

In keeping with the overall aims of this book, my analysis is mainly concerned with the contextual ways in which whiteness operates and, in particular, its historical patterns and continuities.[10] Viewed through this conceptual lens, how might one understand the racialized dimensions of the citizen journalism practices described above? While recognizing that this particular form of citizen journalism may have the potential to disrupt the "us" and "them" dichotomies that otherwise permeate mainstream reporting, the approach I take also demands that we interrogate the exclusionary limits of who can safely and effectively take part in such reporting.[11] Certainly, in critically examining this type of citizen journalism, some questions that arise are ones posed by Sara Ahmed when she asks, "Who gains access to the lives of strangers, who is allowed into their space, and whose documentable knowledge of the strangers hence expands?"[12] Further underpinning this interrogation are the racialized aspects of embodied presence. By this I am referring to what I call "the compelling story of the white, First World activist in the war zone." As I have shown, when activists succeed at drawing the attention of mainstream media or the Western public, it is usually the activists themselves, and not the sites of the conflict they are in, that become the focal points of the story. In many cases, activists are featured in what journalists refer to as human interest or "soft" news stories which often focus on people rather than events. Typically, when reported on in such stories, the activists are asked about their intentions, the reactions of their own families, and are held up as exemplars of global citizenship. Underpinning these stories is a clear inference that it is the experiences and perspectives of those from the First World that are of primary interest.

Moreover, underlying the fact that gunfire lends credibility to their reports is an unspoken presumption about the inequality between Western and non-Western lives. What makes the efforts undertaken by these activists so compelling is that, by exposing themselves to danger, they concretely and immediately challenge the inequality between lives.[13] As shown in Chapter Two, the activists'/humanitarians' experiences are deemed newsworthy because of what Didier Fassin refers to as the sacredness attached to their lives, as compared to the sacrificial lives of the local civilians.[14] The value attached to their lives, Fassin argues, garners access to international media.[15]

One of the racialized dynamics that makes this activism effective is that white and First World activists are taken to be rational actors who are fair-minded about the politics of the region. To put it differently, and borrowing from Richard Dyer, unlike the people from the regions on which they are reporting, these activists are not seen to have the perceived bias of being from a certain race; they are "just human."[16] From the excerpts above, it is clear that some of the activists saw themselves this way, believing themselves to be objective observers, capable of less-biased accounts than the local people. Such displays of authority appear to mimic the role of what Sara Ahmed calls the "all-knowing stranger."[17] It also illustrates what Joseba Zulaika has referred to as an "ironic predicament" because although the public is interested in hearing their accounts and they are positioned as experts, often what little they know about their situation comes from the local people they are speaking about and whom they are supposed to be representing.[18] In many instances, the activists' narratives reveal that they understand themselves to be intrinsically equipped for the role of neutral observer and reporter.

To examine the relational and discursive aspects of whiteness as a racialized positioning in such instances of transnational activist citizen journalism, I adopt Davies' and Harré's methodological approach which pays attention to the ways in which people are positioned in discursive practices and the way in which the individual's subjectivity is generated through various positionings.[19] Davies and Harré contend that how we make sense of the world and our places in it can sometimes be revealed through how the self is positioned within story lines. The main tenet of this methodology as it applies to the discussion that follows is to examine the activists' narratives for what they understand their actual or metaphorical role to be. Importantly, Davies and Harré point out, these processes of discursive positioning are not necessarily intentional.

Returning to the themes that emerged in the activists' narrative and the ways in which they explained their political and moral commitments, one begins to see that some understood themselves to be arbiters of trustworthiness and uncritically assumed roles that involved moral judgment. Moreover the activists' determination to obtain the truth, however well-intentioned, often resulted in what Jean-Klein has described as an "investigative tenor," insofar as they often doubted what they were being told and felt the need to discern the authenticity of the personal stories they heard.[20] Most helpful for the purposes of understanding this dynamic is Said's observation that racialized binaries "naturally" set up the Westerner not only as a spectator, but also as a judge of the Others' behaviour.[21]

What is significant here is not whether they were in fact being told the truth. Rather, it is the notable absence of a critical understanding of how, as Jean-Klein points out, such documenting practices can be "hierarchical, paternalistic and coercive exercises which ideologically cloak these aspects of themselves."[22] Certainly, this could be said of the group of activists in Iraq who, as a means of overcoming people's reluctance to be interviewed by them, approached people more informally, and in social situations. I contend that their determined approach, however well intentioned, was not only paternalistic and coercive, but also raises ethical questions about informed consent.

What can also be gleaned from the interviews is that the activists who were attuned to the asymmetrical character of their roles as citizen journalists justified this positioning through their participation in "alternative" or "independent" journalism, as well as their anti-war political stance. In other words, discourses of exceptionalism could easily be detected in some of their narratives. This was clearly evident in Jerry's narrative insofar as his is a rich example for considering the presumed independence and innocence of citizen journalism. In fact, the proud way that Jerry described his work directly echoed much of the literature on citizen journalism, which largely identifies the practice as a means through which power will change hands and marginalized voices will be heard.[23] For example, in his book *We the Media: Grassroots Journalism by the People, for the People*, Dan Gillmor offers many examples that persuasively illustrate how the Internet enables people to speak out and access a diversity of news and opinions.[24] Although Gillmor concedes that at present, grassroots journalists are comprised of elite Westerners, he argues that the citizen journalism phenomenon "will give new voice to people who've felt voiceless."[25] His overall contention is that journalism is becoming more grassroots, democratic, and pluralistic. Moreover, he argues that the communication network will become "a medium for everyone's voice."[26]

In undertaking journalism work as an activist, Jerry clearly perceived himself to be outside of mainstream and hegemonic knowledge production practices. Although he was critical of attitudes he perceived in mainstream reporters in Iraq at the time, accusing them of feeding off crises to send good stories home, what enabled him to differentiate himself from professional journalists were his activist identity and his political views. He believed that because he was explicitly anti-war, he was able to transcend the seduction of voyeurism and sensationalism.

In many ways, Jerry's narrative exemplified those of many of the activists I interviewed, which squarely corresponded with what Tilley and Cokley refer to as the "three main mythological metanarratives" around citizen journalism: the myth of the Robinson Crusoe Citizen, the myth of the Noble Citizen, and the Myth of Perfect Plurality.[27] These activists understood their practices within a false dichotomy in which citizens speak the truth, while commercial media do not. Tilley and Cokley explain further: "The discourse from citizen journalists about citizen journalism suggests it provides greater truthfulness, less bias, more open access to information, more 'freedom' to report what is seen, and greater plurality of perspectives, especially counter-hegemonic perspectives."[28] Yet, several studies on journalism have refuted this claim. For instance, in her study of Iraq-war weblogs that were posted in the spring of 2003, Melissa Wall found that despite the fact that they saw themselves participating in an alternative and independent medium, the bloggers represented the war in a way not much different from representations in mainstream media.[29] This false sense of independence and freedom from censure exists in mainstream journalism as well. Writing about foreign war correspondents, Mark Pedelty points out that although most see themselves as maverick investigators who set out to uncover hidden truths, they have no more freedom than conventional journalists.[30]

Studies on the production of documentaries in public broadcasting add insights and raise further questions about the independence of the citizen journalism evident in Jerry's narrative, especially with respect to the blurred distinction as to whether he was working as a volunteer *with* and not *for* the CBC. Indeed, a historical study of the broadcast tradition in Canada by David Hogwarth reveals that since the mid-1930s, broadcasters have come to view documentary programming as a uniquely efficient way of telling stories about the nation.[31] Keenly aware of the costs involved in the production of documentary features, broadcasters developed new technologies and equipment specifically designed to cover "events where they happened and when they happened."[32] Hogwarth writes: "Only by means of a 'documentary factory,' according to some program supervisors, could the corporation produce the enormous and steady volume of material required by its public service mandate."[33] Moreover, he explains that when dealing with "controversial issues," they sought to cover a range of views while "not themselves expressing an opinion."[34] This suggests that the opportunity which the CBC granted Jerry and his teammates was not unique, but a common and economically efficient practice that has long been in use. By having an activist such as Jerry broadcast his reports from Iraq, the CBC arguably covered the requisite antiwar point of view for a "balanced" newscast in a very cost-efficient way. While Jerry saw the CBC helping him to achieve his goals, David

Hogwarth's study suggests that it was more likely to have been the other way around – he was helping the CBC.³⁵

That the CBC is the main public broadcasting network in Canada also raises significant questions about national identity. Barry Dornfeld's (1998) work reveals that the production of public broadcasting shares a great deal with processes that Benedict Anderson identified when describing nations as "imagined communities."³⁶ Furthermore, as a Crown Corporation, the CBC was created in an effort to resist US cultural domination of Canadian media and has therefore always served as a major instrument of the production of Canadian culture.³⁷ Thus, if one accepts the view that the representations of "public affairs" are never outside of the dominant force of the state, then one must question the subversive potential of the reporting practices of activists like Jerry.³⁸ In other words, despite his commitments, he cannot be assumed to have escaped interpellation by the state.

Lastly, in exploring issues of voice and who speaks for whom, Sarah's experience demonstrates that the material conditions of a particular geopolitical context require what some feminist scholars have referred to as a *situated* practice.³⁹ Her narrative shows that a fixed set of "dos and don'ts" for activists who are acting as citizen journalists is inappropriate because it can lead to a misguided understanding of what it means to use First World privilege effectively. It also highlights the paradox that would arise if, in a situation like in Iraq, activists refused to become spokespersons for local people on the basis of some fixed notion of what an antiracist practice entails. In other words, while in Iraq, had Sarah and her teammates refused that role of intermediary on the basis of an abstracted antiracist principle of refusing to speak for the Other, they would have been of little help to the Iraqi people who, within the violent conditions of war and occupation, could not access information, nor be heard.

To reflect on these larger questions about the politics of "voice," it helps to draw from feminist scholars who have long demanded that attention be paid to the effects of domination and subjugation that result from speaking. For instance, Ella Shohat contends that "voice" can be effectively used in achieving solidarity. The point, she argues, is to notice how speaking for is "rooted in global structural inequalities that generate such representational practices."[40] In other words, while it is hazardous to speak for someone, Shohat makes a distinction between that and speaking alongside someone.[41] Similarly, Sara Ahmed's discussion of feminist ethnography has particular resonance for these questions insofar as she offers ways of thinking about efforts to avoid dominant imperialist positioning. She clarifies that the most significant question is not whose voices can speak, but whose voices can be heard.[42] Drawing from Spivak, and extending Mary Louise Pratt's discussion of imperialist ventures into foreign spaces, Ahmed challenges the idea that the best way to avoid speaking for others is to avoid speaking at all.[43] Ahmed argues that such a position is a form of cultural relativism that functions, paradoxically, to confirm the privilege of those who are refusing to speak.[44] Ahmed's point is a persuasive one because it shows that to unreflectively assume a position of silence can defeat antiracist intentions. Instead of shallow understandings and simplistic solutions, then, what these scholars call for is a complex understanding of the effects of power that emerge through practices of speech.

SUMMARY AND IMPLICATIONS

The analysis presented here refutes the simplistic resolution that people with First World privilege must not participate in citizen journalism as transnational solidarity activists. Instead, in examining up close some of the contradictions that arise in citizen journalism efforts, it aims to identify some of the nuanced ways in which relations of racialized power might be better negotiated in specific circumstances. The example of Sarah's narrative, coupled with a theoretical discussion of the politics of voice, shows that Western activists can respond in ways that are responsible and useful. In considering the politics of voice, this chapter also illustrated how contextually specific judgements and practices are necessary, but difficult for activists to negotiate.

In highlighting some limitations of certain citizen journalism practices, this critique is premised upon the belief that representational practices, especially those motivated by social justice aims, must be continuously and critically examined. As I have shown, it is a racialized privilege and power that keeps the activists at the centre of the reporting and documenting efforts in which they are engaged. Furthermore, through an analysis of the activists' efforts to document, disseminate, and speak for the Other, I have illustrated that the power relations in which these efforts are embedded are often hidden by notions of neutrality and exceptionalism. Indeed, the pitfalls that the activists encounter, despite their good intentions, reveal the extent to which, as people from the First World, they are inscribed with authority and neutrality. Most importantly, they suggest that activists must carefully consider the complex ways in which their practices may inadvertently reproduce the very relations they seek to disrupt.

CHAPTER FOUR

Race-Conscious Transnational Activists with Cameras: Mediators of Compassion

What difference does it make where the antirace is performed, by whom, and in whose company?

Vron Ware and Les Back[1]

In her book *Regarding the Pain of Others*, Susan Sontag traces how photographic pictures are largely believed to provide evidence of "truth" in advanced capitalist democracies.[2] She and others have shown that when accompanying written or oral text, photographs reinforce ethnographic and journalistic claims on authority, independence, authenticity, neutrality and objectivity.[3] Sontag points out that this especially applies to photographs taken by amateurs because they are considered more authentic, or less "staged."[4] Wendy Kozol suggests that this is because on their own, witness testimonies can be discredited whereas visual documentation has historically retained great authority as juridical evidence.[5] Moreover, Catherine Lutz and Jane Collins argue that pictures of Westerners abroad "serve a validating function by proving that the author was there, that the account is a first-hand one."[6] These studies all variously show that visual images are an effective and efficient means of conveying experiences of suffering, violence and oppression. They offer an immediacy and level of persuasion that words on their own cannot.

Cameras are powerful tools for transnational activists attempting to draw attention to injustice. Building on the discussion in the previous chapter of the activists' representational practices, in this chapter I focus specifically on efforts to publicize human suffering through visual documentation. My objectives here are two-fold: to examine how one transnational activist negotiated ethical dilemmas about spectatorship and First World gaze, and to consider the potential of the uses of visual documentation as a tactic for subverting global white hegemony.

This chapter explores how individuals constitute themselves as ethical subjects through their representational practices and through the meanings they attribute to their actions. It draws from writers who have challenged the idea that ethical conduct, justice-oriented aims, and the desire to alleviate or witness suffering necessarily diminishes power structures.[7] The specific notion of ethics I am working with mainly emerges from the work of Foucault, who posits ethics as a practice or a "manner of being."[8] This particular definition of ethics is most relevant for my purposes because of its emphasis on the cognitive, rational, and intellectual dimensions of ethical subjectivity, particularly as it relates to the practice of self-determination.[9] Furthermore, ethics for Foucault are seen as embedded in, or "parasitic on" prevailing systems of knowledge and power.[10] Arendt's theorizing on moral responsibility complements Foucault's notion of ethics and further informs my analytic.[11] She is concerned with individual conduct and behaviour, and the process of determining right and wrong in order to "judge or justify others and themselves."[12] Morality, for Arendt, concerns the individual in his/her singularity. The answer to the question, "What ought I to do?" she explains, depends in the end on "what I need to do to be able to live with myself."[13] I am specifically interested in the *effects* of the activists' practices in relation to their understandings and constructions of themselves as ethical. I use the term "race-conscious" to refer to the activists' attempts to negotiate their practices vis à vis understandings of their privileged position.

NEGOTIATING ETHICAL DILEMMAS
AROUND PHOTOGRAPHY

To explore the ethics of photo-taking and representational practices, I will present a detailed analysis of the narrative of one activist who will be identified as "Bill." Bill is someone who would be considered a seasoned activist. He had first done accompaniment work in Central America in the 1990s, and eight years later in the Occupied Palestinian Territories. Through these experiences he became very cognizant of his role as a white man from the First World. What is compelling about his narrative is that it offers insights about issues of white gaze over time and in two distinct contexts. On the one hand, the incidents he recounted revealed contextually negotiated responses to the problematics of photo-taking. On the other hand, the issues of white gaze that he encountered were consistent in both geographical sites. Together these reveal the on-going *process* of becoming ethical in one's activist practice.

The first experience he recounted was a story about how he learned a lesson about the invasiveness of his photographic practices, given his positioning as a privileged person from the First World. This lesson took place in Central America where he was accompanying high-profile local human rights activists who were under threat. The specific situation he described was a meeting where these activists were strategizing. As their accompanier, he was present at the meeting:

> I went up with my camera and I asked if I could take a picture of them meeting. It was sort of a symbolic thing. The second I asked, she [Maria] said, "OK sure" and [then] she turned to ice. It was embarrassing. At that point it was too late because I had already asked, but I immediately twigged that she had absolutely no respect for me ... It was pretty humiliating for me. I felt bad ... It was a lesson for me.

This incident helped Bill understand something about his presumptions about his role as a well-meaning solidarity activist and changed his sense of entitlement about taking photos. He then went on to describe how, when he left the meeting feeling embarrassed, he went outside where he saw an opportunity for another photo. Having learned his lesson, he changed his approach to photo-taking:

> I saw an interesting looking local peasant ... So I brought my camera up to my eye. And it's interesting – I brought the cam-

era up, and I thought, "No, I should ask that person's permission before I take his picture. I'm not going to repeat this error over and over again. I'm not here as a tourist, I'm not here to take pictures." Even though I wanted to use the pictures for good things in Canada, to put on slideshows, I thought, "I can't do this kind of thing." So I brought the camera back down again, and I turned away.

Newly aware of the invasiveness of taking photographs of people at will, he explained that from then on, instead of just taking photos when he wanted, he paused first and considered the implications.

The most poignant dilemma he spoke about happened on his trip to Palestine, while doing ambulance accompaniment in the city of Hebron in the West Bank during a curfew. Typically during curfews, life comes to a complete standstill. Palestinian residents remain under house arrest, businesses are closed, and streets are empty. Sometimes curfews last for weeks. Curfews in Palestine have been characterized as a state of constant confusion because the rules constantly change.[14] The curfews may be lifted briefly (often with little or no notice) for a few hours to allow residents time to get food, water, and supplies but are often re-imposed, again without notice, causing havoc as civilians rush to return home. Ambulances are permitted to operate during curfew, but they are stopped continuously and searched in lengthy security checks and can be denied access or detained; thus, ambulance accompaniment is a common activity for First World activists because their presence is believed to help reduce delays so that ambulances can get people to hospitals more quickly.[15] Bill spoke about how during ambulance accompaniment he was often tempted to ask the ambulance drivers to "stop the ambulance, take him back half a block" so he could take a picture, but that he couldn't bring himself to do it and had to remind himself that the main purpose of his activism in that situation was to help take people to the hospital.

The particular incident I want to explore in some detail took place on the last night of Bill's ambulance accompaniment before returning to Canada when he came across the body of a dead Palestinian man. From what he and the people he was with could piece together, the man had walked into town to get groceries, and when the curfew came down he waited until dark to try to walk home, but he was spotted and shot dead. When Bill and the paramedics saw him, he was lying on the ground bleeding with his groceries strewn about. Bill explained:

> And I guess he walked down the road and he was just out in the middle of the road and they machine-gunned him. So there were some containers of food, there was some pita bread; there was a bunch of cigarettes, and this poor old man lying there.

Feeling helpless and quite obviously moved by the sight of the man's body left on the road, Bill sought to do something that might be useful. His plan was to put on slide show presentations when he returned to Canada just as he had done after his trip to Central America and, describing this scene as a "classic shot," he said that he believed this photo would have an impact. What is evident from his narrative is how Bill was weighing the educational potential of taking the photo against the recognition that the photograph could promote a voyeuristic gaze. It is his struggle that offers important insights into his dilemma. Writing about photojournalism, John Taylor reminds us that determining proper conduct when it comes to portraying bodily harm is not a straightforward matter.[16] He points out that in relation to violence, it has become widely considered unacceptable to look at the misery of others out of curiosity.[17] Bill's struggle here can therefore be understood in terms of what Taylor refers to as the photographer's need to discern between different types of looking. Drawing on Sontag, Taylor explains that any form of looking which has "no closed circuit of mutual permission" may be considered dubious. Bill's concerns about the absence of permission can be seen clearly in the following excerpt in which he struggles with whether his desire to capture the violence is in bad taste:

> I stepped back and I looked and I thought, you know, "I should take a picture." But Jeez – you know, – I thought, "Would the old man want his picture taken?" You know, "What am I doing here, taking a picture of this poor old man, this humiliated old

man on the street?" My first thought was, "Am I here to protect these guys or am I here to get amazing pictures?" Because it would have been an amazing picture ... Because it was my last day there, of all the shots I had, that one [photo] would have just been such a chronologically perfect wrap-up, to show this poor old man lying there.

Not knowing what to do, he asked for advice:

So I ask the [Palestinian] paramedics; I said, "Should I take his picture?" And they said "No, no the flash might attract gun fire."

The struggle he was facing was about knowing that such photos are effective for raising awareness. It was, therefore, hard for him to pass up this photo opportunity because he believed it would "be powerful, [and] would do a lot of good back home." In the end, he went back the next morning to take the photo. Since by the time he returned the body had been removed, Bill photographed the scene:

I took a picture of his food and cigarettes and the blood on the ground ... And since coming back to Canada, I have shown the slide and I said, "This is a murder scene" and I explained what had happened. I said, "So that this man didn't die for nothing, you must know his name." And I read the guy's name, I tell his age, and that he was a grandfather, and I talk about the family he left behind.

Clearly, this rich narrative raises a number of complex points on race-conscious activist practices, and photography.

MEDIATING COMPASSION

It is clear that it was deeply unsettling for Bill to be taking the photo of the man in the street: his temptation to use the camera to record the violence conflicted with the recognition that he would be promoting a voyeuristic gaze. Perhaps some of his discomfort comes from the congruencies that Sontag describes between war-making and picture-taking.[18] In her view, "shooting a subject and shooting a human being" exist on the same continuum, and so a man who has already been shot may have seemed *too* vulnerable a subject.[19] Bill's repeated questions of "What am I doing here?" and his asking himself, "Would this man want his photo taken?" reveal a struggle about the fact that the man could not have a say in it. Arguably, then, because it involved a dead body, the ethical questions this situation raised were exacerbated by his inability to gauge consent. Nevertheless, his sense of "duty to record" won out.[20] The strong desire to take the photo came from the recognition of the power of visual reportage and how dead bodies are an effective means of sensitizing the world to terror and violence.[21]

I want to draw attention to how power operated in the negotiation of Bill's dilemma, which was resolved in two ways. First, and very significantly, not knowing what to do, he followed the advice of the Palestinians he was with. This was a way to heed his racialized power, an effort to be respectful, and recognition of his inability to make an appropriate decision given his lack of knowledge in the area. Second, by not photographing the body itself, Bill was able to avoid feeling uneasy about exploiting the dead man and displaying him for spectatorship. It is important to bear in mind that Bill did not intentionally or strategically avoid photographing the body. Rather, the Palestinian paramedics advised him not to take the photo for safety reasons, not ethical ones. Indeed, it is fair to assume that if the Palestinian paramedics had agreed, he would have taken the photo of the man. Nevertheless, his dilemma and the photo itself are worth interrogating on several counts.

What difference does it make whether or not the dead body is shown in the photograph? To answer this question, I rely on Wendy Kozol's writing on the ethical dilemmas around depicting embodied spectacles of suffering.[22] Kozol studies the work of photojournalist Melanie Friend who, driven by the refusal to perpetuate voyeurism, uses an alternative representational strategy for images of war and trauma by photographing tranquil domestic scenes largely absent of people. These images are then juxtaposed with oral testimonies about violent acts.[23] The careful and purposeful renegotiation of conventions of representation in Friend's photography leads Kozol to ask: "Without the body, how do we witness? In losing the spectacle, we lose the voyeuristic privilege of the gaze but do we also lose knowledge of the trauma itself?"[24]

In considering how this question might be answered with respect to Bill's photo, several factors need to be considered. To begin with, there is the important recognition that the death of this Palestinian would not likely have come to the attention of Western audiences. As Mark Pedelty puts it, it lacked sufficient "political value" because it was the "wrong body."[25] The story of a presumably innocent and non-threatening civilian who was killed does not fit easily into the one-dimensional discursive representation of Palestinians (like most Arabs and Muslims) as do terrorist threats and dangers. Publicizing the violence enacted on this man, regardless of whether his body is depicted, is therefore already a highly political act.

Second, it is important to consider the process of publicly mourning the death displayed through the photo. Here, it helps to return to the piece by Judith Butler on the differential grievability of lives (discussed in Chapter One), on the politics of compassion, and on other people's suffering.[26] In it, she raises questions about our exposure to violence, especially in the contemporary global situation, and she critically evaluates the conditions through which certain human lives appear more vulnerable than others. Addressing herself to a North American readership, she demands that we ask: "Who counts as human? Whose lives count as lives?"[27] Ultimately, what makes a life noteworthy enough to warrant grief? The crux of her argument is that grief and mourning are not private matters. Rather, she believes that it is important to consider why only some lives become publicly recognized as "grievable."[28] By troubling the fact that some lives are worth noting and others not, Butler asks us to consider *the ways* in which such stories find their way into the media, if at all. For instance, she asks us to simply notice why names are attached only to some of the deaths we hear about.

Following this, it is easy to see that Bill's efforts certainly succeeded in making the Palestinian man's life publicly grievable. By displaying his photo, talking about his tragic death, and recording the name of the victim as well as his personal history, Bill makes the Palestinian man familiar – makes him human. But does he manage to disrupt or subvert what Butler calls "a hierarchy of grief"?[29] For this we have to consider the photograph itself and the specific ways it was strategized and set up as a politically potent educational tool.

Kozol argues that racial and gender categories are encoded within visual perspectives, and she offers several examples of widely circulated photojournalist images to support her argument.[30] It is the example she provides of an image that appeared in *The New York Times* in September 2000 that is most directly related to my purposes because it relies very specifically on the same masculinist, heteronormative, and racialized tropes as the ones in the photo Bill took. In Kozol's example, the photo in question depicts a Palestinian father and his son huddled against a wall, and it is published alongside a caption explaining that the boy was killed right after the photograph was taken. Kozol suggests that this image was successful in drawing sympathy for the *Intifada* (or Palestinian uprisings) in the Occupied Territories, even if temporarily, because of the heteronormative domesticity it secured. She explains:

> Alone, the father could be figured as a terrorist. Even the boy could look threatening in another context. But, as father and son, within the narrative framework of traumatic loss, the Palestinian cause is momentarily (for this narrative is rarely seen) figured as innocent victims.[31]

It is because of this framework, she argues, that the photograph succeeded in interrupting the usual racialized interpretations of Palestinian men as terrorists.

The same conventions are in effect in Bill's photo – perhaps revealing why this seemed to him to be such "a classic shot." In the photo, race interlocks with gender and heteronormativity to produce the Palestinian man as a sympathetic subject and the viewers as compassionate observers. Furthermore, it relies on similar tropes of domesticity to represent the violence that Palestinian people face. The food strewn about the scene renders the victim of the shooting an ordinary man out getting groceries for his family. Also significant for Bill was the fact that it was an older man, a grandfather. This fact enabled Bill to accompany the photo with compelling information about a normative gendered domesticity. Even without the body, therefore, the trauma could be conveyed through a shared heteronormative understanding of family.

Lastly, does the potential for eliciting compassion and educating through this photograph override the racialized problematics of a voyeuristic gaze? To get at this, I return to the idea that photos must be interrogated in terms of their intended audience and form and consider how "seeing" is projected on to audiences.[32] The particular audience in question here is one comprised of Canadians. What does it mean for a Canadian to be photographing this body and displaying this photograph to a fellow Canadian audience? I argue that it is not the public displaying of this photograph that one needs to be concerned with, but rather that it is the way the photograph is mediated by Bill that counts as both an antiracist *and* a hegemonic move. To explain this I make several interrelated arguments about how Bill understands what can be referred to as the *racialized politics of grief* vis-à-vis his audience and himself.

Photos have a mediating function that enables a distancing while at the same time creating closeness to events far away.[33] In showing this photo as part of his experiences abroad, Bill, the Canadian activist, thereby serves to narrow the geographic distance between "us and them," and his awareness-raising efforts can therefore be considered (at least provisionally) antiracist. What I want to point out, however, is that the process of mediating this experience serves a much more important function to understanding race-conscious practices. To "mediate" in this instance implies interceding, arbitrating, and interpreting, and it is a deeply racialized role. If, as Sontag argues, a viewer's response to photographs and the meanings he or she attaches to them "depends on how the picture is identified or misidentified," it is Bill's narration of the story that produces meaning in this case.[34] Moreover, his narrative reveals he knew that whether or not his audience would be affected by the photo depended on him. In other words, the pedagogical potential of the photo needed him as the Canadian witness of the event and not the violence of the event itself. This is why it was significant to him that he came across the man's body and the photo opportunity the scenario presented on *his* last night in Palestine. The main subject of the story told through the photograph, therefore, is not about the dead Palestinian but is about Bill, the Canadian who photographed him.

Sherene Razack wants us to question how public displays of suffering and compassion help us to understand ourselves nationally.[35] She reminds us that the Canadian who travels abroad, witnesses horror, and comes back to tell about it is a familiar figure. Using the example of Canadian General Roméo Dallaire who attained hero status because of his public calls for humanitarian interventions into the genocide in Rwanda, Razack points out that the situation began to matter to Canadians only when it was presented through Dallaire's eyes.[36] Furthermore, the Rwandan genocide became General Dallaire's personal story of trauma and despair. Playing on Sontag's *Regarding the Pain of Others* title, Razack asks if such moves cannot be better understood as "stealing the pain of others?" Moreover, the consumption of Dallaire's story by Canadians, she argues, forges a powerful national consciousness through a dynamic of identification. That is to say, because he cared, then by extension as Canadians, so must we. This imagined bond with Dallaire, Razack explains, enabled Canadians to feel good about their own high moral capacity for humanity. "In this way," Razack writes, "trauma narratives furnish middle power nations such as Canada with a home-made, that is to say a specifically *national*, version of the politics of rescue."[37] This in turn feeds the Canadian national imaginary in which we position ourselves as having an exceptional propensity for compassion as observers of global suffering.

What does this imply for antiracist activist practices? It is important to recall that the stated purpose for taking the photo was formulated as a deliberate strategy to raise awareness and therefore did not disguise itself, as many photographic practices do, as a neutral act. Here, the display of suffering was consciously deployed to draw out a compassionate response that would otherwise have been largely absent. Whether or not this political tactic is fruitful as an antiracist practice needs to be considered through writings on the politics of compassion. Within this literature, there exists a wide range of ways that notions of compassion, empathy, and sympathy have been defined, conflated, and compared.[38] I use the perspective offered by Hannah Arendt as a heuristic device for my argument because of the contrast between pity and compassion that it affords. Whether or not Bill's political tactic is fruitful as an antiracist practice, Arendt would argue, depends on whether his photo elicits compassion or pity.[39] The important distinctions between the two centre on their relationships to the sufferer. In Arendt's view, a relationship of compassion is more or less an equal one and implies a sharing of suffering. Relationships of pity, on the other hand, re-enact the power differentials between the viewer and the sufferer, rather than disrupt them. In her interpretation of Arendt's argument, Elizabeth Spelman writes: "Insofar as pity, unlike compassion, is not a matter of co-suffering, it heightens rather than erases differences between the non-suffering and the suffering."[40] With this in mind, I return to Kozol's question about whether the story could be told without the body.[41] In this situation, the dead body was not necessary to convey trauma because it was never the trauma suffered by the man who was shot dead that mattered, but the white body that witnessed it.

Most troubling for Arendt, on the subject of the moral and political implications of other people's suffering, were public declarations of the suffering. She believed that declarations about the suffering of others inevitably degenerate into pity, "which accentuates the distance and inequality between those in pain and those exhibiting feeling for them."[42] Spelman points out, "By making one's feeling public, one offers proof of the depth of one's connection with those who are in such great pain and thus the right to speak about and for them."[43] Therefore, while showing the photo does serve the important political function of making this man's death known, it is the photographer's difficult experience that the photo primarily captures. In displaying it, his own shock and pain is witnessed. Following this, I argue that the slideshow elicited both pity and compassion. Put differently, the Western viewers likely pitied the man who was shot, but it was not his suffering they shared. Their compassion, rather, was pointed at Bill, the Canadian activist.

Lauren Berlant posits that using the politics of personal feeling as an entry point for tackling social justice is altogether misguided.[44] She warns of the dangers of framing other people's suffering in sentiment because in simply *wanting* to do the right thing the spectator is less inclined towards action, while, paradoxically still remaining virtuous. Building on this, I argue that the visual practices of the slideshow produce and sustain hierarchy insofar as they secure spectators' and victims' relational roles. Within this relationship, attention is conveniently averted away from the spectator and rests exclusively on the victim. This enables the spectator to simply and unproblematically be compassionate without needing to consider the ways their own bodies are implicated in the spectacle.

I believe that in some significant ways, the slideshow Bill presented does challenge understandings based upon Western information systems by offering an alternative perspective. The practice of showing these slides and narrating them as a white, First World activist, however, perpetuates and reinforces notions of victimhood and vulnerability of the constructed Other. It also inscribes morality to the noble, white activist telling the story. If the ability to elicit compassion among bystanders depends on a white mediator, such activists' practices are far from counter-hegemonic in their effects. Assigning humanity to the Other is, after all, whiteness in its finest form.

CONCLUSION

To act against injustice is an increasingly onerous task. Zygmunt Bauman attributes this to a heightened collective awareness of the amount and the gravity of suffering in the world. With this recognition, people inclined towards activism are disheartened by the knowledge that their efforts are not likely to make "a real difference," and/or are immobilized with a sense of not knowing "where to start and how to proceed from there."[45] Yet despite these pitfalls, committed activists like Bill make the decision that it is better to act than to do nothing. In singling out activists' photography practices in this chapter, I run the risk of obscuring the "bigger" ethical issue – that is, the implications of choosing to do nothing. Bill did not only take photos, he facilitated the transportation of sick people to hospitals. My aim here has not been to elide this important fact or to judge the activists' practices, but to present the "messy complexity" of moral activism and to examine how *they* determine right from wrong.[46] I have shown that ethical decisions the activists make are very complexly weighed in terms of their effects on racialized power relations.

A second objective was to consider how power might be disrupted and/or reproduced through activists' photography practices. Bill's interventions succeeded at interrupting power insofar as he consciously refused to objectify the Other. His photography did not (at least overtly) compromise or simplify the situation in Palestine to which he was seeking to draw attention. However, where his practices did succumb to the existing global order of power and injustice pertains to the ways his positioning as narrator and mediator of the situation inescapably deflected the public's attention back on to him. Moreover, and perhaps most significantly, in displaying this photo and the ethical dilemma that went with it, the activist constituted himself as a knowing subject and as a moral agent, and with this, First World hegemony was re-secured.[47]

This analysis is meant to inform activist practices in a way that is cautionary. In revealing that representational practices raise important questions that extend beyond identity politics, this chapter calls upon activists to critically consider how they may be positioning themselves or being positioned as the objects of empathy. While certainly the activists' "ethical quagmires" regarding their visual documentation practices reveal a cognizance of the problematics of displaying the Other to a Western gaze, less attention tends to be paid to how they inadvertently display themselves in the process.[48] The critical questions that activists must ask relate to the ways the images they display enable their audiences to imagine themselves and the activists as caring and compassionate. In other words, their representational practices must constantly be interrogated not only in terms of who will be consuming the images they show, but also in knowing that by showing certain images, they may inadvertently position themselves as the white hero/saviours. The quote taken from Vron Ware and Les Back presented at the start of this chapter asks: "What difference does it make where the antirace is performed, by whom, and in whose company?"[49] What I have tried to illustrate is that *"the who"* makes antiracist practice possible, while paradoxically and simultaneously limiting this very possibility.

CHAPTER FIVE

Conflicted Commitments: The "Fine Line Between Advocacy and Imperialism"[1]

I was struck by the extraordinary ease with which (especially white) individuals can slide from awareness of whiteness to the lack thereof, related to that slippage, from race-consciousness to unconsciousness and from antiracism to racism.

Ruth Frankenberg[2]

One of the lines of inquiry followed in this book is how First World transnational solidarity activists negotiate and manage their dominant positioning in relation to their social justice commitments and understandings. Specifically, I am interested in how individual activists understand and reconcile their roles vis-à-vis racialized power.

The eighteen activists whose experiences are examined in this book represent a range of motivations and perspectives.[3] They were associated with various faith-based, women's, and/or political groups, each with a particular mandate and political/philosophical orientation. Their political views and commitments ranged from anarchy to pacifism, and they had been involved in various activities that ranged from front-line direct action, to more behind-the-scenes advocacy type of work. The majority of the activists who were interviewed (twelve of the eighteen) had travelled to Palestine with groups including the International Women's Peace Service (IWPS), Ecumenical Accompaniment Program in Palestine and Israel (EAPPI), Christian Peacemaker Teams (CPT), and the International Solidarity Movement (ISM). The remainder travelled with

Project Accompaniment (PA); Peace Brigades International (PBI); the Iraq Peace Team (IPT), and independently to countries including Nicaragua, Guatemala, Mexico, Indonesia, and Iraq.[4]

Despite the different contexts they were in and the organizations they were with, the activists shared some important commonalities. For one, they all responded to the call to participate in this study, which indicated that they thought of themselves as "international solidarity activists," and that they considered their experiences to be ones that fit the criterion in the original call for research participants of having "travelled to another part of the world to promote peace and/or to protest military violence." Most significant, however, is that they all shared the idea that their presence might somehow help people who are suffering, and all were committed to trying to eliminate or reduce violence and oppression in the world. Most of them had also travelled with a Canadian passport.

As I have noted in previous chapters, these activists were, by and large, self-conscious about their power and positioning and wanted to contend with issues of power. The call for volunteers to participate in interviews explicitly indicated that I was interested in knowing how they "negotiated issues of race and national identity," and several activists who responded said they were drawn to the study precisely because of this focus. They believed that the interview might provide them with an opportunity to discuss issues and concerns that they had long been grappling with but that are not often talked about. Being primarily concerned with the activists' negotiations with racialized power, this chapter focuses specifically on their accounts of difficulty, ambivalence, doubt, or strategy, and hones in on excerpts from the interviews that relate directly to these struggles and qualms. As I will show, when reflecting upon their experiences, activists expressed great ambivalence and recounted many tensions that emerged for them on a day-to-day level. In fact, many of the activists who participated in this study had concerns about how racialized power relations are perpetuated through the actions and the presence of First World accompaniers/observers like them. One of the goals of this chapter, then, is to document some of these tensions.

At the level of analysis, I am concerned with the activists' "self-making" practices. This notion of self-making derives from Chris Weedon's definition of subjectivity as a process through which "a combination of conscious and unconscious thoughts and emotions make up our sense of ourselves, our relation to the world and our ability to act in it."[5] The specific self-making practices I am interested in are the ones pertaining to how the activists have come to terms with white privilege, and how the processes of these self-making practices shape their senses of selves.[6] Informing this exploration are studies that have shown that the process of coming to terms with, or acknowledging one's racialized privilege is difficult and fraught with contradiction, and that the (re)productive tensions of whiteness that exist within antiracist practices entail ambivalence, doubt, and ethical struggle.[7]

CONFLICTED ACTIVISTS: DISCOMFORT AND DOUBT

Before proceeding to specific accounts, it is important to point out that in the materials published by the groups that organize these trips, declarations of awareness of privilege and articulations of power imbalances abound. Indeed, although there is some variance in the wording used, virtually all groups that coordinate these trips assert emphatically that they are acting in solidarity *with* and not *for* the people they are assisting. The groups also convey principled efforts to work through collaboration. For example, describing their educational project in Indonesia, Peace Brigades International (PBI) declares that they approach their work in a way that avoids "simply teaching the Western, 'correct' approaches to locals."[8] The International Solidarity Movement (ISM) goes further than Peace Brigades in this respect by overtly stating that one of its principal assumptions is the "need to move from an arrogant 'saviour' model of activism, to a real 'solidarity' model." On an older version of their website, they explained: "Part and parcel of this, is the belief that internationals cannot behave as if they are coming to teach Palestinians anything about 'peace' or 'non-violence' or 'morality' or 'democracy', or anything else that many in the West typically (and arrogantly and mistakenly) be viewed as the exclusive realm of Western activism and values."[9] Moreover, the ISM strives to ensure this through its Palestinian-led organizational structure.

Other gestures of seeking to balance power is evident in the fact that the Christian Peacemaker Team's (CPT) apartment in Iraq was situated outside of the "Green Zone" (a designated safe area in which most foreign journalists and visitors stay) and instead was located in the neighbourhoods where Iraqis live. This was purposefully done so that the members of the CPT would live as the locals do. Similar efforts are made by PBI. As one activist explained, although the local people were sometimes puzzled by the fact that the activists did not have a car or live in a "fancy" house, it generally helped the activists to be perceived in a positive light. Moreover, she said it went a long way to increasing people's trust because it demonstrated that the activists were not there for financial gain.

Despite these principled approaches, many of the First World activists I interviewed, it seems, could not help but re-enact a colonizing role, or what Linda Alcoff calls a "global, racial vanguardism."[10] In day-to-day terms, this typically manifested in the activists telling local people how to act or offering them instruction on effective protest strategies, especially more "radical" ones. For example, Dan, an activist in Palestine with a faith-based organization, had serious concerns about the long-term implications of the interventions of some First World activists. To illustrate his point, he described a scenario in which, in response to a confrontation with Israeli military troops, a group of First World activists broke down a gate and then proceeded to form a human chain as an act of civil disobedience – an action he chose not to take part in. His concern was about the detrimental effect this action could have on the Palestinians in the long run. In his view, the protection that the First World activists offer is very short-lived and therefore very tenuous. As he put it, "We leave the village after three months. If you provoke the military, who gets the brunt of it afterwards? By participating in it, we are encouraging villagers to do the same, except *they* will be remembered."

Dan was also critical of what he believed to be the "extreme" behaviour that some First World activists display. He attributed such behaviour more to an overbearing presence than political strategy. One example he gave was about Palestinian children throwing stones at the Israeli military in defiance and resistance. He observed that First World activists often encourage the youth to throw stones in a misguided effort to empower them. Since Israeli soldiers are less likely to retaliate against the youth when the foreign activists are present, some took that to mean that their role was to support the youth's resistance by encouraging stone throwing.

The issue of Palestinian children throwing stones was also a contentious one for Chris, a long-time member of the ISM. His experience there taught him that many Palestinian parents were against their children participating in this activity and were concerned that the children might be influenced by the First World activists' behaviours, which could further endanger them.[11] He flippantly described some of the attitudes displayed by the First World activists as wanting to be more "hard-core" than the Palestinians. He explains: "You have Palestinians who did not want us standing with the stone throwers because they don't want you to be encouraging the kids to be doing that. Because they don't want their kids being killed. And a lot of internationals didn't have respect for that sentiment." What is evident from Chris's observation is that in their attempts to offer a meaningful intervention, many of the activists enact dominance. The issue of stone throwing raised by both Dan and Chris also reveals an undertone of First World "knowing," and raises larger questions about the First World activists' involvement.[12] Such issues have beleaguered activist groups for decades. For example, one of the issues that ISM members navigate daily is the role internationals should play in the ongoing debate over Palestinian tactics in resisting the Israeli occupation.[13]

The most significant point is that many of the activists seem to naturally assume a paternalistic position over the Palestinians. Another activist named Lisa observed a tendency for some members of her group to have an attitude of wanting to come "help these poor people." Chris similarly spoke of activists who unreflectively assumed the position of "saving the Palestinians" and who, as he put it, were convinced that "Palestinians need white people to be around to protect them from harm." In his view, the specific role that white activists play when providing physical accompaniment was not only ambiguous but also problematic and inappropriate because it created a saviour/victim situation: "It has weird dynamics in terms of using privilege ... this notion that Palestinians need white people to be around to protect them from stuff – it's kind of weird. I personally don't know how I feel about that ... it's not work I felt comfortable doing." He also observed that some activists did not adapt, integrate, or even interact with the Palestinian people, which made it difficult for the Palestinians to trust them. He said, "There were lots of internationals who would never interact with people on a day-to-day level, like on the street. [The Palestinians] were like, 'Who are these people in our community? What are they doing here? How come they don't talk to us?'"

For Chris, the activists who were unaware of their privilege were not only annoying, they were burdens – especially in dangerous situations when the fears and tensions amongst the Palestinian population were high. Chris also spoke of the ways some activists were unaware of their privileged position and had inappropriate expectations and demands. He explained that First World activists who lacked self-awareness and self-restraint "expect[ed] certain comforts" and thereby unknowingly added to the stresses of the people they were supposedly there to assist and support.[14] Chris attributed some of these problems to the recruiting practices of some of the groups, which in his view were too loose. According to him, this meant that the people who join do not necessarily have skills or experience in solidarity movement activism, but rather just have the financial means to travel.

A few of the activists spoke about feeling uneasy with the special treatment and the prestigious status they received. In a journal entry, Lindsey wrote: "Who am I to be meeting with high level officials and diplomats?!!" The same sentiment was echoed by Jason, who spoke of being uncomfortable at an event at which he was automatically given special treatment as though he were a dignitary and placed at the head table, he believed, only because he is white. Sandra said that her whiteness gives her a status that makes her uncomfortable but that she tries to use it to either intervene with soldiers or to get into places and meet with important people whom she would never have access to at home.

Chris recounted incidents when, as a white Canadian activist in Palestine, the Israeli soldiers treated him in ways that suggested camaraderie and kinship, even while they detained him, in contrast with how they treated the Palestinian activists: "The soldiers, the way they'd relate to me when they'd detain me, was very different from [the ways they treated] the Palestinians. They'd always try to start conversations with me. They'd see that I was from Canada, so [for example] one soldier talked to me about his girlfriend in Toronto, just like, you know, like we could be chums." Several activists said that they had eventually found themselves wondering if accompaniment work is in fact even helpful. Others said they recognize that despite their intentions to assist, support, and protect those who are under the threat of violence, their efforts frequently fail.

In a curious reversal, what some of the activists discover is that they become the ones being cared for and protected. For example, one of the most significant apprehensions that Chris expressed about the roles of First World activists in Palestine was his observation that they were the ones, ironically, who often needed help and protection, rather than being the ones to offer it. He explained that being unfamiliar with the political situations and conditions they were in, and, in most cases, not having even basic language skills to get by, the activists' roles were frequently reversed so that the people they were purportedly there to assist had the added burden of being concerned for them.

Joanne observed similar dynamics taking place in accompaniment work in Guatemala. She said: "And of course, that's another great irony of accompaniment – the people you're accompanying worry about *your* security and *your* health and *your* well-being all the time, and that's one of the amazing things that happens is that people are very concerned for you. You're there supposedly to be in concern for them but they're concerned about you." Here again, we see that one of the fundamental goals of transnational accompaniment-observer activism is thwarted.

In sum, these narratives suggest that First World accompaniment activist presence does not necessarily accomplish what it sets out to do, and that, in fact, it sometimes does more harm than good. Chris had strong feelings about this contradiction, to the point of questioning the accompaniment strategy altogether. He was not convinced that, in the context of Palestine, having First World activists around did indeed facilitate access or reduce the day-to-day fears and frustrations of Palestinians living under occupation. Based on his observations and on those of some of the community organizers in Palestine he worked with, he estimated that the presence of activists was only effective in about 50 per cent of the situations they were in. A specific example he gave was related to ambulance accompaniment. He explained that during curfews, white internationals would ride in ambulances with the medical workers as a means of facilitating access and offering some protection. Yet, it seemed to him that the Palestinian medical workers were stopped *more* frequently and detained for longer periods when they had an international accompanier than when they did not. While it is not possible to know whether his anecdotal observations are accurate, what is important is that he came to question whether the strategy of accompaniment worked. As he put it: "Sometimes it complicated the work, sometimes it facilitated it. But it's not clear that having internationals there is one hundred percent a good thing; or that it always simplifies things."

Similarly, Tanya recounted an incident that occurred when Palestinian farmers requested "internationals" to help them harvest olives as an example of First World activists' tendency to "take matters into their own hands without taking the time to fully plan what it was that they want to achieve." She explained that although the request was for simple accompaniment, the activists who were there instead began to argue with the soldiers who were refusing entry to some people: "At first the farmers, who are used to that happening, just sort of waited and were standing around. But then some of the internationals sort of forced the issue with the soldiers by yelling at them and blocking them. And it's hard to say if the actions of the internationals resulted in the gate being closed longer. It definitely didn't make the situation any better." In her view, the aggressive stance taken by the activists ironically resulted in hindering the Palestinians rather than helping them because it increased the hassle and difficulties that they faced at this border.

Sandra confessed that no matter what she did, she constantly questioned whether she was in fact helping Palestinians, adding that she suspected that the presence of activists like her did not end up easing the situation. She characterized this as a feeling of hopelessness and expressed concerns that the international presence set up a dependency, and at the same time, stated that, "in the end we are not really achieving the goal of ending the occupation." Similarly, while Lisa maintains that it is necessary to be there in order to be able write and speak about the situation first-hand, in terms of the daily solidarity work on the ground, she said, "It's very hard to see changes or usefulness of our presence." Moreover, Lisa came to the humbling recognition that as First World activists, they do not hold as much power or are taken as seriously as they might think. She noted that "Palestinians see us as impotent, partially because we are. Children make fun of us. Israeli authorities don't care what we do or think."

Many of the activists who expressed concerns or doubts spoke about the incongruity of offering a supportive presence instead of more material resources. Since the activists were often assumed to be rich and powerful, people frequently asked them for money or for help in obtaining funds. These types of requests destabilized the activists because they greatly conflicted with their understanding of their role of offering solidarity and emotional support. As Lisa explains: "People would prefer that we were a development agency or a humanitarian aid organization. We're asked to build schools, pave roads, give people money for medicine, operations, etc. We have to explain that we're here to support resistance, but it's not always a comfortable situation." Joanne, who worked in Guatemala, explained that the group she was with discouraged giving financial help to individuals. In her understanding, this guideline was put in place in an effort to avoid creating awkward situations between the activists and the people they were there to assist. Her narrative indicated that while this made sense to her, she was deeply conflicted about it. She explained, "That's often very painful for people because you just want to help but oftentimes it's one of the difficult things that people need to learn in accompaniment: that inevitably it causes more problems because you loan people money and then they can't pay you back, and then they feel bad and guilty and so on." Joanne went on to express further ambivalence and difficulties about feeling both powerful and powerless vis-à-vis money. She spoke about how the relative perspective on wealth she encountered created a strain in some of the activists' relationships with local people:

> I think one of the major contradictions is that it was very hard for them to understand that you personally weren't rich, and of course by their standards, you *are* rich. And they always ask you how much your airfare costs. Which is, of course, a thousand

dollars, let's say, or seven hundred dollars, or whatever, it is an unthinkable amount of money for them. They would never have that kind of money ... And so people expect you to be able to give money to projects, or find money at home. There is this perception that either you personally or the organization you are coming from has wealth. And so to say, "No I'm not here with money," was something that people had to really deal with and come to understand.

She admitted that despite the fact that she did not give money, she felt that she was not able to transgress the charity-like relations that she tried to avoid, adding that no matter how hard she tried, she just ended up feeling like she was involved in "donor/recipient dependency relationships."

Lindsey, who was with PBI, similarly described feeling uncertain about whether her group's presence was useful when she realized that she was not able to fulfill the practical needs of the local groups she was there to assist. She wondered if assisting them with obtaining funding and financial resources would have been a more useful service to provide. Sarah, who went to Iraq with CPT, said that people came to their office with a variety of needs for medical treatment that CPT could do little about. Likewise, an activist named Tanya who travelled to Palestine with ISM said that she did not have an adequate way to explain to people who came to her asking for help in getting visas, leaving the country, or obtaining financial aid, that it was assistance that she could not provide for them. She said that she would just try to explain that that was not what she was there to do, although she wished she could.

The activists' narratives here suggest that they began to question the fundamental value of their efforts when they came to see that they were not assisting people with their most basic and pressing needs. While on an intellectual level they could reason that the policies of not offering material assistance were needed, once they were confronted with requests and could see the dire necessity for some key resources, their convictions about the strategy of accompaniment waned.

Some activists also struggled with larger socio-political and ethical questions around solidarity relationships in general and contemplated effective ways to work in solidarity that diminished power differences, dependency, and white hegemony. For example, Monica questioned more broadly what it means to be working in solidarity, asking what "ultimately does it accomplish?" She struggled with her decision to go to Palestine versus working in solidarity movements in Canada, stating, "I can't figure out what's the most humane thing for me to do: fight the US administration from here, or go over there and literally put my body between the Israeli soldiers and Palestinians."

Tanya was challenged to think about what she was there to accomplish when confronted by frustrated Palestinians. She said that although, overall, the Palestinian people she encountered were supportive of the First World activists being there, in times of particular distress they expressed some anger at the activists:

> Some days you meet people who just lost a family member, or their house was just demolished, or something equally traumatic has happened, and they will let you know exactly how they feel and will tell you how it is all your fault – it's all your government's fault. And they'll ask you why you are there, and tell you there is nothing you can do ... So when things like that happen, then you wonder what exactly you're doing, if you're doing good, if you're not having any effect, or if you're actually doing harm in the situation.

Although some other activists reacted very defensively to these types of charges, for Tanya, these encounters raised legitimate questions about the presence of the activists. She said that she could completely understand why they would feel that way.

Some of the individual activists' narratives indicated that they were also cognizant of the cultural consumption and appropriation that this form of solidarity travel is embedded in. For example, Monica stressed that for her, this activism did not mean "going there and trying to live someone else's life," and that it was important to remember "who you are at all times," that is, remind herself that unlike the people she was assisting, she could "go home to [her] privileged life" afterwards. Such recognitions of differences in power by members of dominant groups have been identified as a very first step to social justice and signify that the activists operate, to some extent, through an awareness of their "location."[15]

The views examined here identify some of the pitfalls of dominance that First World activists tend to fall into and revealed that for many, this activism is riddled with ambivalence, doubt, and complex ethical struggle.[16] Whether it was the overbearing First World activists endangering the local people, a false sense of importance attributed to them, the ironic predicaments they find themselves in where they are the ones needing protection, or their fears that their presence may be doing more harm than good, we learn from their insights that the strategic deployment of racialized power is, at the very least, difficult to manage, and worse still, can easily contribute to furthering injustice.[17] In fact, some of them are conflicted *because* they understand that their interventions are enveloped in historical relations of power and that these legacies are virtually inescapable. In other words, their observations suggest that their positioning as First World activists is, in many ways, *overdetermined* as dominant and authoritative. Moreover, their bodies sometimes betray their antiracist intentions insofar as they are accorded special treatment whether they want it or not. Indeed, that many of the activists are conflicted about the ways their presence and interventions weave in and out of complicity and resistance indicates that accompaniment-observer solidarity activism is indeed a muddled, ambivalent, and contradictory interpersonal process.

COMFORTED ACTIVISTS: INTENTIONALITY AND EXCEPTIONALITY

Having shown that many activists were conflicted by their dominant positioning, it is equally important to examine how some of these activists were able to quell their conflicts, concerns, and the ways in which they negotiate, minimize, and otherwise manage that power.

One of the questions asked in the interviews pertained to how the activists made the initial decision to travel to do accompaniment-observer activism, as opposed to working in solidarity from their home countries. Many of the activists justified their decisions about going abroad through what they perceive to be "honourable" motives and objectives. As Lisa put it, "I thought my presence as a white American would reduce violence against Palestinians. I understood the problematic nature of this but saw it as a way to use my privilege somewhat positively, or at least protectively." This type of response reflects what Barbara Heron refers to as "intentionality."[18] The well-meaning intentions behind their choices to go were also evident in the ways in which several activists stressed that the trip for them was merely a starting point for ongoing commitment and activism at home. For them, the problematic of travelling to various parts of the world to make changes "over there" was lessened by the fact that they *also* continue to work extensively in solidarity projects when at home. Terry, for example, said that he was attracted to the Iraq Peace Team project because of its emphasis on continuing the activism from Canada. He explains: "It was designed to have people come into Iraq, spend a few weeks or a month, and then go back home, and that's where the work was really to start. And that was definitely my experience. That's the approach all of us took ... To build up the movements here, that was reason why we were going." A related and recurring theme around their good intentions was the notion of collaboration. The activists repeatedly asserted that their work was *not* a repetition of the colonial/imperial pattern of going to teach (as in missionary work). A typical sentiment was articulated by Elizabeth, who commented on how the organization she belonged to was one that "partners with the Palestinian people."[19]

Related to this, in response to a question about whether or not they ever wondered if they should "be there," several activists stressed how important it was to them that the local groups had requested their presence. The ambivalence is best captured in Lisa's response: "Did I ever think I shouldn't have gone? Absolutely not. Did I ever think I shouldn't be there? Absolutely."

For many, the apprehension about their "right" to be there was alleviated by the idea that they were invited, and they were greatly comforted by the knowledge that they were wanted and needed. For example, Joanne responded to the question about whether or not she ever wondered if she should be there, as follows: "That I should be there? No. I didn't have any question because we were invited there by the Palestinians, as compared to just showing up on the doorstep. So I think that because I was invited there, that that makes a difference." Indeed, the activists' reassurance that they were wanted and greatly appreciated by the local people was a great source of comfort to them.

To best understand these narratives, and the racialized systems of racialized power in which they operate, it helps to draw upon Ruth Frankenberg's work on the discursive repertoire of race. Frankenberg highlights the dual desire to assert essential sameness through what she describes as power-evasive discourses *and* race-cognizant discourses, and stresses that there is much overlap between them.[20] One of the important observations she makes is that within this discursive repertoire, even articulations of racism are structured through a liberal elision of power differences. In a section of her book aptly titled, "Now you see it, now you don't," Frankenberg observes that there are strategic ways white people talk about race that are more "pleasant" and "safe," but that this type of language necessarily evades power. Like the women in Frankenberg's study, some of the activists' narratives examined here suggest a similar dynamic in operation. While many of them acknowledged their dominant positioning, they reconciled dominance with notions of partnership. This, according to Frankenberg, reflects a *desire* to see society in terms of universal sameness and individual difference.[21]

Similarly, Audrey Thompson writes that to escape the recognition that whiteness is a position of dominance, white people will sometimes demonstrate that they are exceptional, different, or better than other racist white people.[22] Thompson adds that this separating strategy often takes the form of comparative statements that discursively shift attention to those who more obviously warrant criticism, or, as she puts it, "whites who really have a problem," to show themselves, in contrast, to be "good" white people.[23] The narratives I analyzed were replete with discourses of exceptionality, especially with respect to the ways the activists understood themselves in comparison to other First World activists. Not only are their investments in what it means to be ethical actors revealed in these narratives, but also the ways they construct themselves as "better" – a stance that enables them to reconcile their discomforts and doubts.

One way some of the activists comforted themselves about their misgivings was by drawing a distinction between themselves, other activists, and international development workers or missionaries. For instance, Elizabeth explains that although she was there with a Christian faith-based group, she had to have a clear understanding that she was not going as a missionary to convert Muslims. Similarly, Joanne, who has participated in both development work *and* accompaniment-observer activism, separates the two. She admits that the distinction is not always clear for her, but that she has "less ambiguous feelings" about accompaniment work.

The ways in which the activists expressed criticisms of other solidarity activists or groups further reveals how they sought to feel better about their own presence. Often, their criticisms were not of individual activists but of the groups they belonged to, and came down to a perceived liberal/radical divide. This was particularly true for those who went to Palestine where there were several groups working closely together. Before exploring these criticisms, it is important to highlight that while this "divide" existed at an ideological level, it did not impede the groups' ability to work together toward the common goal of reducing violence.[24] In other words, despite ideological differences, the activists from different groups often banded together to form a critical mass. This was most evident in Palestine where ISM, CPT, IWPS, and EAPPI collaborated and, in fact, often conducted joint trainings and actions and were strongly and clearly united in their overall anti-violence/anti-occupation mandates.[25] My point in highlighting the differences here is to ask what the activists gained from characterizing themselves as better than *other* activist groups who were deemed more problematic.

The ISM drew the most criticism, both from its own members and from members of other groups. This can be attributed, in part, to ISM's reputation of attracting a radical membership. Several activists criticized the ISM in ways that enabled them to construct themselves as non-dominating First World actors. For example, Ruth, who went to Palestine twice, once with the ISM, and then with IWPS, said that she had difficulty with ISM because they were too "gung-ho." Monica, who was with IWPS, said she had heard criticisms from some Palestinians that the ISM, "was a little like Wild West activism." For Elizabeth, there was an important distinction between being there as a witness and demonstrating on the front-lines. She described the difference in approaches through a detailed example of a demonstration at which she and her team members passively took part: "We're there to support the Palestinian and the Israeli activists doing their front-line work, rather than ourselves being on the front lines ... The ISM people were in the lead there when it came to confronting the soldiers ... they were even more 'there' than the Palestinians ... And so I guess that's kind of a philosophical tension." She also made a distinction between respectable, rational, and more strategic activists and those who are more emotional and self-serving. While Elizabeth contends that the strategies used by the ISM were effective in terms of getting media coverage, and that their skills and demonstration tactics enabled them to get results in ways that her own group could not, she is nevertheless critical of members of the ISM for their attention-seeking tactics.

Many of the Canadian activists' notions of themselves as better or as exceptional also emerged through ideas about national identity. As explored in Chapter Two, this activism is embedded in nationalism, despite its transnational claims. Interestingly, Canadian nationalist imaginings helped several activists see themselves as exceptionally benevolent, particularly when they compared themselves to Americans: "Oh, let me tell you!" Elizabeth laughed. "Canada has a good reputation in the West Bank. So they'll ask where you're from, and you'll say, 'I'm from Canada.' And their response is a big smile. God forbid you are from the United States. But as a Canadian it's just wonderful; it's all good. So for my own national identity it was a good thing. I had a Canadian flag on my packsack so I made sure everybody knew." The genuine exuberance Elizabeth expresses here captures her conviction about the merits of being Canadian. Although the majority of activists were not as emphatic about the merits of being Canadian, they were nevertheless comforted by the thought that they were better than Americans.

In several instances, there were compelling points of tension in their narratives with respect to being both critical of the Canadian government, while at the same time feeling proud to be Canadian through their activism. For example, Lindsey said that she came to develop "a greater appreciation for the differences" between Canadians and Americans, while still being critical of the problems that exist in Canada. Joanne also declared that she was not nationalistic and yet, she said, in some ways she brought a "proud to be Canadian" sentiment on her trip to Guatemala, all the while recognizing that the Canadian government was playing a direct "disgraceful" role in Guatemala at the time. She then goes on to redeem Canada for the role it is playing, by pointing to some hopeful discussions that took place with the Canadian embassy. This, she added, made her feel, "happy to be connected with a place where there was at least a chance that we could influence our government's policy toward Guatemala." Dan stated that although he did not have great trust in Canadian foreign policy before becoming an activist, he came to appreciate something about Canadian national identity in relation to the Americans he met. What makes these claims about Canadian national identity important from a critical race point of view is that these notions also enable the activists to position themselves as exceptional or as better than other First World activists. Most significant for the purposes of this analysis are the ways these narratives show how self-making practices are tied to national identities in a way that is mutually constitutive.[26]

RECONCILING DOMINANCE

Together, these narratives illustrate that the activists work hard to manage the power that comes with being from the First World. Through their experiences, many activists became highly attuned to racialized power dynamics and sought to be ethical antiracist actors by trying not to assume positions of superiority and authority. As I have shown, many of the activists were able to reconcile some of their ambivalence around their dominant positioning through notions of intentionality and exceptionality. By feeling wanted, and viewing themselves as being in partnership with the people they were assisting, the activists were able to alleviate some of their anxieties about their participation in these ventures. Also, by throwing the activists' mechanisms of seeking comfort under a critical light, I want to propose that it is instructive to contemplate their need to feel good about what they do. Again, Audrey Thompson's work on the growth, loss, and risk in white antiracism is helpful here.[27] She suggests that white activists would be less inclined to take part in antiracist efforts if they are overly self-critical. In other words, some activists need to feel that their actions are righteous in order to do the work. Similarly, Barbara Heron points out that while a conviction in the goodness of the actions must be preserved, it is nevertheless a pitfall of privilege because to avoid thinking of themselves as racist (and therefore immoral), white people will presume themselves to be antiracist in ways that may limit their antiracist understandings.[28] "Regardless of how 'nice' or 'good' we may be," Heron writes, "we are discursively produced to see and understand relations of power, both globally and at the micro level, in ways that mask our own complicity and thus enable their operation."[29] I want to propose, then, that the comfort the activists feel is not on solid ground, and is in fact perpetually at risk. It seems that one of the results of being positioned in contradictory ways, as people who both have racialized power and who divest themselves of it, is that they can never fully achieve the comfort they seek.

SOME PALESTINIAN PERSPECTIVES

It is important to reflect on how the presence and support of solidarity activists is perceived by those on the receiving end of it in Palestine. Since several existing publications document the successes of this activism and celebrate the bravery and altruism of those who take part in it, the discussion here is specifically geared towards considering more critical views. While bearing in mind the important ways in which these activists offer support and intervene, I want to now consider some of the ways in which the white/Western activist presence presents challenges and the tensions that arise from it. The findings of a study by Nadera Shalhoub-Kevorkian and Sana Khsheiboun provide a useful entry point for this discussion.[30] They interviewed Palestinian women who were survivors of Israeli demolition practices on how they perceive "human rights" activist interventions in their communities.[31] Although the women's responses did not necessarily focus only on foreign activists, but rather examined the presence of human rights activists more generally, including Israelis, they nevertheless offer some important considerations that strongly resonate with the questions I am exploring. Furthermore, the candid views expressed by the women in this study rarely make their way into scholarly inquiry on transnational solidarity practices. For this reason, and because they challenge the predominantly self-congratulatory tone of most writing on solidarity and humanitarian initiatives, it is important to examine them closely.

Some of the women interviewed felt that human rights' actions and organizations succeeded at raising global awareness on their situations and spoke of being helped by them in very practical ways. For instance, some recounted how the activists were integral in facilitating their otherwise restricted mobility by obtaining permits for them to get to their universities for classes or to hospitals for medical care.[32] For the vast majority, however, the presence of the human rights activists in their day-to-day lives has become a source of great strife. Many of these women described the arrival of activists and organizations in their communities as an invasion of privacy and held feelings of hostility and resentment towards them.[33] For some of the women these feelings emerged out of dashed hopes when the activists were not able to prevent the demolitions of their homes, revealing that a sense of despair and disappointment clouded their views. That said, their feelings about the presence of human rights activists in their communities appear to extend beyond hope and despair, and instead point to some more generalized dynamics about the fraught power relations that the activists' presence creates for them. For example, a humiliating sense of being pitied was a common theme in their narratives and more specifically, feeling like they were the objects of the activists' sympathetic but somewhat patronizing gaze. As one woman put it: "They are all foreigners – they know nothing about our society. They just come to conduct studies and write about us ... to feel sorry for us. And I do not want anyone to feel sorry for me.[34] Another woman said, "I felt they came to look at me, take pictures of my demolished house, and observe me while in pain."[35] Already, these views challenge the prevalent idea that the activists are always welcome and wanted, as well as further revealing how invasive photography can be in these contexts, even when it is done with the best of intentions.

More importantly, Shalhoub-Kevorkian and Khsheiboun's study reveals a more deep-rooted weariness that has set in for Palestinians as a result of the burgeoning NGO industry that has overtaken their communities in the past forty years.[36] This point is best illustrated by first pointing out what some have called the exponential mushrooming of "civil society" organizations worldwide and how that has impacted communities such as those in Palestine.[37] As one Palestinian organizer observed, "every second person you meet there is part of a human rights NGO." Furthermore, the distinctions between social movements and NGOs are increasingly unclear. For instance, some NGOs understand themselves to be part of social movements despite the fact that they are complicit with, are funded through, and or co-opted by governments and states. These perspectives clearly raise important further questions about what has recently been termed the "NGO-ization" of social movements. That is, the increasing institutionalization and professionalization of foreigners (often paid) to help those who are suffering in zones of conflict and instability.[38] The impacts of this NGO-ization of their daily lives and political struggles greatly impacted the women interviewed for Shalhoub-Kevorkian and Khsheiboun's study. They indicate that the increasing prevalence of these human rights activists has prompted a growing cynicism about whom these organizations and initiatives actually benefit. Moreover, the women in the study are disturbed by how the very conditions of military occupation which oppress them, also give purpose, and (in some cases) careers and income for those assisting them. In other words, some of them believe that sustaining what they perceive as the "human rights industry" has become more significant than empowering those whose lives are most impacted by the occupation.[39]

To glean further insights on the ways in which power operates according to one's subject position in this site of activism, four Palestinian community organizers located in Palestine who work with First World activists were interviewed.[40] Specifically, they were asked about the challenges that come up for them when working in solidarity with First World activists and how they perceive and negotiate the asymmetrical relations of power that arise for them in these solidarity projects.[41] These particular organizers were approached because they all had many years of direct experience with groups like the ISM and had been in leadership roles in the training and mobilizing of foreign activists.

Like the women from the Shalhoub-Kevorkian and Khsheiboun study, all four of the organizers stressed that there are both positive and negative aspects to the Western activists' presence. They also expressed appreciation and respect for the majority of activists they had met, whom they believed were motivated through an earnest desire to stand in solidarity with Palestinians. They did, however, also identify some important challenges. For example, all four of them mentioned the difficulties that arise when activists arrive without any idea about the history of the struggle, the culture, or the politics. While this was identified as a challenge, it was not presented as a problem. They all seemed willing to accommodate these differences, to educate and inform them, and to accept that many people went there to learn.

Another important point raised by one of the community organizers pertained to the increasing numbers of activists and some alternative ways the resources now used for travel could be otherwise spent. She explained:

> The money that was spent on those people and their tickets, which is not a little, could have been used on tangible things. For example, we have schools that have broken windows. I think we need to rethink this program. For instance, rather than have fifty participants come to create pressure, ten are enough. The remaining people can be directed to work with local organizations to rehabilitate the land or the water cisterns. The cost of a ticket for one can be used to build a water cistern for a Palestinian family and we know that the next war is going to be over water ... The amount of money would be better spent, rather than just to profit the airline companies.

She went on to reflect upon some of the burdensome impacts that the large numbers have had on the community's resources:

> Of course the huge numbers of people also put additional burden on the local people. For example, at Birzeit University we were required to do community work and we would often go

help the farmers with the olive picking. Well, at the end of the day, they would put out food for us that probably cost more than the olives we had picked. If ten [activists] went, then it was manageable, but when fifty [activists] would go, then it would mean that every family in the village would have to contribute something. So it was a real burden.

Another compelling point raised by one of the community organizers centered on what the activists understood their roles to be. In his experience, when the activists came to be rescuers or protectors, then problems arose. He also explained that some assumed the role of trying to bridge gaps between Palestinians and Israelis. This type of attitude was not only frustrating at an ideological level, but at a very material one as well. He explained that the stresses that come up in such situations simply cannot be afforded in light of serious life and death stakes. As he put it, "It is not [like] waving a flag at a [demonstration] in your city where the worst you can get is a police officer pushing you away. It is way beyond that." In his view, to be helpful, the activists needed to have an unambiguous understanding that they were there only to support Palestinians. He explains: "You are not here to bridge the gap and to bring people together. You are here for that specific task – you are with Palestinians against the occupation, period. If the people come here and accept the idea that they are here to partner with the Palestinians in the struggle [or] if they come here with the clear point of view, then there are no problems." When asked about how he thinks Palestinians in general feel about the activists being in their communities, his response corroborated the ones of the Palestinian women mentioned earlier. He said: "People are warm and welcoming. But also the annoying thing is their [the activists'] eyes are always on you; whatever you do wrong is registered. And that is why people feel that their privacy is invaded all the time."

One of the organizers questioned what is accomplished when, as she put it, "we show the world that people are standing in solidarity with us." She has come to believe that organizing in their home countries would be a more effective way to act in solidarity with Palestinians. As she explained, "A demonstration in France calling for the rights of the Palestinians is better than sending all of those [French] people to Palestine."

The Fine Line Between Advocacy and Imperialism 115

A curious and unexpected theme that ran through all four of the interviews relates to tourism. In soliciting the views of Palestinian community organizers to consider what tensions come up for them in their work with solidarity activists, I discovered that their concerns centre not only on activists, but also on tourists who increasingly come to the Occupied Territories on political reality or observation tours. More interestingly, it soon became evident that for these organizers, the distinction between activist and tourist was not always very clear. For example, two of the organizers described some of the activists as treating their time in Palestine "like it was a vacation." As one of them put it, "It's like paying a visit to somewhere like a tourist, but instead of being interested in the shrines [tourist sights], you are more interested in the people."

Exploring this theme further, I discovered that political tourism is a growing trend and one that is seen by many Palestinians as an effective means of getting their message out. In fact, two of the organizers who were interviewed were now involved in offering political tours – a venture increasingly seen as reasonable. As one Palestine-based organization called Alternative Tourism Group explains in their tour guide, members of their community can be self-empowered by conducting their own tours as a pragmatic way of setting the tourist agenda (i.e. narrating their own histories) while at the same time bolstering their economy with the tourist dollar.[42] Indeed, the fascinating overlaps between tourism and activism bear further consideration, and it is to this trend that I return in the Afterword section of this book.

SUMMARY:
ON FINE LINES AND SLIPPAGES

What can be gleaned from the perspectives of the activists is that the strategy of deploying a white/Western presence is not one that necessarily achieves what it sets out to do. Stories of overbearing Westerners endangering people and of activists being cared for and protected by the people they are purportedly assisting very clearly indicate paradoxes and contradictions that occur "on the ground" of this activism. Furthermore, this research supports Simona Sharoni's observation that solidarity projects are often defined by those carrying out the act of solidarity rather than by the people whom one is in solidarity with, thereby pointing to the imperative for respecting the local leadership in these projects.[43]

The activists' concerns therefore offer important insights into the imperialist relations of power in which their interventions are embedded and show that they are riddled with ambivalence, doubt, and complex ethical struggle. Yet, many were able to mitigate discomforting concerns about their presence. By viewing and portraying themselves as wanted, helpful, and as well-meaning, some were able to reconcile their concerns about the racialized dominance they enact through their presence. While the implications of these findings will be discussed in Chapter Seven, the goal of this chapter has been to illustrate the very "fine line" between the advocacy and imperialism of these interventions. Indeed, in showing how the activists oscillated between being conflicted and being comforted, and all the related ambivalence that comes with these encounters, one can see, in very concrete ways, Frankenberg's observation on the easy slippages from antiracism to racism.

CHAPTER SIX

"Split Affinities": Gender and Sexual Violence in Solidarity Movements[1]

An Internet flyer that reached the desk of a right-wing Israeli newspaper journalist in 2010 led to heated feminist debates and what has been described as "a media storm."[2] The flyer advertised a sexual harassment workshop for young Israeli women activists who were involved in direct-action solidarity against the occupation in the *Sheikh Jarrah* neighbourhood of East Jerusalem.[3] The very need to hold such a workshop, the journalist argued, was evidence of the widespread sexual harassment of young women activists by Palestinian men with whom they were in solidarity. In response to these accusations, Yvonne Deutsch, a long-time feminist anti-occupation activist and one of the workshop facilitators, tried to contextualize the issue by pointing out that since sexual harassment exists everywhere as part of widespread violence against women within patriarchy, there is no reason to assume that the field of direct action against the occupation would be immune to its occurrence. She also added that the young Israeli women activists being invited to the workshop were not only coping with harassment from Palestinian men but also with harassment from the Israeli army and policemen. This information, in Deutsch's view, was of little interest to the journalist. The simple fact that such a workshop was being held, rhetorically and ideologically equipped him with "a new way of attacking the Palestinians." He saw the workshop as evidence of their danger.[4]

A right-wing feminist lawyer named Roni Aloni-Sadovnik subsequently entered the debate, first blaming the workshop organizers for silencing sexual harassment and eventually accusing them of covering up a rape that occurred in the *Sheikh Jarrah Solidarity*

Movement. In response to these accusations, Deutsch clearly denied any knowledge that a rape had occurred.[5] She also pointed to the absurdity of being accused of trying to silence women concerning sexual harassment when she and her colleagues had organized a workshop specifically addressing the issue and to create opportunities for discussion.

This incident brings to the foreground a number of contentious issues with respect to race, gender, sexual violence, and solidarity struggles. First, it captures the wide assumption that movements for social justice are "pure" spaces in which violence does not take place. Second, it illustrates the tensions and factions that exist within feminisms, especially with respect to interlocking issues of race and gender. In this case, we see the leftist anti-occupation Israeli feminists attempting to address the issue of sexual harassment in ways that do not perpetrate racism, while their right-wing liberal counterparts accuse them of selling out feminism and colluding with patriarchy. Third, and most importantly, it captures a dilemma that many women-solidarity activists have faced for years and in myriad political contexts. That is, it illustrates how women in solidarity struggles often find themselves wary of addressing sexual-violence issues because to do so gives those in positions of power reasons to further justify racist oppression. As the incident above reveals, the attempt to offer a workshop to discuss the issue of sexual harassment became grounds to circulate the racist views that some men, in this case Palestinian, are particularly prone towards the violent treatment and degradation of women.

This chapter reflects upon these issues in depth. Specifically, I will utilize the idea of "split affinities" first coined by feminist scholar Valerie Smith to characterize the inner conflicts that arise from the impossibility of choosing sides between gender and race.[6] Drawing from the interviews I conducted with women activists, I demonstrate that it is not just race, but race as it interlocks with gender, that situates the activists in particular and precarious ways. Building further upon the theme of the discontinuities that arise within transnational accompaniment activism, I consider here the gendered dimension to deploying an embodied racialized presence. In illustrating some of the competing tensions at the convergence of racism and sexism that come up in this form of activism, I argue that given the different systems at play, race (whiteness) gives the female activists power while, simultaneously, gender disempowers them. Furthermore, in showing that gender plays a significant role in the ways activists are positioned, and in shaping their experiences, I argue that this site of activism is a very masculinist one, particularly its aim of "offering protection." The necessity of representing themselves as *not* vulnerable is exacerbated for women who are participating in the role of offering protection. To define this transnational activism as a masculinist space is to take into account, firstly, that the notion of activism itself is gendered through the dichotomy which posits active as male and passive as female. Furthermore, that this activism is transnational also symbolizes the masculine insofar as within a local/global binary, the global is often understood as masculine while the local is taken as feminine.[7] Put simply, the world of activism is still very much "a boy's game" and to participate in it, women need to be "one of the boys." As such, women activists simply cannot deploy privilege in the same way the men activists do, and they are required to calculate their strategies much differently.

GENDER AND SEXISM IN SOCIAL MOVEMENTS

Feminist theories contend that being unconscious of one's physicality is not a luxury afforded to women who are constantly aware of the threat of violence and that racialized embodiment is always mediated by gendered positioning.[8] How do these gendered dimensions of embodied experience unfold in activist contexts? Some have argued that, symbolically, women's bodies in protest and social movements signify spatial transgression into a masculinized space. For example, Margaret Laware's work on the Greenham Common Peace Camp shows how the women activists used their bodies "as a subversive tactic to rhetorically challenge the real and symbolic boundary markers that the [nuclear missile] base represented" by literally and figuratively transgressing boundaries and by being visibly "out of place."[9] Laware refers to such tactics as an *embodied rhetoric*. Similarly, sociologist Cynthia Cranford studies gendered aspects of social movements, and she points out that the inclusion of women's (and children's) bodies in protests is effective because it helps to frame social justice not only as a male politic, but also as a "family" concern.[10] Moreover, in Cranford's view, such tactics work at upsetting the gendered and racialized hegemony insofar as the women actors transgress from private spaces into public ones. This kind of view also emerges from Sasson-Levy and Rapoport's study on the Women in Black movement which shows that the public is more disturbed when female bodies express dissent.[11] We also learn from the work of Kathleen Blee that sexism persists within "mixed" gender groups.[12] For instance, the above mentioned study from Sasson-Levy and Rapoport offers particularly salient insights about the positioning of women in mixed-gender groups through a comparative analysis of two Jewish Israeli movements (one of which is Women in Black), both against the occupation of Palestine, showing that in the mixed gender group, the women "were the doers/the men the thinkers," despite the fact that the women were leading intellectuals, activists and scholars.[13]

When social movements are strategically cross-racial, the sexualized dynamics that emerge through them seem to take on a particularly complex form. Writing about the US civil rights movement, Dierenfield reveals some important insights into its sexist and sexualized dimensions and explains that despite some informal bans on cross-racial intimate relations in the movement, cross-racial sex was commonplace.[14] Moreover, from Dierenfield's study, we learn that some black men in the movement used white women's commitments to antiracism as a manipulative tool and challenged them to "prove their lack of prejudice in bed," and that some of those who resisted were labelled "racists" or "white bitches," while others succumbed out of liberal guilt.[15] Becky Thompson also addresses some of the racialized dynamics and issues of sexuality between black men and white women in the US civil rights movement and explains that they were particularly contentious because, "for many historically sound reasons, [they] hindered white and black women from seeing each other as allies."[16]

SAFETY, PROTECTION, SEXUALITY, AND THE GENDERING OF ACTIVISTS' BODIES

Based on the interviews I conducted, the ways in which gender interlocked with race to structure the female activists' experiences varied greatly and shifted according to their particular contexts.

Several activists conveyed to me that they were treated better than the "local" women. A few of the women, particularly the older ones, believed that an upshot of being "foreign" was being treated like an equal to men because in certain contexts they were respected and listened to more than they were accustomed to in Canada. For example, Sandra found herself organising mainly with Palestinian men, because, she explained, more men than women spoke English where she was. Consequently, she, and some of the other Western women activists she was with, believed that the Palestinian men regarded them more as equals than the Palestinian women did.

Referring to her solidarity activism in Guatemala, Joanne described her gendered position by saying, "If you are a [white] woman, you are respected as much as a man." Natalie, who was in Palestine, had an anecdote that captured a similar dynamic. She said: "We were at somebody's house, and so the women prepare the coffee and bring it to us, and we're treated, in a way, like we are not equal to the women in the household. Not just because we are visitors, but our status as women is very different – as Westernized women, as women who have this kind of professional role or whatever it is, that provides another way of relating to men that's not part of that culture in the same way." This elevation of status as women occurs through what Barbara Heron has identified as a hierarchy of gender/race between subordination and domination which allows Western women who venture into Others' spaces to claim social identities unavailable to them under Western patriarchies.[17] Furthermore, Heron's work shows that in foreign spaces, white women are considered as *more* equal to men, and can therefore be invited to participate in the subordination of the "local" women.

Another pronounced gendered dynamic that emerged in the interviews pertained to how the women activists' bodies were sexualized. Women activists who were considered physically attractive were strategically utilized in situations to negotiate with military forces.[18] Chris said that at checkpoints in Palestine, for example, the ISM leaders would sometimes send "the pretty young girls to talk to the border guards." Women activists' flirting with the border guards was regarded by several activists to be an effective negotiating tactic. As Paul observed in at least one situation, it may have prevented them being arrested: "the leader of this group, he picked me as the oldest one in the crew, and he picked out a girl, she was quite pretty, and he sent us up to negotiate with this captain who was about to arrest us. And we went up there and she did most of it and I stood there, and she chatted him up a bit, and mollified him and so we didn't get arrested, fortunately." Although such strategies may indeed facilitate access in some instances, they also raise questions about the types of contributions women activists are seen to make. Lisa observed that the movement is merely a microcosm of society and as such, there is no reason to think solidarity activism would not reproduce sexism, classism, and heterosexism. She said that many of the white male activists use their male privilege in various ways, and that some display machismo. Sandra noticed that the international male activists tended to be judgemental of the sexism amongst Palestinian men, yet they did not take responsibility for their own sexism and patriarchal attitudes.

Women's bodies also played a particular role in organized demonstrations. The following excerpt refers to a strategy of "layering" the visible markings of race and gender hierarchies. As Jason explained, "It is [like] layers. They put the Israeli Jews who are pro-Palestinian at the front of the demonstration. Next in line are the internationals, and then behind them are the Palestinians ... And usually they put the women at the front and the men at the back, because the women might not get shot." In this description, race symbolically and materially interlocks with gender and relies on gendered tropes which render women more vulnerable and less of a threat; their bodies serve more effectively as buffers than men's bodies, and for this reason, they are put at the front.

While these narratives about gender offer glimpses into the interlocking aspects of this form of activism, the complex ways that notions of safety, protection, and sexuality are inscribed onto the white female activists' bodies become most evident in their narratives about sexual violence. By sexual violence, I refer to a continuum of experiences ranging from unwanted sexual attention to rape. I focus on the experiences of three women in particular, one who was in the Middle East, one in Indonesia, and the third in the United States.

Before proceeding to this examination, I want to note my own apprehensions about this topic. My main concern stems from the inadvertent but very real possibility that I may perpetuate the colonial myth that white women are especially prone to sexual violence. In focusing on white women's experiences of sexual violence in "foreign" spaces, I am equally concerned about eliding the prevalence of sexual violence that women experience in their daily lives in their own communities and thereby erroneously promoting the idea that the primary perpetrators of sexual violence are "those" men. Furthermore, there is the issue of the sexual violence that First World male activists may have perpetrated against women activists or "local" women – a topic that, curiously, did not come up in any of the interviews and requires further investigation.

HARASSMENT AND THREAT

When it came to corporeal danger and safety, the women in the study had a range of experiences. For example, Elizabeth felt that being a woman in Palestine was safer than being a woman in Canada:

> In the West Bank, I felt an extra degree of safety that I don't feel as a white woman here in North America, when it comes to being safe on the street for example. Part of it is because it's a Muslim culture and so men and women tend not to interact in the same way, so that men tend to keep their eyes down, or you don't get harassed or anything like that. And generally there isn't alcohol because it's a Muslim culture, so people aren't out drunk, so that oddly I felt safer there than I do here.

Sandra believed that being "older" was advantageous because the Israeli soldiers did not consider her to be a threat, and so she adopted the strategy of "pulling moral rank" with them, "like – 'I am old enough to be your mother!' type thing." She said that on one level age gains her respect as a woman, but at another level because she is older she felt as though she "disappeared" in the eyes of many of the men she encountered.

To feel safer, some women sought to blend in and not draw attention to themselves as foreign. For example, describing her experiences in Iraq, Sarah explains: "[Because] My hair colour is blond, reddish blond, I did attract some attention that I was aware of ... Of course, devout Muslim women cover their hair. So I did become aware that it was kind of flashy [laughter] to have your hair, blonde like that ... [So] be prepared to keep your hair tied back. Just to blend in. It's not useful to be 'look at me; I'm the foreigner' in that situation. I don't think that's very useful."

Unlike Elizabeth and Sarah who gained a sense of safety while they were abroad, Lindsey and Tanya, both women in their twenties, spoke about the ways, as Western women, they were presumed to be sexually active and available and how that made them vulnerable to particular forms of harassment. Tanya described ongoing harassment from men on the street as an inevitable part of the activism in the geopolitical context she was in:

> I had men grab my bum and say things to me. But I don't know, I think you just have to know how to deal with it and not, it's not like the end of the world. And the way that you respond to it is really important. Like you can be as stern as you want in saying no to people and if they touch you, to slap them back. It will only help you to gain respect in the community because they'll realize that isn't appropriate behaviour towards you. And that you expect to be treated the same way that a man would treat a local woman.

What is noteworthy about this statement is the way she glosses over the fact that men were grabbing her body instead stressing that what was important was the way she responded to it. Thus, she assumes responsibility to avoid, if not prevent, this type of treatment.

Lindsey's trip extended over a period of almost one year during which she experienced various forms of harassment and threats. She spoke at length about the struggles she had forming friendships with men at the beginning:

> I have had ongoing trouble trying to figure out how to interact with young men who want to befriend me because I'm a foreigner. Information from my [local] women friends about what's appropriate behaviour for young men and women is

helpful, but the problem is the men who approach me don't expect behaviour appropriate to a [local] woman. So, they pressure me to give my phone number, go places with them, visit with them, etc. Sometimes I feel exhausted refusing all this while trying not to be rude. I always refuse because some of them have intentions distinctly dishonourable, borne out of TV, and even the most benign are only interested in me as a foreigner, not as a person.

By way of example, Lindsey spoke of a particularly difficult experience with someone whom she described as "a stalker-type individual." This was a man she met and spoke to on a bus who later started showing up at her workplace and house. She explains that she could not figure out "how to tell him to bugger off" because of the sensitive cultural factors. His showing up at her house caused her distress to the point of feeling at times like she was "on the verge of tears all day." She also added that it was hard for her to explain why she was so upset by this, especially because she did not think that he was "really dangerous."

Journal entries written by Lindsey in the early period of her trip suggest that she was sometimes amused by the constant male attention she received on the streets, but that as time passed she grew tired of it. For instance, she wrote: "being a 'beautiful' woman is not everything it's cracked up to be." Lindsey also spoke of incidents of being grabbed on the street, and like Tanya, she too minimized it by saying, "It's just annoying, not dangerous." In her journal she wrote, "There are some men who just want to see what a white woman feels like, I guess." In her letters home, she reassured her friends that she did not go out alone at night and that she did not ever go to unfamiliar areas alone. To further reassure her friends and family, she wrote: "I have the phone number of the UN security advisor, the chief of police, and the Canadian ambassador on me at all times. I have met these people and they will help me if I ever need it. I am probably safer here than I usually am in Canada."

Despite repeated assertions of her safety and her insistence that these situations "were not really dangerous," the details that she reveals suggest the threat was indeed serious. For instance, the female activists on her team were told to always carry a condom as a safety precaution so that in the event of a sexual assault, they might convince their assailant to wear it. As the interview progressed, she disclosed that sexual harassment was a big source of stress, especially at the end of her stay. She explained that for the most part she could "tune it out," but was not able to after a while. She explained that foreign women had to prepare themselves for that constant, unwelcome attention. Although, she wanted to clarify that for the most part the harassment was verbal, adding that some of the comments were "tame," like, "Hey pretty lady, marry me." She felt that for women going there to protect others, such treatment, however mild, can be quite disheartening, and that these experiences impacted how much protection she could offer to the people she was there to assist.

One experience that Lindsey shared with great detail was about an intruder who, on three separate occasions, had tried to break into the house in which she was staying. When I asked how she and her housemates (all white women) responded to these break-ins, she said that they had called the police on one occasion, but that eventually they hired a security guard and increased the physical security of their house. Although they suspected that they were being targeted because they were foreign white women, they were not certain, because at the time, there had been reports of local women being raped in the area. She also explained that this could have been a ploy to intimidate the activists so that they would leave. As she put it: "We weren't sure at the time on whether it was a random psycho guy or it was possible that he was being paid by the army to intimidate us ... because that is also quite a common technique supposedly, to pay local folks to break into people's homes to scare them. So that was an even scarier thought because if that was the case, we could expect it to happen more." She added that when a male security guard or a male member of the organization subsequently stayed at the house, the break-in attempts stopped.

RAPE

The ways that the female activists sought to negotiate their positioning and the gendered complexities that arose for them is perhaps best illustrated through the narrative of Barbara, an activist who participated in the 1964 Freedom Summer campaign of the civil rights movement. Although her solidarity work was long ago and not transnational in the same sense as the activist experiences examined in this book, it nevertheless warrants a detailed exploration because it starts to unravel not only the complex interlocking and competing tensions at the convergence of racism and sexism that come up around racialized and gendered embodiment, but it also offers important insights about the ways some activists try to negotiate their positioning. Furthermore, as I showed in Chapter One, there are many instructive parallels that can be gleaned from examining the civil rights movement alongside the more contemporary transnational solidarity struggles.

Barbara was twenty-one years old and living in Toronto when she responded to an advertisement in a political magazine that was recruiting white people to join the Student Nonviolent Co-ordinating Committee (SNCC).[19] She subsequently went first to Mississippi and then to Georgia where she worked on various civil rights movement projects. During the interview, Barbara disclosed to me that towards the end of the summer campaign, she was raped by a black man who was also a member of the movement. Barbara described her rape as follows:

> One night, people were going down to a restaurant in Atlanta, and I got a ride down. I knew so few people there, and I was just kind of sitting with the group and then people started to go, and I asked if I could have a ride back to the conference location and this SNCC guy said he'd take me back. He dropped everybody off except me, and then he took me to this house in this black neighbourhood ... at that point I said 'Are you going to take me back?' and he said 'No, you could stay at our house tonight.' And then he raped me that night.

She recounted that the next morning, he drove her to the SNCC office "just like nothing had happened." I asked her if she told anyone about the rape, and she said that she had told a friend. Importantly, she added that she did not tell anybody else out of concern that "it would just validate all the things that they [white people] were already saying [about black men]" and added that she "didn't want it used against the movement." She did, however, decide that she could no longer be involved in SNCC and left the next morning.

In narrating this experience, Barbara stressed the changes in the interracial dynamics of the movement that had taken place over the summer. In particular, she shared two anecdotes which illustrate shifting temporal and spatial dimensions with respect to the experience she had as a white woman in the movement. Barbara said that initially and throughout most of the summer, she and the other white activists felt threatened by white people who were opposing the civil rights campaign. One example of this threat took place on her first night of training when the activists were told that the Ku Klux Klan had burned a cross in the yard of the college in Ohio where they were staying. Moreover, the activists were informed that three men who had gone to Mississippi ahead of them were missing and were believed to have been killed.[20] Indeed, in the training sessions that Barbara participated in, the activists had role-played how to respond to attacks by the police or by white people in Mississippi. She had not anticipated any animosity from black activists.

Barbara's senses of fear and safety changed very significantly, however, toward the end of the summer. It is important to recall that, by then, the *Freedom Summer* project had ended, and most of the white students had gone home. Moreover, the end of the summer campaign brought with it a breakdown of the interracial harmony that appeared to be in place at the start, and racial tensions overtook the campaign.[21] Barbara explained that, over time, black activists had begun to challenge the interracial composition of organizations like SNCC and were increasingly compelled by ideas of racial separatism and violence as self-defence.[22] Barbara attributed part of the change in energy to the fact that black activists had endured beatings and jail all summer long and were worn down and hostile. As she describes it, "that does something to people after a while." She described the feeling in the movement at that time as "manic" and said that she remembered beginning to feel afraid of the black men in the movement. One example she gave was a description of how she felt attending a mainly black SNCC convention in Atlanta, Georgia in the fall: "And I remember sleeping in this dormitory and the dormitories were mixed and I remember sleeping with my sheet over my head so nobody would know whether I was a man or a woman. I was scared."

Gender and Sexual Violence in Solidarity Movements   129

In Barbara's view, these changes in the movement help to explain and contextualize the rape that she subsequently experienced. If, as Barbara thinks, the rape was in fact brought about through the shifting cross-racial relations in the movement, then her experience illustrates that changing dynamics within a movement can have a profound and adverse effect on the ways that women are treated within it. More specifically, Barbara's experience illustrates that female activists bear the brunt of these dynamics, often through incidents of sexual violence. While the changes in the Freedom Summer campaign may have also resulted in white men in the movement being seen as opponents rather than allies, and while it is likely that they also faced hostility from black members of the movement, one can presume that, for the most part, hostility did not manifest in sexual aggression toward them.

Barbara said that after the rape, her "self-image had plummeted." She explained that it took her a long time to sort out what happened and to "put it to rest," but that over the years, and through her education and subsequent activism, she came to know that her experience in Atlanta was not an isolated situation, and that the sexual violence she experienced was part of a much wider phenomenom of violence against women.

Despite the very disparate temporal and spatial contexts and the manifestations of their experiences, Tanya, Lindsey and Barbara share some commonalities that pertain to minimizing or silencing the sexual violence that they faced. In the discussion I proceed to next, I identify three specific and simultaneous factors that may be contributing to their responses: the politics of silence in cross-racial sexual violence; the need to prioritize race or state violence over gendered violence; and the need to "fit- in" to masculinist, activist spaces by not seeming vulnerable.

SEXUAL VIOLENCE AND THE POLITICS OF SILENCE

In thinking about race and sexual violence, Sherene Razack contends that one must take notice of the racialized *structure* of the narratives and of how the people in the narratives become "figures" in one central story.[23] In some respects, the scenarios of rape and harassment outlined in this chapter are re-articulations of a familiar black rapist/white victim motif insofar as white women and their assailants represent two sets of figures in the "discursive family" of rape scenarios.[24] In other words, the men of colour in question were marked with the assumption of sexual aggression and threat long before they acted. Conversely, the white women were encoded as being vulnerable to the threat of sexual violence. As a first step to analysis, therefore, it is important to recognize that the activists' experiences of sexual violence were already embedded within historical legacies of gender and race. To this end, I draw from writing on the silence around cross-racial sexual violence, a topic that has long been the subject of controversy and debate.[25]

In 1976, Susan Brownmiller wrote about how white liberals' awareness of racial oppression and compassion for the alleged rapists created a situation where "to discuss rape is to be on the side of the prosecution."[26] In Brownmiller's view, the fear of playing into the hands of racists dictated such responses and resulted in the wrongful absolving of black male rapists. She cites a study in which a young, white victim of rape revealed her reluctance to prosecute her rapist, or even to report the crime, stemming partially from her political belief that the rape was "an extension of the social struggle of black against white or poor against rich."[27] She offers another example of a young white woman who was raped by a black youth who said, "I just can't throw off history. I feel like I'm being used to pay off the old debts to men falsely accused in the South of raping white women."[28] Brownmiller posits such emotional and guilt-ridden responses as irresponsible and anti-feminist. Worse yet, in her view, these women were consciously being complicit, insofar as their responses are an extension of women's traditional role of "making things all right."[29] Brownmiller's book, though hailed as a key text in the feminist canon, has since been widely criticized for sacrificing race for gender and for resuscitating "the old racist myth of the black rapist" rather than problematizing it.[30]

The complexities of the politics of silence in cross-racial rape have been examined in more recent and nuanced analyses. For example, Wendy Hesford contends that we need to contemplate the politics of silence and the embodiment of racialized rape scripts, given the historic power of white women's disclosures or accusations of rape "to unleash violence against black men."[31] Similarly, Mary Eagleton has written, "That in certain historical circumstances, white women's silence about rape could be [considered] a condition for political progress."[32] Both Hesford and Eagleton make their arguments through the analysis of a compelling short story by Alice Walker entitled "Advancing Luna – and Ida B. Wells." The story is about a tenuous friendship between two students who worked together in the civil rights movement in Atlanta. The student who narrates the story is an unnamed young black woman. The other is Luna, a young white woman. The two meet the summer of 1965 in Atlanta at a political conference and rally. The following year, Luna discloses to her friend that a black civil rights activist had raped her the previous summer. She points out that these tensions culminate when, in response to her friend's question about why she didn't "scream her head off," Luna replies, "You know why."[33]

I propose that a dynamic similar to the predetermined racialized script of sexual violence examined by these scholars may have played a role in the women activists' efforts to silence and/or minimize their experiences. Firstly, it is important to consider that as activists committed to ending racism, these women's responses may have been shaped by the bigger political concern of the movement. In other words, since Lindsey, Tanya, and Barbara all saw themselves as being on the same political side as their male assailants, their responses may have some parallels with the responses of women of colour who are reluctant to report sexual violence in their communities in an effort not to perpetuate racist myths about the violence of men of colour.[34] By minimizing or not talking about their experiences, the activists may have been attempting to counter the history of racist allegations against men of colour, and in so doing, perhaps see themselves as making an ethical political decision.

In the narratives presented here, this tension can perhaps be seen most clearly in Barbara's case. Barbara, who, given the time period and the fact that cross-racial rape has long been used to justify lynching, racist violence, and racial segregation, knew full well that "calling rape" would have serious repercussions not only on her assailant, but on the black community as a whole.[35]

Since Barbara's rape predated the "breaking the silence" about sexual violence era that emerged through feminism in the 1970s and 1980s, it is fair to speculate that had her rapist been a white man, she may have responded in the exact same way and not told anyone. Moreover, it could be argued that Barbara's rape was a common acquaintance rape and had nothing to do with race, especially when one bears in mind that her rapist's demeanour of being nice to her the next day and acting as though nothing had happened is consistent with the behaviour of most men who commit acquaintance rape.[36] Additionally, we know that in cases of acquaintance rape, the victim's distress is compounded by a sense of betrayal which helps to reveal why the fact that her assailant was a man in the same movement was likely both confusing and particularly hurtful. It is not possible to know whether or not Barbara's rape was racially motivated. Nor does it matter. What is important is to draw attention to the role that race undeniably played in shaping her experience and the possibilities that were available to her. The historical circumstances Barbara faced presented her with the very difficult task of reconciling ethics, politics, and self-care. Indeed, Barbara's stated reasons for not reporting the rape, her concern that it would set the movement back, clearly reflect the racialized and gendered dynamics that surrounded it. Her decision seemed to be based, at least in part, on how black men were already perceived.[37]

PRIORITIZING RACISM AND "SHELVING" SEXISM

A second and related way of explaining the interlocking dynamics of race and gender as they play out in these sexual violence scenarios is the widespread, implicit understanding that only one system of oppression can be tackled at a time. Although, on the whole, transnational solidarity groups declare a commitment to anti-sexism in their frameworks, the primary mandate they are driven by is one that sets anti-state violence or antiracist violence as its goal. Thus, although sexism is acknowledged in the movements, it is not given priority. I argue that conceptualizing these systems of domination as separate results is limiting the possible responses to sexual violence. Put simply, I suggest that although they may be permitted to talk about sexism in the abstract (and perhaps even challenge male colleagues on sexism) female activists must not talk of actual experiences of sexual violence that happen during their activist experiences.

Writing about Native American women activist communities in the US, Andrea Smith reveals that a prevailing idea amongst the activists is that they are "Indian and women – in that order."[38] In other words, they are oppressed first and foremost as Indians, not as women.[39] Furthermore, Smith argues that this notion is perpetuated in documents and theories which articulate Native women's activism in ways that are overly simplistic. The crux of Smith's argument is the need for theories that focus on the ways state/colonial violence and gender violence *constitute one another*. Such a conceptualization serves as a helpful entry point for theorizing the activists' experiences of sexual violence.

First, Smith's work helps us to see that although struggles against patriarchy and state colonialism must not be understood to be separate systems of domination at the level of theory, the reality is that on the ground of activism, they often *are* separated.[40] The need to focus on one issue at a time in the day-to-day work of activism has been documented in other decolonizing struggles as well. Given the urgency in places like Palestine, for example, women activists are expected to pour their energies into the struggle against the state, in spite of any feminist commitments and concerns they may also have.[41] Thus, while taking care not to elide the vast differences in histories, contexts, subject positions, and power between Native women activists and white-women- solidarity activists, I believe that a parallel can be drawn between the two groups. Like the Native women that Smith is writing about, some of the female activists see themselves as involved in a struggle against state and colonial powers. Furthermore, as allies, they likely adopt the position of the women activists with whom they are working in solidarity. In this sense, many are likely to see themselves as "anti-state activists first, women second." This prevailing idea creates the conditions whereby women "shelve," or set aside feminist issues while focussing on the "real" issue, that is, racial/state/colonial violence. The split affinity dynamic is thus clear. The female transnational solidarity activists must choose between, or prioritize, either racial justice *or* gender justice. Yet, the danger of such a dualistic analysis, Andrea Smith reminds us, is that it "fails to recognize that it is precisely through sexism and gender violence that colonialism and white supremacy have been successful."[42] More importantly, for the purposes of the analysis presented here, within such a paradigm, sexism *within* movements cannot be addressed.

SEEKING LEGITIMACY IN THE MASCULINE SPACE OF ACTIVISM

A third power dynamic that is operating through the activists' accounts of sexual violence pertains to gendered discourses of fear, control, and power. Bearing in mind that the activists largely think of themselves as disembodied when it comes to race (as argued in the introduction to this book), it is clear that traces of this notion of a universal disembodied self may seep into the realm of gender as well. The liberal notion of the universal subject, in which men and women are purportedly not differentiated, is incongruent with the women activists' confrontations with their embodied differences. As such, they minimize these differences in order to construct themselves as rational, autonomous, and in control. To illustrate this, I begin by drawing from feminist research on fear and violence more generally, and then consider the gendered conditions that emerge in the particular context of transnational solidarity activism.

The type of minimizing displayed in the narratives presented earlier is a common feature of gendered discourses on violence. Drawing from their feminist, poststructural study on gender and fear of violence amongst university students in Edinburgh, Mehta and Bondi report that although female participants said they felt afraid of violence only "occasionally," they adjusted their behaviours and self-regulated their movements in ways that suggested *acute* vulnerability.[43] Mehta and Bondi propose that the tension between what the women say and the way they live is a way to feel self-empowered. They explain: "To report feeling afraid only 'occasionally' may itself be a part of taking up a position in a discourse that constructs excessive emotionality (particularly fear) as 'irrational,'" and associated with passivity – all states associated with powerlessness – and hence rationality and control of fear as empowering.[44] Like the women in Mehta and Bondi's study, the narratives of sexual violence articulated by the women activists I interviewed suggest that they may find it desirable and necessary to think of themselves as unafraid.[45] In order to be "one of the boys," one cannot be vulnerable or "violatable." As Mehta and Bondi put it, "the negotiation of danger is in many ways the negotiation of power."[46] Writing about men of colour who seek to be one of the white boys, Razack observes a similar dynamic.[47] She states: "The terms and conditions of membership ... [are such that] men of colour must forget the racial violence that is done to them."[48] Razack explains that to secure belonging, the men of colour must deflect attention away from their shortcomings as less than ideal men. Thus, one of the ways men of colour gain respectability is to deny racism. In the context I am discussing, a comparable situation is in place. To gain respectability and be taken seriously within the masculinist space of activism, women must deny and/or minimize the sexual violence to which they are subjected. Thus, to participate in this activism in a way that is legitimate is to contribute to the denial of sexism. Bearing in mind, too, that the activists see themselves as responsible for others' physical safety, it is easy to see why the women must convey fearlessness. In sum, the ways in which the women activists minimize threats and fears of violence are thus shaped by their "investments" in being seen as having power.[49]

CONCLUSION:
INTERLOCKING SYSTEMS OF GENDER AND RACE

In hindsight, since sexual violence was an unanticipated theme that emerged in the interviews, I wonder what else might have arisen if the topic had been pursued more systematically. In other words, although I consistently inquired about how gender shaped the activists' experiences in all the interviews, it might have been instructive to also ask very explicitly about experiences with sexual violence. As such, one can assume that there are additional gendered aspects pertaining to sexual violence that did not necessarily come up in the interviews, but that certainly warrant further investigation.

These challenges and limitations notwithstanding, this analysis exposes one of the contradictions at the core of accompaniment-observer activist projects; that is, that the white body is safer and can therefore lend protection to differentially racialized bodies. When gender is taken into consideration, we see that the threat and experience of sexual violence profoundly affects the female activists' experiences, thus illustrating the complexities that arise in relations of solidarity with respect to the gendered aspects of embodiment.

To consider the implications of these gender relations, it is important to recall that to bypass the dominance of male leadership, women in the civil rights movement, the anti-Vietnam war movement, and the anti-occupation of Palestine movement (to name only a few), have found that women-only groups work best.[50] That said, there is ample evidence to suggest that women-only groups, though they may create more of a space for addressing questions of gender and sexual violence within movements, inadvertently let men off the hook for having to deal with these issues.[51]

More generally, the issues addressed in this chapter point to a larger debate currently found in many types of social movements. Many of the concerns raised here can be found written from a personal perspective on Internet postings with headings like "Keep quiet for the cause."[52] Some of the few resources published by organisations and currently circulated on the Internet offer further insights into the ways in which these issues are currently being addressed, as well as some of the barriers to implementation. For example, dealing head on with the issue of sexual violence in activist communities of colour, a report published by INCITE! entitled "Gender Oppression. Abuse. Violence. Community accountability within the people of color progressive movement" reveals the complexities and sensitivities that are being sought.[53] The tone of this report reflects a politic in restorative justice while taking into account the needs of the survivor and the non-exclusion of the abuser from the community. Basically, the model advocates that the abuser take responsibility/accountability and commit to ongoing education about gender and violence.[54] Another report published by affiliated activist organisations, Philly's Pissed and Philly Stands Up, also reflects an approach that seeks to work with the perpetrators of sexual violence to get them to take accountability for their actions with the emphasis to rebuild trust within activist communities by working with all parties. They call their work "revolution through trial and error."[55] A pertinent point is that the activists do not want to engage with or rely on the state to resolve problems that exist in their communities. Together, my interviews with women activists and these sites all point to the need for more scholarly investigations into sexual violence in social movements and the particular complexities around silence that it presents.

CHAPTER SEVEN

Liberal Universalism and Pragmatism: Implications for Decolonizing Solidarity

There is no reason at this moment to be hopeful about the outcomes of these debates and struggles, but the past gives little reason to conclude that such struggles can never achieve tangible gains for those most concerned.

Frederick Cooper[1]

What struck me most forcibly about Yusif and Mahmud's sentiments were the uncomfortable questions they provoked about what we - as privileged westerners are actually doing when we record narratives of violence or try to bring these subaltern histories into view.

Diana Allan[2]

As the chapters in the book thus far have shown, the political efficacy of accompaniment-observer activism largely depends on being seen and recognized as white/Western, and therefore as distinct from those being targeted by violence. In effect, it is a politic of embodied racialized practice insofar as activists' bodies serve as symbolic markers of whiteness. This book began by questioning why race is rarely explicitly acknowledged in this activism despite the blatant ways in which it is mobilized. In this chapter I return to this question to theorize how that comes to be.

The experiences of the activists I interviewed indicate that the symbolic and material actions that they participate in, ranging from giving eye-witness accounts to accompanying people through checkpoints, are explicitly organized around the meanings inscribed onto their bodies and often entailed purposefully distinguishing themselves from the people they were there to assist through markers of race.[3] For instance, those who had fair skin and blond hair were displayed front and centre in demonstrations.[4] Conversely, activists whose physical traits could be read as Other (i.e. dark hair and eyes) were strategically paired with an activist who was more "white-looking." Some of these ways in which whiteness was strategically enacted and deployed suggest that their strategies rely on "gradations of whiteness" – a perceptible continuum in which certain types of whiteness yield more power than others.[5]

As stated at the start of this book, the term "internationals," which is commonly used to refer to accompaniment-observer activists, obscures the racialized power differences in this activism. It is clear that it is not merely "international" bodies with the privilege of access and mobility that enables them to be effective in this activism, but the power that is specifically attached to white/Western bodies. Additionally, the term "human shields" encompasses a key aspect of this analysis given the centrality of the body and racialized power. When used in the contexts of transnational solidarity activism, it is a term that suggests a highly racialized hierarchical differentiation whereby one (white) body stands in front of another to protect it from violence.

Given the dramatic and dangerous imagery it connotes, the term "human shields" is often used by journalists to describe accompaniment-observer activism. However, most groups organizing transnational solidarity activisms object to the use of the term. For instance, the kidnapping of the four Christian Peacemaker Team (CPT) activists in Iraq in December of 2005 put the term "human shield" in the media spotlight and provoked strong public reactions, as seen in an online debate posted on the CPT website in February 2006, while the four men were still in captivity. In this debate, Claire Evans, a personnel coordinator for the organization, discusses the CPT's work in Iraq and clearly states that she sees the term as altogether problematic because "it places the people being protected in the role of victims, and the people doing the shielding as rescuers."[6] Evans further explains that because the term "human shield" can also refer to civilians being taken by force and used as shields by those in the military, members of the CPT are concerned that using the term might wrongly suggest that they condone such practices.⁷ Yet, CPT's distancing itself from the term "human shield" is somewhat tenuous if not contradictory, given the group's motto of, "getting in the way," which, according to a CPT publication, conveys "multiple meanings including the practice of stepping between aggressors and victims."⁸

Like the CPT, the Iraq Peace Team (IPT) organization also sought to disassociate its actions from the term "human shield." Their website states, "The Iraq Peace Team is not affiliated with Human Shield projects. Though we hope to remain in Iraq in the event of an attack, we don't consider ourselves 'human shields.' IPT exists to stand in solidarity with the peoples of Iraq ... [IPT] refuses to incorporate military language or ideas to describe the peace witness of Iraq Peace Team members."⁹ Other terms that emphasize the embodied aspects of what I have been referring to as transnational accompaniment-observer activism are also contested. Groups such as the Peace Brigades, for example, use the term "unarmed bodyguard" to capture the embodied protective aspect of the activism, yet many members of the Peace Brigades reject this term.¹⁰

The tensions around the terminology used to describe transnational accompaniment-observer activism can be seen in the narratives of the activists who took part in this study. With the exception of two, all of the activists who were interviewed explicitly objected to the use of the term "human shield." The two activists who did think that the term applied to the work they had done and believed that it aptly defined their role and their experiences were both with the ISM. This is likely due to the fact that the ISM makes explicit that one of its main objectives is to provide protection through the use of international bodies (as discussed in Chapter One). However, this was not the view of all ISM members; some did express discomfort around the term even though they had, for example, been placed in the houses of suspected suicide bombers in Palestine – actions that were clearly designed to use the foreign body as a symbolic shield. This is also apparent in the case of ISM member Rachel Corrie who died while using her body in an attempt to prevent the bulldozing of a home. Although media reports referred to her as acting as a "human shield," in her own writing Corrie describes herself as a "human rights observer, documenter, or direct-action resister."[11]

There is also a gendered dimension to the responses about the terms utilized to describe their work insofar as the two activists who readily used the term "human shield" were both men. In contrast, when explaining their discomfort with the term, the women from a cross-section of groups expressed a strong dislike for the term because of the "drama," "bravado," "risk," "adventurism," and "macho" connotations it has. For some of them, the term misleadingly suggests quite literally being in the direct line of gunfire and therefore does not accurately reflect their experiences.

Although the desire to distance themselves from language that may have militaristic connotations and from gendered notions of bravado helps to explain why "human shield" is such a contested term, I propose that part of the reason it is largely refuted also has to do with the activists' imagining themselves as disembodied universal subjects. In fact, the activists often appeared to want to minimize differences between themselves and the people to whom they were offering protection, and they preferred terms like "accompaniment" and "witnessing" to describe their actions. The following explanation of the term "accompaniment" that appeared in an online newsletter article published by a group called Doctors for Global Health helps to explain why those terms are more agreeable than "human shield." Modelling itself after the principles of Peace Brigades International, this group explains that they adopted the "accompaniment" model because they believe it suggests a "mutual respect and walking alongside each other; giving and receiving; learning from and sharing with each other."[12] The notion of "accompaniment," then, is valorized because it connotes a horizontal rather than vertical positioning, allowing those doing accompaniment to consider themselves as equals in a partnership.

Importantly however, in many cases, the activists' rejection of the term "human shield" and their adoption of alternative terms such as "witnessing" or "accompaniment" had little to do with the actual actions in which they took part. The following explanation from a CPT member best captures this inconsistency. In explaining why she did not think of herself as a human shield, Sarah said:

My teammates did it, but they considered it witnessing; not shield, witness. Maybe there is a subtle line there. During the invasion in 2003, they camped out on the grounds of a water treatment plant, which was also close to a children's hospital. They camped out there not as shields so much, as saying, 'you're bombing my friends, you're bombing us.' You know, meaning, 'I'm no more worthy of life than my friends in this neighbourhood.' It's not quite shield but it may appear that way.

Although it is clear that Sarah seems to interpret the idea of being an equal as incommensurate to acting as a shield or bodyguard, it is difficult to see the distinction she tries to make, which she admits is "subtle." Moreover, one can glean from her description that the activists were indeed shielding rather than witnessing in this instance because they were using their bodies as protection. Sarah also said that she considers the expression "human shield" to be a "put down" because, she said, it is "kind of mindless."

Other activists gave more fervent oppositional responses to the term "human shields." Terry and Tanya variously stated that they found the term offensive because it reduces their value to being merely a physical body. Terry's objection was around the idea that all human shields essentially do is sit or stand, whereas, he emphasized, his group participated in much more meaningful activities such as talking to people and sending stories back to their home countries. In other words, to be thought of as "just a body" was taken to be a de-valuing of the multi-faceted dimensions of the work. Similarly, Tanya preferred to depict herself as having a range of skills and principles to offer, stressing that her moral and emotional characteristics and commitments were much greater than a mere physical presence: "To me the term 'human shield' seems to mean that you are just there as basically an object, and there are so many other things that we do other than just, like, standing there. Like we have interaction with the community and we do lots of other things. You know, getting involved in the community, and meeting people, and stuff like that."

These articulations reveal that the activists explain, deny, or minimise processes of racialization in seemingly contradictory ways. On the one hand, the fact that they travel to offer protection through their embodied presence is clearly indicative of their recognition that they are unequally positioned with respect to those they are seeking to assist. On the other hand, through various discursive moves, they appear to disavow this knowledge. The tensions around the terminology point to what is arguably the most pressing current challenge for social justice activism: the conceptual and discursive parameters of liberal universalism. Drawing on some theories on race, liberalism and social movements, in the following section I will argue that the activists' abilities to acknowledge how power is inscribed onto their bodies is largely constrained by a paradigmatic notion of a raceless, universal, white subject. Indeed, I propose that because transnational accompaniment-observer activism is a site in which activists purposefully "trade" with their whiteness, it is a compelling site for exploring the conceptual parameters of liberal universalism and how it ubiquitously limits antiracist and decolonizing practices.

RACE, EMBODIMENT, AND THE PARADOX OF LIBERAL UNIVERSALISM

Explaining that the egalitarian ideology of liberalism has unquestioningly become the hegemonic political outlook of the modern age, political philosopher Charles Mills points out that the ubiquity and attractiveness of liberalism is that it is premised upon the virtues of equality and fairness.[13] Arguing that race has "underpinned the liberal framework from the outset," Mills asks us to notice, however, that the key issue of racial equality is remarkably overlooked by liberalism.[14] According to his argument, because articulations of racism actively contradict the tenets of liberalism, racism can only be noticed (if at all) in ways that dismiss it as an anomaly. Critical race theorist David Theo Goldberg has similarly written on the paradox of race that transpires within liberalism.[15] Defining liberalism as the defining doctrine for modernity, Goldberg argues that since it is formulated through ideals of equality and individualism, racism is both denied and naturalized through it. One of the first requirements of a liberal conception of justice is the tenet of universalism through which people are to be considered as individuals and equals. Goldberg defines universalism as the idea that a subject "is divorced from the contingencies of historicity as it is from the particularities of social and political relations and identities."[16] The liberal conceptions of individualism thereby transmit and reproduce white supremacist systems of thought in ways that perpetually reinstate the status quo. This results in a type of "conceptual hegemony" which "turns not only upon the totally imposed order of terms in defining the social subject, but upon the subject's acceptance of the terms as his or her own in self-definition and conception."[17] In other words, liberalism posits all human beings as equal and in so doing, erases or minimizes the ways in which people are differently positioned within racialized stratification systems.[18]

A related paradox on how race is understood and articulated within liberalism pertains to the disembodiment of universal subjects. It has been argued that the "ideal" body, which functions as the norm, is white/Western, male, and history-less insofar as it can step outside of historical events such as colonialism and slavery, and that this "dehistoricizing" of white/Western male subjects is often linked to notions of disembodiment achieved through movement.[19] In other words, because of its ability to move, the white/Western body "dematerializes" or is "unmarked."[20] Furthermore, those racialized as white are constituted as having the more advanced ability to think in the abstract, which is largely attained through the white body's freedom of movement.[21] This notion of the universal white subject is constructed against the idea of blackness, which is always trapped within the body. As the writings of Frantz Fanon have variously shown, the experience of blackness is first and foremost embodied, marked, and fixed in place.[22] Connected to the idea of disembodiment and white subjectivity are Christian philosophies of transcendence through which "black people can be reduced (in white culture) to their bodies and thus to race, but white people are something else that is realized in and yet is not reducible to the corporeal or racial."[23]

Postcolonial and transnational feminist critiques on the elision of historicized difference and theories on race and the body have long argued that in modernity, the universal white subject is constituted as without history and as disembodied. Moreover, we learn from feminist scholarship that within the liberal paradigm, Western understandings of power differences are frequently articulated in terms of universalism, as in "we are all women (i.e. the same) and so our struggle is one." It has also been shown that efforts to transcend universalism's notions of commonality by paying attention to "difference" are not necessarily effective in acknowledging power differences.[24]

Together, these critical writings bring out several significant points regarding the liberal tenet of universalism and the paradoxes to which it gives rise. First, within liberal discourses, to condemn racism demands that race be articulated in ways that render it benign. Second, the quagmire of universalism's "dehistoricizing" of differences is antithetical to addressing issues of racialized power insofar as it presupposes a "level playing field," thereby eliding different racialized positionings. These studies thus help us to understand the widespread attraction to euphemisms like "international" and discomfort with the notion of "human shields." Since within the parameters of liberal universalism, it is considered morally wrong to set oneself apart on the basis of race, it becomes difficult for the activists to articulate their presence in explicit terms. Moreover, the idea that race should not make a difference becomes confused with the fact that it does.[25]

The site of this study, then, is a particularly salient one for uncovering the seductive pull and force of liberal discourses of universalism because it reveals how raceless discourses persist even when racialized differences are consciously deployed. Indeed, this illustrates just how remarkably regenerative and virtually inescapable the paradigm of liberal universalism is.[26]

THE IMPORTANCE OF FRAMING

I have been arguing that the activists' narratives are limited by the disavowal of racialized embodiment within the core liberal principle of universalism. Paradoxically, then, the activists act out against racism and injustice, while adopting a language that elides the racialized differences. This raises a larger question about the significance of liberal discourses in antiracist practice.

Does it matter if activists articulate their work in terms that make race explicit, as opposed to in terms of raceless liberal universalism? If activists travel to conflict zones with the righteous goal of ending war and violence, one could argue that it makes little difference how they understand or articulate their work. Some offer the perspective that at the ideological level, one cannot afford to be choosy. This point of view has been put forth in some studies that have argued that the primary way to effect change is through a sustained movement or a critical mass, which means being less concerned about what the activists perceive the philosophical and political goals to be.[27] David Goldberg offers a different view, contending that the discursive framing of antiracist activism is of utmost importance. He explains: "For the liberal, the standard of non-discrimination necessarily entails a commitment to nonracialism, to ignoring race. Antiracisms, on the other hand, recognize the possibilities of multiple manifestations of racist exclusions, of exclusionary resurgences and redefinitions, of newly emergent racisms or expressive recurrences, of different discursive impositions or terminological transformations."[28] The important difference, then, is that transformative possibilities lie *only* in approaches that are explicitly framed in antiracist terms. Others have similarly shown that the development of race consciousness and responses to racism depends on available political discourses in temporally specific contexts. Writing about the US civil rights movement, Paula Brush highlights the significant discursive shift that came about when the Black Power movement emerged and insisted upon articulating their activism in terms of white cultural hegemony, instead of "equal rights."[29] In so doing, Brush explains, the vision of the civil rights movement reached beyond the goals of integration and the creation of a raceless society and truly gained power and momentum when it took the power to define its own political framework and goals.

These theories suggest that in the absence of a clear, radical political agenda, antiracism movements, especially those which rely on the deployment of white bodies, can discursively reinforce rather than transcend global white hegemony. Consequently, despite their important day-to-day actions and interventions aimed at reducing racialized violence, so long as activists work from a raceless premise, the antiracist potential of accompaniment-observer activism is limited. Furthermore, the conceptual bind of universalism that the activists find themselves in represents one of the primary paradoxical constraints of this activism. Indeed, this site of activism is particularly fruitful for uncovering the force through which such liberal discourses operate because it reveals how discourses of racelessness flourish even in contexts when differently racialized bodies are the central tactics being used.

IMPLICATIONS: DO WE GO?

In identifying the barriers, challenges, and concerns that come up in transnational solidarity activism, my goal has been to inform anti-racist and decolonizing practices. The picture that emerges from my investigation suggests that transnational solidarity activism is fraught with *contradictions and paradoxes* with respect to race and power. In fact, as I have shown, the discursive, symbolic, subjective, and material effects of accompaniment-observer activism *reinforce* rather than transcend or disrupt global white hegemony. I want to consider the implications of this claim in terms of ethics and practical challenges, as well as to propose some decolonial alternatives.

The first question that this study raises is whether people from the Global North should be participating in this activism at all. During times of war, conflict, global inequity, and interdependency, privileged people from the global North are increasingly being called upon to act in solidarity with those who most suffer the consequences. Knowing that we have mobility, resources, and authority, should we exercise these privileges to offer protection to those being targeted by racist violence? Sometimes when critical analyses reveal the insidious ways racism permeates in well-meaning interventions, there is a tendency to think that it is best for people in dominant positions to stay out of the issues altogether. If we cannot truly form relationships of solidarity that are based on equality, the logic goes, then maybe it is best not to intervene at all.

This type of reasoning, I argue, denies complicity, and obscures the ethical issue of choosing not to act at all.

The ideas put forth by Hannah Arendt inform my assertion.[30] In Arendt's view, being human entails taking responsibility for the crimes committed by others. To shirk this responsibility, as Arendt plainly sees it, is to be complicit. Working with the ideas of Arendt and others, Zygmunt Bauman explores questions of moral responsibility in the contemporary context. Challenging the distinction between perpetrators and bystanders or on-lookers, Bauman argues that one of the important similarities between the two is that they both operate in denial.[31] Moreover, he emphasizes that violence and oppression could not succeed without bystanders. As he puts it, perpetrators *count on* bystanders in order to accomplish their goals.[32] He writes: "Would the perpetrators – the "real culprits" – engage in their evil deeds if they could not count on the indifference and non-interference of all those around? If they did not know for sure or at least have good reasons to believe that the witnesses were not likely to turn into actors?"[33] The instrumental role that apathy plays in violence and oppression is the very reason Bauman is concerned that denials of responsibility in the form of "there was nothing I could do" are rapidly on the rise.[34] Also persuasive is Sara Ahmed's argument that the question is not whether we should intervene, but *how* we intervene.[35]

How, then, to intervene? Sherene Razack has insisted that transnational interventions must be approached in ways that take responsibility for the ways that we, as people from the First World, are increasingly implicated in the injustices we want to end.[36] For Razack, this entails careful consideration of how people might be *equipped* for such interventions. One of the ways people might be better equipped for their roles in transnational activism is to understand it in terms of what has been referred to as "a principled pragmatism."[37] This means that activists need to recognize that certain global conditions demand that they utilise whatever available options exist, including those that are not necessarily transformative. Goldberg points out, for instance, that during the civil rights struggle in the US, priorities were set according to what was believed to be most viable, and that while fully cognizant that certain campaigns were likely to reinscribe racialized relations, black movement leaders, nevertheless, mobilised them as strategic first steps.[38] This pragmatism has been likened to a sceptical realism in which one can recognize the hegemonic outcomes of certain actions in which they partake.[39] Others have used the term "constructive complicity" to capture a parallel sentiment. Drawing on Spivak, de Jong explains that such an approach recognizes the power imbalances that such relations of solidarity and support are borne out of.[40] Similarly, we learn from Bernice Johnson Reagon's earlier writings on cross-racial coalitions in the US second-wave-feminist movement that black women were starkly aware of the power relations and the inherent threat that comes with solidarity relationships.[41] To dispel sentimental notions about black women *wanting* to team up with white women, Reagon points out that their requests for solidarity were often grudgingly made and prompted by absolute necessity.

In the context I have been examining, a principled pragmatism would begin with the realization that groups who are being targeted by violence and oppression and calling out for assistance from members of the dominant groups understand the hegemonic risks involved in these arrangements, but are nevertheless hard-pressed to implement them. The few points of view of Palestinians shown in earlier chapters suggest that the current calls for international solidarity activists being made by communities under siege are operating out of a similar pragmatic. The requests for First World activists currently put forth by Palestinians in the Occupied Territories, for example, are likely borne out of careful calculations on the immediate and the long-term effects that such a presence can have. As Charmaine Seitz observes, the Western presence is welcomed by many Palestinians because it means "their children can play outside without the same fear," at the same time as they continue to strategize and contemplate alternative resistance strategies.[42]

In emphasizing the pragmatism behind these calls for solidarity, my intention is to make clear the fallacy that oppressed groups seek out cross-racial coalitions out of a desire for cross-border intimacy or friendships. I believe that such an understanding may also reduce the possibility of misunderstanding such transnational solidarity relations as hopeful examples of the "beyond borders" discourse that has gained much currency in the First World in recent years.

The issue of pragmatism plays out very differently, however, when it is applied by those in dominant positions of power. In other words, although principled pragmatism may be necessary for those calling for solidarity, it is important to caution against what some have described as the "ideology of pragmatism" that increasingly shapes social-activist approaches. Indeed, when employed by those in positions of power, pragmatism brings with it some important dangers. For instance, writing about anti-globalization and anti-imperialist social movements, Aziz Choudry points out that such an approach facilitates the compartmentalization of issues. As he explains, adhering to an ideology of pragmatism conveniently justifies not confronting root causes and structures of social inequality, such as imperialism and capitalism, and instead gives activists permission to concede that limited gains are all that can be hoped for.[43]

First World transnational solidarity activists must try, then, to hold two seemingly contradictory presuppositions together: that their practices are embedded within racialized systems and therefore reproduce relations of power, and that their interventions may nevertheless be needed. What must be recognized is that what they can offer is not heroic or revolutionary in any sense, but rather is a terribly troubled role put in place through white supremacy and made necessary only because of the urgency of certain global crises.

CHALLENGES

In reflecting further upon the question of how Western activists might be better equipped for transnational interventions such as the ones examined here, and to raise important considerations for those who are faced with the task of weighing the costs and gains of such pragmatic interventions, I want to turn my attention to some of the specific and concrete, practical, and conceptual challenges that came up in this study. To begin with, from Rachel Corrie's example, we learn that the political power that transnational activists represent diminishes when they are not regarded as truly white. A similar observation was made in the US civil rights movement when its leaders came to see that white activists had more of an impact if they did not associate too closely with black people.[44] Very basically, this meant that white activists had more efficacy when they portrayed themselves as simply being against violence, or for equal rights, as opposed to being seen as radicals who were explicitly on the side of black people.[45] Thus, it is critical for activists to remain mindful that the political viability of this strategy wanes when the neutrality that is associated with whiteness is called into question. Thus, for strategic purposes, it is more politically effective for activists to maintain a very pronounced white identity – one untainted by relations with the Other.

The issue of sexism and sexual violence in transnational solidarity activism raised in this study has important concrete implications as well. Put simply, it demands recognition that women are differently positioned in this activism and that their bodies are not afforded the same safety and protection. In keeping with and extending the previous point about what Corrie's example reveals, it is equally important to recognize that Western activists of colour also face threats because their bodies hold less power than those of white activists in certain geopolitical spaces, regardless of their First World passports.[46] Together, these concerns point to the need for those organizing these delegations to better prepare for and ensure the safety and support of women activists and activists of colour.

One of the complex dynamics of transnational and cross-racial solidarity that this study brought to the fore is the concern that some white activists walk away from these transnational encounters with a fortified sense of innocence. Although many of the activists I interviewed were greatly concerned about their dominant positioning, my analysis revealed that even the most committed and critical of activists are easily scripted (or script themselves) into the roles of "the compassionate and neutral observer," "the truth auditor," "the peaceful Canadian," and so on. The analysis I have offered emphasizes how these figures are so prominent in the racialized imaginary that they can be reinstalled despite activists' careful vigilance. The example I offered of James Loney in Chapter Two captures this challenge. While Loney did manage to disrupt and subvert the Orientalist-captivity narrative he was being scripted into, he did so with struggle and slippages. In other words, with few notable exceptions, conventional tropes of imperialist benevolence profoundly shape this activism and are in turn, perpetuated through it.

ALTERNATIVES: ENCOUNTERING THE ENCOUNTER AND DECOLONIZING SOLIDARITY

How, then, might transnational solidarity activism be reconceived to better attend to the racialized power dynamics with which it is embedded? A decolonizing approach would require careful rethinking of the Western epistemologies, like liberalism, in which we are embedded. Frantz Fanon long ago argued that injustices are achieved through "a string of philosophico-political dissertations on the themes of the rights of people to self-determination, the rights of man to freedom from hunger and human dignity" and attributes the success of these discursive processes to the fact that they are adopted as truth both by colonizer and colonized.[47] Building on Fanon, more contemporary decolonial theorists have argued that our very conception of justice is deeply linked to Western philosophical traditions that render us unable to see how discourses of "rights" are inextricable from imperial projects. For instance, Walter Mignolo argues that what is taken to be "universal" is in fact deeply Eurocentric and cautions that when using these discourses uncritically, social justice efforts are likely to constitute a continuation of the Western imperial trajectory.[48]

These decolonizing approaches have important implications for pedagogy and education. Indeed, the vast majority of existing pedagogies and educational theories in social justice education remain faithful to the liberal paradigm and are underpinned by essentialist, modernist, universal, and naively idealistic principles.[49] Despite their best efforts, these approaches produce subjects, knowledge, and values that fortify existing power relations rather than challenge them. Thus, a very first step to decolonizing solidarity requires that liberal underpinnings be unravelled through alternative epistemological frameworks in order to transcend the usual presuppositions about the unquestioned goodness of those who advocate for universal rights.

Related to this, I want to propose that we "hear" the rallying cries for solidarity with some healthy scepticism. Although I believe that it is a moral imperative for those of us in privileged positions to respond to calls for solidarity, equally important is to approach these calls with caution. Just as feminists of colour interrogated the term "sisterhood" in earlier feminist movements, we must now examine the term "solidarity" as it is being applied to transnational activism. As I have shown throughout this study, solidarity needs to be conceived as both a central element for effective political movements *and* as a set of practices that rely on racialized and gendered structures of colonialism and imperialism.

One crucial step is to situate these newer transnational networks, organizations, and interventions in a long history of imperialism. For example, as Cooper states, "The current efforts to challenge 'global' capitalism via 'global' social movements ... have precedents going back the late eighteenth century."[50] "Questions of poverty and exploitations that were once imperial," he writes, "have become both national and international."

Another way that transnational solidarity activists might be better equipped for the challenges they face is to embrace the strife that goes with it. Furthermore, while one can take hope in the solidarity commitments these activists demonstrate, we should not be too quick to praise and celebrate them merely on the basis of their motivations and actions. Instead, it is the uneasy inner struggles that many of the activists faced *because* of their motivations and actions that deserve praise and recognition. As anthropologist Diane Nelson has suggested that "solidarity is in part enjoyment and about forms of self-fashioning that may not be very self-reflexive."[51]

One hopeful example of the ongoing efforts to decolonize solidarity can be seen in the work of Projet Accompagnement Solidarité Colombie (PASC).[52] As a Canadian organization that works in solidarity with communities in Columbia, this group has committed to decolonizing its solidarity practices, and its members have been actively addressing issues of power and privilege in their work.

They identify the decolonizing project as a continuation of the anti-colonial feminist movement developed by women of colour and Third World feminists, among others. In framing their work through this lens, they seek to acknowledge their feminist and anti-colonial political positions with the goal that it will contribute to enriching the practices of international solidarity. For instance, in documenting the history of their group, PASC members explain that when they first met to decide which resistance struggle to support through a long-term solidarity project, they chose Columbia simply because someone at the meeting had just returned from eight months there. Recognizing the arbitrariness and the privilege of being in a position to make such a choice, they explain that PASC's commitment to supporting disenfranchised communities in Colombia was thus a matter of chance, and that the circumstances surrounding the struggling communities in Columbia conveniently, yet randomly, coincided with their personal goals.

Lastly, to respond to the question of how transnational solidarity activists might be better equipped to contribute to decolonizing solidarity, I want to borrow from Sara Ahmed who proposes that Westerners must enter transnational encounters with the Other with "a strong sense of what it means to be 'in it,' and how 'being in it' is the site of both differentiation and hierarchisation."[53] When encounters begin from an "in-it-ness," Ahmed adds, the encounter allows us to see that the differences between us involve power and antagonism.[54] What Ahmed is arguing is that Westerners ought to set the objective of seeing the encounter for what it is (as opposed to what we want it to be), and in so doing, try to make a difference in how it is already constituted.[55] In raising this point, I do not mean to elide the fact that most social justice activists have a strong understanding of their privileged positioning – indeed, many of the activists I interviewed did. I nevertheless maintain that implicit in much of their understandings is the idea that, because they see themselves as allies, and because of their antiracist commitments, they somehow expected to avert this encounter. This was mostly evident in the dilemmas they narrated which suggested that they were caught off guard to find themselves in situations already structured by race.

I want to end by asking: What, then, might be gained if those who participate in this activism "go in" with the clear but difficult understanding that their encounters will unequivocally be overdetermined by race?[56] Or, put differently, how might the activists narrate their experiences and their self-perceptions differently if they entered into the solidarity relationship knowing *fully* that it is a colonial encounter? Might an unambiguous and conscious grasp of the ways in which our bodies and identities are marked through colonial histories pave the way for truly transformative decolonizing solidarity practices?

AFTERWORD

Solidarity Tourism and the Depoliticization of Activism

I think my soul is nomadic .... I've always stared upward at airplanes cutting white paths through the sky and wondered where they're going. I've always been jealous of migratory birds.

Rachel Corrie[1]

Given the EZLN [Zapatista National Liberation Army]'s emphasis on discursive combat and its care in leaving non-combatants unharmed, the uprising has only served to enlarge Chiapas's appeal as a tourist destination.

Steven Flusty[2]

At the start of this book I was interested in a small subset of thoughtful, exceptionally committed, and socially conscious people who travel to conflict zones with the explicit intent to participate in social justice demonstrations and activism. Yet, I end the book on the topic of tourism to suggest that deep consideration of the increasing overlap between tourism and activism is needed.

The blurring between transnational, direct action activism and tourism first became evident to me when I solicited the views of Palestinian community leaders to consider tensions arising for them in their work with Western solidarity activists. I soon discovered that they make little distinction between the radical activist who goes there with the objective of protesting the occupation of Palestine and the sympathetic/curious tourist who happens to take part in an observation tour or a demonstration while they are there. Indeed, I was surprised to see that although they were being asked questions about "activists," they kept using the terms "tourists" in their responses, revealing that for many of them, the activist and the tourist are one and the same. On further contemplation, I could see how this merging of the two figures was not only possible, it was inevitable.

A newspaper article published online by *Haaretz*, an Israeli English-language newspaper, offers some compelling insights into the troubling conflation between activism and tourism. Referring to this trend as "occupation tourism," the author writes about an Italian teacher who led a reportorial photography workshop for ten students from Rome.[3] The group is in Bil'in, waiting for the weekly demonstration against the separation fence. The teacher is described as saying, "For us it is like a vacation," at the same time as he takes a photo of an Israeli holding a gas mask. Another older tourist from France at the same demonstration is described as snapping photos with his digital camera, each time an explosion goes off, "in an attempt to capture the perfect shot." He is quoted saying that he loves coming to Palestine and sees his presence there as showing support for Palestinians. A third tourist quoted in the article is a twenty-six-year-old art student from Japan, who says, "I saw a movie about Bil'in on YouTube and I decided to come here." He adds, "I wanted to see the fence, the people, the soldiers." According to the author, along with other tourists, the three watch a group of about 150 demonstrators being assaulted by stun and tear-gas grenades as they make their way from the center of Bi'lin towards the fence.

The growing presence of tourists in Bil'in has of course sparked criticism and accusations of treating the region as a "safari park."[4] Others are more optimistic in thinking that through this exposure tourists would leave "more committed to the struggle." Other types of tours are perhaps less controversial, but are just as popular. For example, Rotem Mor, who describes himself as a long-term activist, now organizes "reality tours," including one called the "East Jerusalem Political Overview Tour," which shows the difficult realities of life in East Jerusalem such as the wall, settlements, home demolitions, evacuations, and more.[5]

While this kind of tourism in Palestine has become the topic of many fascinating in-depth studies, I briefly draw attention to it here to invite reflection on the implications of the blurring between

Afterword

tourism and activism. Indeed, as some of the quotes suggest, one can spend an afternoon during their holiday taking part in a demonstration and think of themselves as having acted in solidarity. The excerpt from Corrie's writing presented at the start of this chapter clearly suggests that at least part of what impelled her to go to Palestine is a *wanderlust* common in youth of privileged countries. In highlighting this aspect of her motivation, I want to draw attention to the increasing inseparability between travel and the desire to do good.

Good intentions and strong commitments notwithstanding, there is cause for concern about young people traveling to war zones with the formidable mandate of demanding justice and saving lives. Indeed, as some on-line discussions have revealed, there is some indication that this type of travel appeals to privileged Western youths who are bored with backpacking and merely seeking adventure. One of the tourists in the aforementioned news story further said, "When there is an international presence here, the army attacks the Palestinians less." This reveals that for him, being a tourist brings with it the virtues of offering a protective embodied First World presence and, in turn, illustrates the perilous kind of conflation to which I am drawing attention.

While it is heartening that the word "privilege" has become part of the everyday lexicon, and many people now understand that they are differently positioned in social systems according to the race, class, and gender privileges they incur, there is also reason to worry about how such an understanding is sometimes mobilized, especially through travel.[6] More and more people from the West seem to think that a virtuous use of their privilege is to use their passports to travel to "hot spots" to participate in various forms of activism or volunteerism around the world.[7] We must ask, however, what constitutes ethical and subversive social justice interventions for those who have the privileges of carrying a passport from a powerful Western nation-state? The 2007 arrest of three Canadians who displayed a large "Free Tibet" banner on the Great Wall of China is one case in point. It sparked heated debates amongst activists and political commentators about the contradictory tensions that arise when privilege, travel, and activism come together. Many activists insisted that such actions are meaningful attempts to alleviate oppression because they model a "without borders" politic. These activists argue that actions such as this one are concrete and admirable ways of putting Western privilege to good use. Indeed, one of the activists arrested in China stated that as someone who has the privilege of holding a Canadian passport, she was prompted by a sense of duty and obligation to demonstrate against global injustice.[8] Others believe that such brazen acts are prompted by Western arrogance. Indeed, some political commentators argued that the release of the activists, just hours after their arrest, due to the intervention of Canadian officials, is evidence of a dangerous misuse of privilege. As one newspaper reporter asked, "Does our [Canadian] passport entitle us to charge into foreign lands, smugly demanding they right what *we* view as wrong in their society?"[9] Similarly, a posting on the discussion forum of *Rabble.ca*, a popular independent/alternative media Internet site, pointed out the duplicity of such actions: "I am waiting for the Chinese to go to the States and unfurl banners that say Free Hawaii and Free Puerto Rico. Or maybe to Canada to say 'Free the First Nations or Free Quebec.' Some of us Westerners sure do know what is good for the rest of the world."[10] Indeed, there is also ample evidence indicating that those who do not necessarily think of themselves as activists, and whose primary motivation is leisure, are being drawn to conflict zones. This trend invites us to consider the ways in which conflicts are becoming commodified and consumed. Writing on the persistent figure of "the tourist," feminist theorist Caren Kaplan explains, the "tourist travels, crosses boundaries, is freely mobile, consumes commodities, produces economies, and is, in truth, commodified to a lesser or greater extent."[11] In fact, it is a salient illustration of the kind of depoliticization that increasingly undercuts some social movement initiatives as well as trivializes the impacts of violence on the effected communities.

The coupling of tourism and social justice is certainly a curious one. Tourism is one of the biggest culprits of global inequality while activism, by its very definition, seeks to challenge those inequalities. One would assume that the two activities would be diametrically opposed to one another. Yet, opportunities for activist tourism have proliferated in recent years under the banners of "solidarity," "revolutionary," "justice," and "reconciliation" tourism. Given what is known about the exploitative economic, cultural, and environmental aspects of tourism, it is becoming harder and harder to justify. In recent years, public awareness of the ways tourism contributes to the economic and environmental demise of the Global South has become more commonplace, and in response, various forms of responsible "alternative," "eco," or "pro-poor" tourist options have proliferated and are steadily on the rise.[12] While one can take hope in the fact that conventional tourism is being questioned and is losing its appeal, we should not be too quick to praise and celebrate these so-called "alternatives."[13] Further to this, it is important to note that some of these newer "alternative," altruistic and ethical-political forms of tourism are increasingly being offered by both governmental and non-governmental organisations (NGOs). These trips, rapidly on the rise, offer opportunities to combine tourism with political education, volunteerism, activism, and or/advocacy abroad. As Deborah McLaren puts it, "While social activists are developing new tourism strategies, concerned tourists are changing their focus from relaxation to activism." [14]

One example is a US-based NGO called Global Exchange that offers "reality tours for politically conscious travellers" and claims that these tours "can and do change the world." In recent years, this organization has offered such educational tours to approximately thirty different destinations, mostly countries in the Global South. Typically, these package tours draw white, middle-class people, mainly from the US, last ten to twelve days, and consist of visiting various local communities to see and learn about the social conditions in which people live as a means of raising awareness about global power imbalances. Global Exchange's Reality Tours emphasise social movements to stress the resilience and resourcefulness of the local people. Their tours explore grassroots movements, offering travelers an opportunity to meet people behind the scenes, "from Zapatista in Chiapas and young people in Cuba to women organizers in south Africa and Vietnamese facing injustices created by capitalism. Tourists are now monitoring elections in Mexico, speaking out on behalf of indigenous peoples being forced from their lands by oil companies."[15] In short, this NGO offers tourists the attractive title of "citizen ambassador," which primarily affords Westerners a quick and easy feel-good way not only to reconcile their discomforts about tourism but also to reconstitute themselves as cosmopolitan and ethical beings.[16]

The idea that travel can be a means towards social change is not new. In recent years conditions brought about through globalization, including electronic communication and cheaper airfare, have facilitated the increase of such journeys. As a result, solidarity tourism is being undertaken with increased fervour and unprecedented frequency. More importantly, the idea that tourism can be infused with good proliferates in and through neoliberal trends of various NGOs. There we find very unambiguous claims about the benefits of travel/tourism ranging from modest claims that it can make "a positive change" to far more righteous declarations that when done responsibly, travel can be the impetus for world peace. Indeed, the idea of global citizenship and acting or intervening across, without, or beyond borders has become an axiom so imbued with righteousness that it tends to remain largely outside of the purview of critique. Whether it is to help out through international development volunteer work or to raise one's awareness on an exposure tour to conflict/war zones, the idea that these efforts abroad help make the world a better place remains largely unquestioned. One exception to this is a feature story that appeared in Briarpatch Magazine asking readers to imagine a reverse scenario in which you arrive at work one day and find a new co-worker has joined your team:[17] "He comes from abroad, and he'll only be working with you for a little while – after graduating from university, he wanted to come to a different country and volunteer for a spell, just to gain experience and 'help out however he can.'"

Ethically and/or politically motivated travel including "reality tours" in the slums of India, government sponsored "development youth internships" in Rwanda, educational trips to Nicaragua, or some of the above mentioned educational/observation trips to Israel/Palestine require that we ask: is it better to travel to the Global South on, for example, a "solidarity tour" rather than simply as tourists? If so, better for whom? Indeed, the "political correctness" of solidarity tourism not only allows us to avoid being an arrogant First World tourist, but also persuades us that by taking part in it, we can contribute towards social justice at a global level.

Certainly these trips are part of a larger trend, one that has created the conditions whereby, as Chouliaraki observes, "'doing good' has never been easier."[18] These trips must be understood as emerging alongside ubiquitous "humanitarian" concerts, celebrity appeals, and "send-a-text-to-donate-a-dollar" campaigns. Indeed, as Chouliaraki's and others' work have shown, these consumerist strategies demand that we consider what they tells us about contemporary Western understandings of solidarity and morality, and the marketing thereof.[19]

It is important to note that the distinctions between social movements and NGOs are increasingly blurred, or more accurately, that NGOs are being framed as social movements.[20] One example of this trend, Me to We, which is premised on what its founders describe as "an ingenious business model," is primarily concerned with selling merchandise and offering volunteer tours.[21] The description on the website reads: "Me to We transforms consumers into world changers, one transaction at a time."[22] Me to We is an affiliate of the well-established international development charity organization called Free the Children.[23] What is interesting about these two organizations is that despite the fact that their interventions fit squarely within depoliticized models of aid development and charity, and that they adhere to a blatant neoliberal framework (including receiving millions in corporate funding), they nevertheless mobilize and co-opt language that suggests radical politics and change, brazenly using terms such as "action/activism," and "social justice," to describe the work they do. Indeed, at their events one can find auditoriums of youth wearing t-shirts, holding up signs, and shouting out the organizations' catchy slogans such as "We are the revolution."[24]

More important still are the ways in which such NGOs are complicit with or co-opted by profit-seeking businesses. Thus, not surprisingly, claims about the virtues of more ethical types of travel can now as readily be found in the private tourism sector as well. In October of 2009, the Frommer's travel publishing magnate released a new guidebook entitled *500 Places Where You Can Make a Difference*. It is a good example of the overlap between for-profit and not-for-profit industries. Though it is a book sold for profit, many of the travel options it lists are offered by not-for-profit NGOs. Responding to the growing trend of volunteer tourism, it promises to inspire readers with travel choices ranging "from caring for orphans in Delhi, India, to teaching English on the beaches of Salvador, Brazil ... or building a school in Madagascar." With these 500 options, would-be tourists are promised the best of both worlds: they can see the world "in extraordinary ways" while at the same time serving the communities they are visiting.[25]

The interesting confluence between big business and solidarity or justice travel is also evident in a September 2008 special issue of the Condé Nast Traveller magazine, which typically specializes in luxury and high-end business travel. This issue was devoted to what it referred to as "the new soft power" of socially responsible travel, declaring that "travel is making all the difference in lives and places across the planet."[26]

The analysis I have offered throughout this book proposes that these trends be examined in terms of racialized power relations. The starting point is simply to ask: how is race addressed either implicitly or explicitly in the narratives or structures related to these forms of travel? More specifically, we need to interrogate "anti-conquest" discourses (i.e. "we have a lot to learn from them"),[27] notions of reciprocity and exchange, the racialized assumptions about who can witness and testify, and perhaps most important of all, a questioning of the access, mobility and the right/entitlement to travel. In sum, there is a need to question what such encounters *do* in terms of producing First World subjectivity.

Indeed, an analytic that keeps a close eye on race is useful for uncovering the ways in which First World subjects are constituted through these encounters. The nuanced reading I am proposing would, of course, need to take into account several complicating factors. For instance, it would require theorizing the increasing numbers of people of colour who are second-generation members of diaspora communities in the West who are travelling to "ancestral homelands" to volunteer, and how the complexities of their experiences relate to the racialized category of First World subjects.

Another complexity that needs to be considered is the fact that members of marginalized communities can be self-empowered by conducting their own tours as a pragmatic way of setting the tourist agenda (i.e. narrating their own histories) while at the same time bolstering their economy with the tourist dollar.[28] As Steven Flusty's writing on the mutually constituting effects of tourism on the Zapatista movements in Chiapas, Mexico has shown, the "dichotomy between political authenticity and commodityhood is a false one."[29] He argues that the arrival of tourists who were sympathetic with the Zapatista agenda made the seemingly opposed value regimes of tourism and transformative social change not as discrepant as one might first assume. In fact, he believes that certain forms of "commodity-ness can become effective unconventional methods that transport and translate uprising[s] into the larger world."[30] Indeed, the challenge is to hold these different aspects in tension with one another and avoid facile conclusions of good or bad. The goal in considering the North-South racialized relations of power that are furthered through solidarity tourism, then, is to simultaneously disrupt taken-for-granted assumptions about its virtues *and* identify instances (albeit rare) when it appears to offer meaningful disruptions to the existing neo-colonial order.

Notes

INTRODUCTION

1 The title is borrowed from a newspaper article by Ashifa Kassam, "Passport, or carte blanche to raise hell?" *The Star*, 1 September 2007, http://www.thestar.com/news/insight/2007/09/01/passport_or_carte_blanche_to_raise_hell.html.
2 This quote was written in an email that Corrie sent to her family from Palestine days before she was killed. These e-mails have subsequently been published in a number of on-line and print sources including Stohlman and Aladin (eds.), *Live from Palestine*.
3 "Join the 2010 Olive Harvest Campaign," International Solidarity Movement, 29 August 2010, accessed 11 March 2011, http://palsolidarity.org/2010/08/14103/.
4 "Oaxaca Solidarity Network – February '07 Humanitarian Delegation," CASA Collective, January 2007, accessed 11 March 2011, http://www.casacollective.org/story/reposts/oaxaca-solidarity-network-february-07-humanitarian-delegation.
5 Project Accompaniment Solidarity Colombia website, accessed 13 March 2011 from http://www.pasc.ca/spip.php?article59.
6 In the case of Peace Brigades International, the calls are ongoing because they continuously organize international volunteer accompaniment delegations to a number of countries. They have been in operation since 1982. "About Protective Accompaniment," Peace Brigades International, accessed 11 March 2011 from http://www.peacebrigades.org/sobre-pbi/about-protective-accompaniment/?L=1%3FL%3D0.

7 "Oaxaca Solidarity Network – February '07 Humanitarian Delegation," CASA Collective, January 2007, accessed 10 March 2011, http://www.casacollective.org/story/reposts/oaxaca-solidarity-network-february-07-humanitarian-delegation. Emphasis mine.
8 "How We Work," Peace Brigades International, November, 2001, accessed March 11, 2011, http://www.peacebrigades.org/about-pbi/how-we-work/.
9 A discussion on these terms is provided in Chapter Seven.
10 Mahoney and Eguren, *Unarmed Bodyguards*.
11 Ibid., 251.
12 Ibid.
13 Ibid.
14 Ibid. Similarly, colonial histories created a dynamic whereby Spanish activists in Central America and British activists in Sri Lanka were less warmly received than activists from other countries.
15 Ibid.
16 Geraldine Pratt and Philippines-Canada Task Force on Human Rights, "International Accompaniment and Witnessing State Violence in the Philippines," 768.
17 Weber, *Visions of Solidarity*, 55.
18 Thompson, "El Testigo Verdadero Libra Las Almas," 182. Thompson also observes that there was virtually no communication between the white activists and the communities they were assisting, and that the activists "rarely knew how either to identify or confront their own race and class privileges." She exposes some of the contradictory ways cross-racial alliances were reified through the white-dominated organizations that participated in the campaigns.
19 Mica Pollock, "Using and Disrupting," 193.
20 I am grateful to Indu Vashist for this insight. These activists were from countries including Japan, Malaysia, Pakistan, India, Iran, Indonesia, New Zealand, Kuwait, and the UAE. Moreover, many on this delegation had problems with visas and, in some cases, were detained along the way. For example, Indian activists originally were not given permission to cross into Pakistan, while Egypt refused visas to Iranian members to enter Gaza through its Rafah border. Also noteworthy is that this delegation received very little attention, not only from the media but also from its activist colleagues in the West. For more, see: "Asian People's Movement For Gaza," Asia to Gaza, 2011, accessed 11 March 2011, http://www.asiatogaza.org/., and Nita Bhalla, "Asian aid ship to Gaza fraught with chal-

lenges, say activists" *Reuters*, 12 January 2011, accessed 10 March 2011, http://in.reuters.com/article/2011/01/12/idINIndia-54098920110112?page Number=2

21 Alcoff, "Towards a Phenomenology of Racial Embodiment," 267–83.
22 Some of these include Anderson, *Weaving Relationships* and Brown, "Christian Peacemaker Teams: An Introduction,". One important exception is Hooker's *Race and the Politics of Solidarity*. However, drawing mainly on political theory, her main thesis is for the need for more interracial solidarity. Some have called for further study and analysis of the racialized paradoxes and dynamics that inhere in accompaniment-observer activism. Weber points out that race issues are rarely examined because there is a reluctance to criticize a movement that is otherwise hailed as honourable. For example, she reveals that many Christian transnational activists believe that their faith helps them to overcome racial, class, ethnic, national and ideological differences because they believe they share a "collective identity," with the people they are assisting based on religion. Weber, *Visions of Solidarity*. See also Nepstad, "Creating Transnational Solidarity," in *Globalization and Resistance: Transnational Dimensions of Social Movements*, ed. Jackie G. Smith and Hank Johnston (Lanham, MD: Rowman & Littlefield, 2002), 133–49.
23 Hans-Ulrich Krause, "About Protective Accompaniment," Peace Brigades International, accessed 5 August 2013, http://www.peacebrigades.org/sobre-pbi/about-protective-accompaniment/?L=1%3FL%3Do.
24 Owing to a body of antiracist writing that burgeoned in the 1990s that shifted the focus from the ways racism hurts people of colour to the ways it benefits white people, the word "privilege" has become part of the everyday lexicon in discussions of issues of race. See Ahmed, "Declarations of Whiteness."
25 What is operating in the euphemistic use of internationals is best understood by addressing the paradigm of liberal universalism. Indeed, within the liberal doctrine, people believe themselves to be equal to all human beings, and in so doing, erase or minimize the ways people are differently positioned within social stratification systems. Writing about the paradox of race that transpires out of liberalism, Goldberg argues that since it is formulated through ideals of equality and individualism, racism is inevitably denied and naturalized through it. See Goldberg, *Racist Culture*.
26 The interviews were conducted between March and May of 2005. The

activists who participated in the interviews consisted of twelve women and six men. Fourteen of them are Canadian citizens who travelled with a Canadian passport. Two had dual American/ Canadian citizenship, but they also travelled with Canadian passports. One is an American and one Australian, each travelling with passports of their respective countries. They travelled with a number of different organizations including IWPS; Ecumenical accompaniment or monitoring program organized by the United Church of Canada (EAPPI or EA); CPT; ISM, Project Accompaniment; PBI; and IPT. Their ages at the time of activism ranged from twenty-one to eighty with roughly one third in each of the following age ranges: 20–30, 30–50, and 50–80. They were comprised of students, a lawyer, a retired minister, a teacher, artists, a former mechanic, and a retired professor.

27 In presenting this narrative interview data, the intention is to go beyond some empirically based methodological conventions of letting the data "speak for itself." Instead, my approach leans towards a discursive and ideological analysis of their narratives to consider the frameworks embedded within.

28 Some of this history and the recent changes will be delineated in Chapter One.

29 "About ISM," International Solidarity Movement, accessed 15 March 2013, http://palsolidarity.org/about/.

30 Ibid.

31 Ibid.

32 "ISM: Home," International Solidarity Movement, accessed 15 March 2013, http://palsolidarity.org/.

33 "About CPT," Christian Peacemaker Teams, accessed 15 March 2013, http://www.cpt.org/about_cpt.

34 Ibid.

35 "About: Mission and Vision," Christian Peacemaker Teams, accessed 15 March 2013, http://www.cpt.org/about/mission.

36 Ibid.

37 Ibid.

38 "Our Work," Christian Peacemaker Teams, accessed 15 March 2013, http://www.cpt.org/work.

39 Ibid.

40 "About PBI: How We Work," Peace Brigades International, accessed 15 March 2013, http://www.peacebrigades.org/about-pbi/how-we-work/.

41 "About PBI: Vision and Mission," Peace Brigades International, accessed 15 March 2013, http://www.peacebrigades.org/about-pbi/vision-and-mission/.
42 Ibid.
43 "What We Do," Peace Brigades International, accessed 15 March 2013 http://www.peacebrigades.org/country-groups/pbi-uk/what-we-do/international-protective-accompaniment/.
44 "About IWPS," International Women's Peace Service: Nonviolence in Action, accessed 15 March 2013, http://iwps.info/?page_id=62.
45 "About IWPS: Nonviolence," International Women's Peace Service: Nonviolence in Action, accessed 15 March 2013, http://iwps.info/?page_id=101.
46 Specific areas include: Mas'ha, Deir Istiya, Azzune Atma, Izbat At Tabib, An Nabi Salih, Bruqin, Awarta, Qalqiliya, and Iraq Burin. See "Villages," International Women's Peace Service: Nonviolence in Action, accessed 15 March 2013, http://iwps.info/?page_id=910.
47 "About IWPS."
48 "About IWPS: Nonviolence," International Women's Peace Service: Nonviolence in Action accessed 15 March 2013, http://www.peacecouncil.net/pnl/02/713IraqPeaceTeam.htm (site discontinued.
49 Ibid.
50 Ibid.
51 At the time of writing, it appears that this organization is no longer active.
52 "About EAPPI: Overview," Ecumenical Accompaniment Program in Palestine and Israel, accessed 19 June 2013, http://eappi.org/en/about/overview.html.
53 Ibid.
54 Ibid.
55 Abbott, "Project Accompaniment: A Canadian Response," 26.
56 Anderson, 2003, 42.
57 According to Robert Miles, the concept of *racialization* can be defined as "a dialectical process of signification." As such, emphasis is placed on the fact that racialization is a *process* as a way to make clear that race is not a fixed category or a naturally occurring phenomena. See Miles, *Racism*, 75.
58 Similar analytical approaches have included an additive model of oppression whereby racism *plus* sexism produces a doubly oppressed woman or "intersectionality" where racism *meets* sexism and produces a certain experience. The concept of interlocking differs in emphasis in that it

stresses the ways the systems of race, capitalism, sexism, racism, heterosexism, etc., rely on and need one another. See Razack, *Looking White People in the Eye*, 11–13.
59 Goldberg differentiates between the often conflated terms of race and racist as follows: "race" (or racial) refers to the various designations of group differentiation. The term "racist" invokes those racial exclusions prompted or promoted by racial reference or racialized significance, whether such exclusions are actual or intended. See Goldberg, *Racist Culture*, 2–3.
60 Thomas and Clarke. "Introduction: Globalization and the Transformations of Race," 2.
61 Arat-Koc, "New Whiteness(Es), Beyond the Colour Line?" 147.
62 Ibid., 148.
63 See also Hall, "New Ethnicities."
64 See Bhattacharyya, Gabriel, and Small, *Race and Power*. Although most of the activists who were interviewed for this study identified themselves as "middle-class," for some of them the travel expenses they incurred for their trips provided a financial challenge, suggesting that there was a significant range in terms of their income levels.
65 Ibid. As Bhattacharyya et al. have insightfully pointed out, the aspects of material social life in which racism is most apparent, such as wars and famines, are also where poverty is most stark.
66 See Michel Foucault and Colin Gordon, *Power/Knowledge*; Foucault, "The Subject and Power," in *Michel Foucault*, 208–26; Foucault, *The History of Sexuality*.
67 Foucault, "The Subject and Power," 212.
68 See Weedon, "Feminisms and the Principles of Poststructuralism"; Henriques et al., "Introduction to Section 3: Theorizing Subjectivity."
69 Foucault, "Society Must Be Defended."
70 Fassin, "Humanitarianism as a Politics of Life."
71 Ibid., 500–1.
72 Ibid.
73 Alexander and Mohanty, "Introduction: Genealogies, Legacies, Movements," xxi.
74 Ibid.
75 Fanon, "The Fact of Blackness." Scholarship that has applied the notion of the encounter to contemporary sites has been most useful in demonstrating racialized dynamics. For example, I am drawn to Razack's contention

that the contemporary racialized encounter remains a moment when powerful narratives turn oppressed peoples into objects, to be held in contempt, or to be saved from their fates by more civilized beings: Razack, *Looking White People in the Eye*, 3.

76 Pratt explains that this usually involves "conditions of coercion, radical inequality, and intractable conflict." Pratt, *Imperial Eyes*, 6.
77 Ibid., 4.
78 Ibid., 7.
79 This approach is captured in Grewal and Kaplan's introduction to *Scattered Hegemonies*, in which they write, "Our critique of certain forms of feminism emerge from their willing participation in modernity with all its colonial discourses and hegemonic First World formations that wittingly or unwittingly lead to the oppression and exploitation of many women." Grewal and Kaplan, *Scattered Hegemonies: Postmodernity and Transnational Feminist Practices*, ed. Inderpal Grewal and Caren Kaplan (Minnesota: University of Minnesota Press, 1994), 2. The alternative that Grewal and Kaplan propose is one that demands that international social movements (such as peace movements and international women's groups) be examined by placing front and centre the inequalities in living standards between nations, unequal access to resources, the legacy of colonialism, and international trade. The concept of transnationality that I employ is also shaped by Inderpal Grewal's cautionary note about how "the international" is often erroneously assumed to be "supra-national," thereby disguising the fact that the concept of internationalism relies on and reifies nation-states for its existence: Grewal, "On the New Global Feminism and the Family of Nations," 510.
80 See Shohat, "Area Studies, Gender Studies, and the Cartographies of Knowledge," 75.
81 This should not be taken to mean that colonialism has ended.
82 Ahmed, *Strange Encounters*, 43.
83 Frankenberg, *White Women, Race Matters*.
84 Ibid., 236.
85 Ibid., 236-7.
86 Hage, *White Nation*.
87 Ibid., 58.
88 Heron, "Desire for Development," 6.
89 For a great discussion on these risks see Chapter One of Dyer, *White*.
90 Arat-Koc, "New Whiteness(es)," 148.

91 Ibid.
92 See Naber "Introduction: Arab Americans and U.S. Racial Formations."
93 Dyer, "The Matter of Whiteness," in *White*; Coleman, *White Civility*.
94 For more on this see Kaplan, "Beyond the Pale."
95 Interview participant "Lisa." All names in this study are pseudonyms.
96 As Chandra Mohanty points out, despite its inadequacies and the fact that it does not line up consistently within physical hemispheres and is therefore empirically imprecise, when used critically, the term "Western" can have political value insofar as it helps to distinguish between affluent, privileged nations and communities, and "non-Western" economically and politically marginalized nations and communities: Mohanty, *Feminism without Borders*.
97 Said, *Orientalism*.
98 Mohanty, *Feminism without Borders*.
99 For more on the connotations of particular terminology see ibid., 222–3.

CHAPTER ONE

1 Suheir Hammad, "On the Brink of War." The Electronic Intifada, accessed 10 March 2011, http://electronicintifada.net/v2/article1272.shtml Retrieved March 10, 2011.
2 Berlant, "Compassion (and Withholding)," 1–13.
3 Hammad, "On the Brink of War." The poem was written on 20 March 2003.
4 The poem ends with these words.
5 Richard Dyer, *White*, 14.
6 Stoper, *The Student Nonviolent Coordinating Committee*.
7 Riches, *The Civil Rights Movement*.
8 Thompson, *A Promise and a Way of Life*, 48 and 59. For more on the gendered aspects of the civil rights movement in the United States see Chapter Four in this book.
9 Ibid., 48; Riches, *The Civil Rights Movement*, 56.
10 Dierenfield, *The Civil Rights Movement*, 103.
11 Riches, *The Civil Rights Movement*.
12 See Babson, et al., *The Color of Law*, 343.
13 Riches, *The Civil Rights Movement*, 80.
14 See Thompson, *A Promise and a Way of Life*; Stoper, *The Student Nonviolent Coordinating Committee*.
15 See Olson, *Historical Dictionary of the 1960s*, 61.

16 Dierenfield, *The Civil Rights Movement*, 107. Importantly, the racialized dynamics that emerged in the US civil rights movement have been observed in the struggle against apartheid in South Africa as well, revealing that the cross-racial tension amongst activists in the US was not an isolated or context-specific phenomenon. For example, organizations such as the African National Congress faced similar difficulties in determining the role white people ought to play in the resistance movement. Offering an analysis of the cross-racial dynamics of this movement, Vron Ware identifies the contentious themes of autonomy versus integration that arise in racially mixed organizations. Like the Black Power faction that emerged out of the US civil rights movement, in South Africa, a black Consciousness group founded in the 1970s condemned the notion of racial integration, asserting that it would inevitably result in the domination of blacks by whites. See Ware, "Mothers of Invention," 133–68.
17 Sandercock et al., *Peace under Fire*.
18 Laila El-Haddad, "Israel Activist Bridges Worlds." Aljazeera.net, 2 July 2005, accessed 4 March, 2011, http://english.aljazeera.net/archive/2005/07/200849130457607I1.html.
19 Andoni as cited in Charmaine Seitz's, "ISM at the Crossroads: The Evolution of the International Solidarity Network." *Journal of Palestine Studies* 32, no. 4 (2003): 53.
20 Ibid. This uprising was the result of Israeli forces attacks, first on Palestinians at the Al-Aqsa Mosque in East Jerusalem (a disputed territory) on 29 September 2000, in which at least four Palestinians were killed, and then, again the next day when they attacked Palestinians who were demonstrating against the brutality they were subjected to the previous day, killing more. Since then, military violence against Palestinian civilians continues to escalate, leading the Israeli military actions to be condemned by Amnesty International and prompting outrage from human rights and anti-war organizations (Amnesty International, 2003 / 2007). Also see Seitz, "Ism at the Crossroads," 50–67; Andoni et al., "International Solidarity."
21 El-Haddad, "Israeli Activist Bridges Worlds."
22 Andoni and Qubbaj et al, "International Solidarity." For more on how the word "international" has become stand-in for "white," see introductory chapter of this book.
23 El-Haddad, "Israeli Activist Bridges Worlds." The ISM emphasises that it is "not an organization, but rather a movement which all organizations,

groups and/or individuals who agree to our principles can join." See http://palsolidarity.org/about, accessed 14 May 2010.
24 Seitz, "ISM at the Crossroads," 50–67.
25 El-Haddad, "Israeli Activist Bridges Worlds." ISM founder Neta Golan estimates that 20% to 25% of the American volunteers are Jewish.
26 This refers to the International Covenant on Civil and Political Rights of 12 August 1949 in which Article 1 requires that parties to the Covenant protect the rights of all individuals subject to its jurisdiction. Moreover, their lives are besieged through mechanisms of military control in the form of watchtowers, barbed wire, concrete block barriers, and flying checkpoints. See Gregory, *The Colonial Present*.
27 See "About ISM" on *International Solidarity movement* website, accessed 11 March 2011 http://palsolidarity.org/about-ism/
28 See Sandercock et al. *Peace under Fire*; Andoni et al., *Live from Palestine*. As a means of expressing dissent, nonviolent direct action is most often associated with Gandhi whose efforts demonstrated that it is an effective strategy for deterring violence or force by denying the aggressor the human assistance and cooperation necessary to exercise control over a population. Non-violent direct action generally refers to three categories of actions. The first is protest and persuasion, such as marches, picketing, and distribution of literature. The second category is defined by non-cooperative actions such as boycotts and strikes. The third method, non-violent intervention, refers to tactics that challenge the opponent more directly, through sit-ins, fasts, non-violent obstruction, and parallel government. See Sharp, "The Techniques on Nonviolent Action," 224; Howard Zinn, ed. *The Power of Nonviolence: Writings by Advocates of Peace*.
29 Judith Butler, *Precarious Life*, 22.
30 Ibid., 32.
31 Daniel Pearl was an American journalist who was kidnapped and beheaded by militant Islamic terrorists on 1 February 2002. At the time of his kidnapping, Pearl served as the South Asia bureau chief of the *Wall Street Journal* and was based in India. He went to Pakistan as part of an investigation into the alleged links between Richard Reid (the "shoe bomber") and Al-Qaeda.
32 Butler, *Precarious Life*, 37.
33 Much more on the gendered dynamics of this activism will be explored in Chapter Four. For this discussion see Kotef and Amir, "(En)Gendering Checkpoints. "The particular organization they are examining is *Check-*

point Watch, a group primarily comprised of Ashkenazi middle-class Jewish women. CPW women's bodies are in other instances (they consider these to be fewer, yet more effective) highly sexualized. They are considered either the sexual objects of the soldiers, or as "Arab's whores." In some instances, women perform bargains with soldiers by flirting. This sometimes results in soldiers allowing Palestinians through checkpoints more easily.

34 Corrie's death is also believed to have marked the beginning of a concerted crack down on "Internationals" by Israeli troops (Sandercock et al., *Peace under Fire*).

35 Other international observers, journalists, and activists have since been injured by the Israeli Defence Force (Sandercock et al., *Peace under Fire*).

36 Klein, "On Rescuing Private Lynch and Forgetting Rachel Corrie"; Schueller, *Locating Race*.

37 In her work, Sarah Stillman has similarly examined the mainstream media play a vital role in constructing certain endangered young women as valuable "front-page victims." Writing about what she refers to as "the missing white girl syndrome," Stillman emphasises the ways in which storytelling is used to bring young female victims of violence into the public imagination and mobilise resources for their protection. See Stillman, "'The Missing White Girl Syndrome.'"

38 Gregory, *The Colonial Present*.

39 Ibid., 132–3.

40 Ibid., 133.

41 Ibid.

42 Nora Barrows-Friedman, Al Jazeera English Online, 8 September 2010, accessed 10 March 2011, http://english.aljazeera.net/indepth/opinion/2010/09/201098123618465366.html

43 In June 2003, about two months after her death, the late Edward Said wrote an essay entitled "The meaning of Rachel Corrie" in which he made public his admiration of the young woman and her actions, given his long-standing commitment to the cause of ending the occupation of Palestine. See also Said, *Peace and Its Discontents*; Said, *The Question of Palestine*; Said and Hitchens, *Blaming the Victims*.

44 Gilroy, *Postcolonial Melancholia*, 81. Gilroy's argument is part of a much broader complex discussion of cosmopolitanism and contemporary challenges to global injustice.

45 See Schueller, *Locating Race*, 174–5. One example she examines is a car-

toon drawing of Corrie sitting in front of a bulldozer with the caption: "stupidity." This cartoon originally appeared in the 18 March 2003 issue of the University of Maryland student newspaper *The Diamondback*.

46 Despite the agreement in their arguments about Corrie, Schueller explains that her overall thesis about race differs from Gilroy's insofar as he sees racial politics as inherently limiting, whereas she believes race politics can be effectively mobilized to promote change (Schueller, *Locating Race*, 3).

47 Klein, "On Rescuing Private Lynch and Forgetting Rachel Corrie"; Kumar, "War Propaganda and the (Ab)Uses of Women."

48 Kumar, "War Propaganda and the (Ab)Uses of Women," 302. Kumar points out that this becomes especially evident when one compares the attention Lynch received to that received by Shoshana Johnson, a black woman who was a member of the same company as Lynch and who was also captured, held prisoner, and was rescued along with others twelve days after Lynch's rescue. While the stories are similar, Kumar writes, "Johnson could not be Lynch" because as a black woman with dreadlocks, Johnson simply cannot "qualify for the status of 'girl next door.'"

49 See Shohat, "Area Studies, Gender Studies," 39. As others have observed, the demand to "choose sides" between "good" and "evil" created the conditions whereby voicing dissent became grounds for suspicion. For example, see Thobani, *Exalted Subjects*.

50 Mother Jones, "About Mother Jones," at the website for *Mother Jones*, 2007, accessed 6 May 2007.

51 Hammer, "The Death of Rachel Corrie."

52 Ibid, 102. For more on this article see Shueller, *Locating Race*.

53 Hammer is alluding to an incident in which ISM members in Rafah acknowledged that they had briefly and unwittingly met with two British citizens who later carried bombs to a café in Tel Aviv (for more on this incident see Seitz, "Ism at the Crossroads," 61).

54 A head scarf worn by some Muslim women

55 Hammer, "The Death of Rachel Corrie," 71 and 73. In addition, a video clip of her flag burning can be accessed on the internet through *Wikipedia*.

56 Ahmed, *Strange Encounters*.

57 At community discussion panels in Montreal, 2007.

58 For details on various memorials and projects about Rachel Corrie see

the website of the Rachel Corrie Foundation for Peace and Justice, accessed 10 March 2010, http://rachelcorriefoundation.org/ rachel.
59 The "MV Rachel Corrie." In May 2010, reports from Israel have indicated that the Israeli authorities will not allow the Freedom Flotilla to reach Gaza with its cargo of much-needed reconstruction material, medical equipment, and school supplies. According to Israeli news sources, clear orders have been issued to prevent the ships from reaching Gaza, even if this necessitates military violence. See http://palsolidarity.org/2010/05/12381 accessed 15 May 2010. MV refers to Motor Vessel; it is the prefix that is used for ships with fuel-burning engines.
60 Ali Waked, "Ramallah Presents: Rachel Corrie Restaurant." YNEt News.com. accessed 3 January 2014 from http://www.ynetnews.com/articles/0,7340,L-3973994,00.html.
61 For example, during its run at the Teesri Duniya Theatre Montreal in December 2007, five "Community Discussion Panels" were held whereby various activists, academics, and artists were asked to offer their perspectives or commentaries on the play.
62 Said, "The Meaning of Rachel Corrie."
63 Ibid.
64 See Abraham, "Tracing the Discourses of Defiance."
65 See Said, *Peace and Its Discontents*; Said, *The Question of Palestine*; Said and Hitchens, *Blaming the Victims: Spurious Scholarship and the Palestinian Question*.
66 See website of Veterans Today. The headline reads: "US Groups Ask Veterans to Demand Obama Stop Delivery of Death Bulldozers to Human Rights Violator." The open letter was posted on this site by Johnny Punish on 1 November 2010. Accessed 10 March 2011 from http://www.veteranstoday.com/2010/11/01/caterpillar-stop-delivery-death-bulldozers-human-rights-israel/
67 The idea of racial imagery as it used here is borrowing from Richard Dyer, *White*.
68 In 2013, ten years after her death, an Israeli court ruled that the death was an accident. For more on this see: http://rachelcorriefoundation.org/ and Beale, "Honouring Rachel Corrie, 10 Years On." *Aljazeera* 2013. Accessed 5 August 2013 from http://www.aljazeera.com/indepth/features/2013/03/2013316131725108877.html
69 That she was the first Western ISM activist casualty in Palestine has also likely contributed to the attention and sympathy she has received.

70 Kotef and Amir, "(En)Gendering Checkpoints," 973–96.
71 Ibid., 986.
72 Klein, "Moving through the Symbols," 257. Klein traces this change to the 1999 protests against the World Trade Organization in Seattle. Also see Brecher, "Globalization Today," 199–210.
73 Corrie, Rickman, and Viner, *My Name Is Rachel Corrie*, 55.
74 The play initially stirred up much controversy and was subsequently banned in New York City, Miami, and Toronto. Calls for banning the play revolved around charges of anti-Semitism and came either from Jewish groups or because of fears that it could upset some members of Jewish communities and were clearly connected to the fact that its content (which was taken directly from Corrie's personal writing) is openly critical of Israeli policies. Commenting about its banning in Toronto, theatre critic Richard Ouzounian noted: "The astonishing thing is that in no point of the play's history has it been the cause of any actual confrontations or demonstrations." Rather, calls for banning the play were motivated by "fear of what *might* happen." After carefully negotiating for the rights to bring the play to Toronto, Canadian Stage Company decided not to stage it for fear of being deemed anti-Semitic (CBC, 20 November 2006).
75 Corrie, Rickman, and Viner, *My Name Is Rachel Corrie*, 57.
76 Ibid., 54.
77 For a discussion of Corrie's writing as a political tourism text, see: Maureen Anne Moynagh, *Political Tourism and Its Texts*.
78 The panels took place at the Teesri Duniya Theatre.
79 These discussions were audio-recorded and then transcribed.
80 Since the play began running, the Corries have often attended the performances and participated in workshops and discussion forums and interviews to promote it.
81 Jimmy Johnson, "Film Review: Simone Bitton's investigative documentary, "Rachel," *The Electronic Intifada*, 16 April 2010, accessed March 10, 2011, http://electronicintifada.net/v2/article11214.shtml.
82 Ibid.
83 Others have also observed the significance of this scene in Bitton's film. See: http://www.thenation.com/article/rachel-corries-memory-israels-image [Accessed 16 March 2010].
84 Ahmed, "Declarations of Whiteness."
85 Hochschild, *The Managed Heart*.

86 Flam and King, *Emotions and Social Movements*.
87 Yang, "Emotions and Movements," 1,389.
88 One important exception to this is Sara Ahmed's work, *The Cultural Politics of Emotion*.

CHAPTER TWO

1 The CPT works with local partners to support those facing violence in a capacity that is often referred to as "third-party nonviolent intervention." The goal of the CPT is to promote a world of non-violence in which all human lives are valued equally. The CPT also has active campaigns in support of marginalized peoples in the United States and Canada (the countries in which the CPT is based); for my purposes, the focus is exclusively on their projects in the Global South. Arguably, however, some of the racialized power dynamics discussed in this essay would apply to local contexts as well, such as the solidarity work with indigenous people in Canada.
2 Brown, "Christian Peacemaker Teams," 14.
3 Lyn Adamson, "Why Peace Teams Risk Their Lives," *Toronto Star*, 29 March 2006. Accessed 28 February 2011. http://www.npcanada.org/Why PeaceTeamsRiskTheirLives.htm
4 For example, the CPT has been credited for the leading role it played in documenting the detention without due process of an estimated 14,000 Iraqis (Adamson, "Why Peace Teams Risk Their Lives," 2006 / 2011). Furthermore, in January 2004, CPT held a press conference on their findings concerning the abuse in Iraqi prisons, four months before the Abu Ghraib prison scandal emerged: Scrivener, "Getting into Harm's Way."
5 For detailed accounts of how each of these events unfolded from the points of view of members and supporters of the CPT, see Brown, *118 Days*.
6 Dearnaley and Trevett, "Aukland Man Held in Hostage."
7 Michelle Shephard, "Horror, Prayers Follow Ultimatum," *Toronto Star*, 3 December 2005, A1.
8 In Canada, then Prime Minister Paul Martin declared: "I can assure Canadians that there is no more urgent priority than the safe return of our citizens," adding that he had "instructed the minister of foreign affairs and the clerk of the Privy Council to make certain the full resources of

the government of Canada are made available to this end: CTV.ca News Staff. "Aid Group Blames U.S., U.K. For Iraq Abductions." *CTV News* online, 30 November 2005. Accessed 28 February 2011. http://www.ctv.ca/servlet/ArticleNews/story/CTVNews/20051129/aid_workers_051129/2005 1129?hub=TopStories.
9 For more on this see my analysis on the public responses to Rachel Corrie's death in Chapter One.
10 Stasiulis and Yuval-Davis, *Unsettling Settler Societies*; Goldberg, *Racist Culture*; Thobani, *Exalted Subjects*.
11 Alexander, "Imperial Desire/Sexual Utopias"; Puar, "Mapping U.S. Homonormativities."
12 Goldberg, *The Racial State*, 105.
13 Isin, "Theorizing Acts of Citizenship."
14 Coleman, *White Civility*.
15 Dyer, *White*, 12.
16 After the rescue, Sooden returned to New Zealand where he had become a resident in recent years, thereby receiving far less media attention in Canada.
17 Official citizenship status as "Canadian" notwithstanding, arguably, Sooden could never come to represent Canada in the same way that Loney did because as many theorists have shown, only those who have white-Anglo-Christian backgrounds are considered "real" Canadians. See Bannerji, *The Dark Side of the Nation*; Coleman, *White Civility*.
18 Fassin, "Humanitarianism as a Politics of Life."
19 Ibid., 505-6.
20 Ibid., 514.
21 Ibid.
22 Ibid., 504.
23 Ibid., 514.
24 Ibid., 515.
25 Ibid., 500.
26 Ibid., 513. Statistics on the war in Iraq indicate that the life of one First World soldier is worth one thousand times the life of an Iraqi.
27 Ibid., 514. He explains that in the process of saving lives, humanitarian action becomes the "dialectic" between the lives of the victims and the lives of those intervening. Drawing from Giorgio Agamben, he makes evident that in such equations, there are "populations" who passively await aid, and "citizens of the world" who come to assist them (505).

28 Ibid., 500–1.
29 Ibid. For more on the distinction between the politics of life and biopolitics, see Fassin, "La biopolitique n'est pas une politique de la vie."
30 Mufti and Shohat, "Introduction to *Dangerous Liaisons*," 5.
31 The fact that the CPT has consistently declared that its members are aware of the risks of working in war-torn nations but that they believe that the threat does not outweigh the potential benefit of remaining had little bearing on these reports. See Gillis, "Just Getting in the Way? Abductions in Iraq Have Given Christian Peacemakers a Higher Profile, but That's Not Helping Their Cause." Macleans.ca, 2005 / 2006; Hurst, "Activists' Action Poses Dilemma"; Weber, "Peace Group Says No to Violence in Hostage Talks"; Scrivener, "Getting into Harm's Way."
32 Scrivener, "Getting into Harm's Way;" Hurst, "Activists' Action Poses Dilemma."
33 Gunter, "The Tyrant's Best Friend"; Burman, "Thanks, Mr. Loney. Just Don't Read The News."
34 Scrivener, "Getting into Harm's Way"; Nafziger and Barrow, "Writing Peace Out of the Script."
35 Shohat, "Area Studies, Gender Studies, and the Cartographies of Knowledge (Copy 2)"; Butler, *Precarious Life*; Osuri and Banerjee, "White Diasporas"; Goldberg 2005, "Killing Me Softly"; Thobani, *Exalted Subjects*; Razack, *Casting Out*.
36 Burman, "Thanks, Mr. Loney."
37 Ibid.
38 Hackett, *News and Dissent*; Hackett and Gruneau, *The Missing News*.
39 Herman and McChesney, *The Global Media*; Dornfeld, *Producing Public Television, Producing Public Culture*.
40 See Kymlicka, "Being Canadian"; Razack, *Dark Threats and White Knights*.
41 Maloney, "Are We Really Just Peacekeepers?"
42 Campbell, "A Dedicated Presence in Iraq."
43 Loney (Interview), *The Current*, 6 June 2006.
44 Ahmed, *Strange Encounters*; Goldberg, "Killing Me Softly."
45 Loney (Interview), *The Current*.
46 Dyer, *White*; Goldberg, "Killing Me Softly"; Coleman, *White Civility*.
47 Ross, "Whiteness after 9/11." In Ross's observation, it is noteworthy that politicians end their speeches with the obligatory divine call "God bless America" because this religious-political form of patriotism not only leaves no room for dissent, but also conforms with the contemporary "Christian crusade" that shapes much of the foreign policies of the West (240).

48 Said, *Orientalism*.
49 Loney (Interview), *The Current*.
50 I am grateful to Sorouja Moll for this insight.
51 Pratt, *Imperial Eyes*.
52 Slotkin, *Regeneration through Violence*; Sturma, "Aliens and Indians."
53 Pratt, *Imperial Eyes*, 86–7.
54 Said, *Orientalism*; Ahmed, *Strange Encounters*.
55 Pritchard and Rose, "Unless a Grain of Wheat Falls," 12.
56 Hunt, "Taken Twice."
57 Author's emphasis. Gulliver, "A Life-or-Death Closet."
58 Said, *Orientalism*; Puar, "Mapping U.S. Homonormativities."
59 The reactions to this decision raise significant questions about the possible benefits of keeping Loney's sexuality hidden from Canadians as well. In other words, it is important to speculate on the ways that knowledge of his homosexuality may have adversely affected Canadians' public opinion on Loney.
60 Gulliver, "A Life-or-Death Closet."
61 Marchildon, "When Silence Is Golden."
62 Yuval-Davis, "Intersectionality, Citizenship and Contemporary Politics of Belonging."
63 Puar, "Mapping U.S. Homonormativities," 71.
64 Puar employs Lisa Duggan's notion of homonormativity which refers to a "new neo-liberal sexual politics" that hinges on "the possibility of a demobilized gay constituency and a privatized, depoliticized gay culture anchored in domesticity and consumption" (Puar, "Mapping U.S. Homonormativities," 68). Also see Duggan, "The New Homonormativity."
65 Puar's point is that the market and legislative "welcoming" of certain heteronormative, class-normative queer subjects occurs at the expense of racialized "terrorist" others, and that some gay/lesbians/queers are "folded into life" through normative lines of citizenship, a process that fundamentally depends upon racialized bodies who are subject to surveillance. What are truly "queer" in this equation are the Arab/Muslim bodies that do not uphold the imperatives of American imperialism.
66 CBC, "Loney Says Camp Closing Because of His Homosexuality." *CBC News*, 20 June 2006. Accessed 28 February 2011.
67 CBC, "Catholic Conference Retracts Invitation to Former Iraq Hostage." *CBC News*, 26 October 2007. Accessed 28 February 2011. http://www.cbc.ca/canada/manitoba/story/2007/10/26/loney-winnipeg.html.

68 Ibid.
69 Brown, *118 Days*.
70 Brown, *118 Days*, xiii.
71 Ibid.
72 Michelle Shephard, "Muslim Groups Call for Release of Canadians."
73 Ibid. A complete list of these groups is appended in Brown, *118 Days*.
74 Razack, *Casting Out*.
75 Carrie Kristal-Schroder, "Free Hostages, Canadian Detainees Urge Open Letter Pleads for Iraqi Kidnappers to Free Hostages as 'Righteous Muslims.'"
76 Nyers, "In Solitary, In Solidarity."
77 Fassin, "Humanitarianism as a Politics of Life," 499–520.
78 Nyers, "In Solitary, In Solidarity," 333–49.
79 Ibid., 346.
80 Ibid., 345.
81 Brown, *118 Days*.
82 CBC, "Ex-Hostage Loney Arrives in Toronto, Seeks Privacy."
83 Designed as a "Freedom caravan," this week-long protest campaign was organized to end in Ottawa with a vigil coinciding with the Supreme Court of Canada hearings on the constitutionality of the security certificates and indefinite detention: Behrens, "Reflections from the Freedom Caravan and Camp Hope." The website for *Homes Not Bombs*. Accessed 10 March 2009. http://www.homesnotbombs.ca/caravan diary.htm. Other interviews that Loney gave that week included an appearance on *Canada A.M.* (CTV.ca, "Loney Feels Terror Suspects Being Unfairly Judged."
84 CTV.ca, June 2006.
85 It is important to note that very early on in the kidnapping, in December 2005, the CPT had made the decision to use the publicity they were receiving to try to spotlight the plight of Iraqis held in detention. However, the press almost completely ignored this emphasis in the interviews and press releases that the CPT had issued (Nafziger and Barrow, "Writing Peace Out of the Script," 140).
86 CTV.ca, "Aid Group Blames U.S., U.K. For Iraq Abductions."
87 CPT, "CPT Statement, 23 March 2006: CPTers Missing in Baghdad Released." The website for *Christian Peacemakers Teams*, 2006. Accessed 23 March 2006.
88 Isin, "Theorizing Acts of Citizenship."
89 Ibid., 16.

90 Ibid.
91 Ibid., 38.
92 Ibid.

CHAPTER THREE

1 The term is used broadly here to refer to the publicizing of political events by non-professional journalists. It is important to state from the outset, however, that the term "citizen journalism" can be misleading insofar as the activists with whom this chapter is concerned do not necessarily fit into the category of "accidental journalists" whose reports are considered to be the "spontaneous actions of ordinary people." Allan, "The Politics of Witness," 374 and 378. Rather, working with NGOs or other civil-society organizations, these activists go to war zones with the explicit purpose of gathering and disseminating reports.
2 See Frankenberg, *The Social Construction of Whiteness*; Dyer, *White*; Morrison, *Playing in the Dark*.
3 A good example that focuses on the context of Iraq is Enders *Baghdad Bulletin*. Enders, a graduate student at an American university who opposed the war, travelled to Iraq to see the aftermath first hand. While in Iraq, he produced and distributed an English-language newspaper of the same name. The book chronicles the eight bi-monthly issues that Enders and his contributors produced.
4 IPT. *Iraq Peace Team*, 2007, accessed 26 February 2007 (italics mine).
5 Adamson, "Why Peace Teams Risk Their Lives."
6 Scrivener, "Getting into Harm's Way."
7 See Thobani, *Exalted Subjects*. Similarly, Ghassan Hage explains that within this climate, those wishing to know and to inquire about the socio-political conditions that may have led to these events are perceived as "inherently suspect, a nuisance if not a traitor" ("'Comes a Time We Are All Enthusiasm,'" 87). See also Jiwani, *Discourses of Denial*.
8 Said, *Orientalism*.
9 Furthermore, as Inderpal Grewal and Caren Kaplan's work shows, the representational practices of these activists demand critical examination because they are intended as a form of resistance. See Grewal and Kaplan, "'Warrior Marks.'"
10 As outlined in the Introduction.
11 Allan, et al., "Bearing Witness.
12 Ahmed, *Strange Encounters*, 68.

13 Fassin, "Humanitarianism as a Politics of Life."
14 Ibid., 514.
15 This also raises important questions on how the white First World activist is, as Toni Morrison points out, propped up by the shadow figures of the people they report on, people who are presented as "dead, impotent, or under complete control." See Morrison, *Playing in the Dark*, 33.
16 Dyer, *White*, 3.
17 Ahmed, *Strange Encounters*, 73.
18 Writing about ethnographers doing fieldwork on violent struggles, Joseba Zulaika highlights the fact that although they are deemed "specialists," they in fact often know very little, and what little they know comes from the local people ("The Anthropologist as Terrorist").
19 Davies and Harré, "Positioning."
20 Jean-Klein, "Alternative Modernities, or Accountable Modernities?"
21 Said, *Orientalism*, 109.
22 Jean-Klein, "Alternative Modernities or Accountable Modernities?," 50. Jean-Klein's work focuses on organized political-observation tourism in the occupied Palestinian West Bank territories during the first Intifada in 1989. She examines issues of authority, objectivity, and neutrality as they emerged in the predispositions of European university students who participated in the tours. Jean-Klein highlights an important hidden dynamic whereby the Palestinian organizers who were dependent on the European student observers' approval assumed the defensive role of trying to prove themselves. Jean-Klein describes the power relations of these political observation tours as a type of "structural coercion" wherein the young student observers judged the Palestinians' activism against a predetermined "gold standard" of European modernity that, she contends, is a contemporary form of Western domination.
23 Allan and Sonwalkar et al., "Bearing Witness."
24 Dan Gillmor, *We the Media*.
25 Ibid., xvii–xviii.
26 Ibid., xiii.
27 Tilley and Cokley, "Deconstructing the Discourse of Citizen Journalism," 108.
28 Ibid., 103.
29 Melissa Wall, "Blogging Gulf War II."
30 Mark Pedelty, *War Stories*.
31 Hogwarth, *Documentary Television in Canada*, 22–3.
32 Ibid., 24.

33 Ibid., 23.
34 Ibid., 24.
35 Ibid.
36 Dornfeld, *Producing Public Television, Producing Public Culture*, 61. See also Anderson, *Imagined Communities*.
37 Herman and McChesney. *The Global Media*. The CBC operates two television networks, four radio networks and two 24-hour news channels in both of Canada's official languages.
38 Hackett, *News and Dissent*, 270–1.
39 See Grewal and Kaplan, "'Warrior Marks'"; Shohat, "Area Studies, Gender Studies, and the Cartographies of Knowledge"; and Mohanty, *Feminism without Borders*.
40 Shohat, "Introduction to Talking Visions," 9.
41 Ibid.
42 Ahmed, *Strange Encounters*.
43 Ibid., 166. See also Spivak, "Can the Subaltern Speak?" in *Marxism and the Interpretation of Culture*; Pratt, "Fieldwork in Common Places."
44 Ahmed, *Strange Encounters*, 166.

CHAPTER FOUR

1 Ware and Back, *Out of Whiteness*, 14 (emphasis mine).
2 Sontag, *Regarding the Pain of Others*.
3 Pedelty, *War Stories*.
4 Sontag, *Regarding the Pain of Others*, 104.
5 Kozol, "Domesticating Nato's War in Kosovo/A," 21.
6 Lutz and Collins, "The Photograph as an Intersection of Gazes," 373.
7 Hannah Arendt, *On Revolution*; Berlant, "The Subject of True Feeling: Pain, Privacy, and Politics"; Spelman, *Fruits of Sorrow*.
8 See Foucault, "Politics and Ethics: An Interview," 377.
9 See Tobias, "Foucault on Freedom and Capabilities."
10 Ibid., 77.
11 Arendt, *Responsibility and Judgment*.
12 Ibid., 50.
13 Ibid., 97.
14 Sandercock et al., *Peace Under Fire*.
15 Ibid.

16 Taylor, "Problems in Photojournalism: Realism, the Nature of News and the Humanitarian Narrative."
17 Ibid., 135–6.
18 Sontag, *Regarding the Pain of Others*.
19 Ibid., 66.
20 Ibid., 52.
21 Pedelty, *War Stories*.
22 Kozol, "Domesticating Nato's War."
23 Ibid., 6.
24 Ibid., 29.
25 Pedelty, *War Stories*, 3.
26 Butler, *Precarious Life*.
27 Ibid., 20.
28 Ibid., 30.
29 Ibid., 32.
30 Kozol, "Domesticating Nato's War."
31 Ibid., 31.
32 Mike Crang, "Picturing Practices: Research Through the Tourist Gaze."
33 Sontag, *Regarding the Pain of Others*.
34 Razack, "A Violent Culture or Culturalized Violence?"
35 Razack, *Dark Threats and White Knights*; Razack, "Stealing the Pain of Others."
36 Razack, "Stealing the Pain of Others."
37 Ibid., 381 (my italics).
38 Berlant, "Compassion (and Withholding)"; Garber, "Compassion."
39 Arendt, *On Revolution*.
40 Spelman, *Fruits of Sorrow*, 65.
41 Kozol, "Domesticating Nato's War."
42 Spelman, *Fruits of Sorrow*, 61.
43 Ibid., 64.
44 See Woodward, "Calculating Compassion," 71.
45 Bauman, *Society Under Siege*, 216.
46 Jasper, *The Art of Moral Protest*.
47 Foucault, "On the Genealogy of Ethics."
48 Hesford and Kozol, *Just Advocacy?*, 9.
49 Ware and Back, *Out of Whiteness*, 14.

CHAPTER FIVE

1. I borrow this phrase from one of the research participants who said this in the interview.
2. Ruth Frankenberg, "The Mirage of an Unmarked Whiteness," 77.
3. For more on the people who were interviewed and the interview process, see note 26 in the introductory chapter.
4. Between them, the activists had made over fifteen trips to Palestine, four trips to Iraq, three trips to Central America, one trip to Indonesia, one to South Africa. This count does not include trips they may have made with non-governmental organizations, or work they did (paid or unpaid) outside of anti-violence or peace solidarity groups. A large number of these activists had made more than one international solidarity trip (to either the same location or a different one) and a few had participated with more than one group. The length of stay varied greatly. The shortest trip was two weeks, and the longest was one year. The average length of the trips was two to three months.
5. Weedon, *Feminism, Theory, and the Politics of Difference*, 32. See also McNay, *Foucault and Feminism*; Hollway, "Gender Difference and the Production of Subjectivity."
6. Alcoff, "What Should White People Do?"
7. Pratt, "Identity"; and Thompson, *A Promise and a Way of Life*. When applied to studies of race, the concept of ambivalence usually brings to mind the work of Homi Bhabha who has used it to show the complex mix of attraction and repulsion that exists between dominant and subordinated groups. With this concept, Bhabha has made an important scholarly intervention into postcolonial studies that disrupts facile notions of identities as unambiguously shaped by colonialism. Bhabha, "Of Mimicry and Man"; Ashcroft et al., *Key Concepts in Post-Colonial Studies*.
8. Peace Brigades International (PBI), one of the longest-standing non-governmental organizations dedicated to protective accompaniment. See the Introduction chapter for more information about this organization. PBI International, Peace Brigades International (2007), http://www.peacebrigades.org/etp/etp.html
9. ISM Canada (2007), *ISM Canada*, accessed 28 March 2007.
10. Alcoff, "What Should White People Do?," 25.
11. This view is shared by one of the ISM's Palestinian founders, Ghassan Andoni, who is strongly committed to nonviolent direct action. Accord-

ing to Charmaine Seitz "Andoni tells his foreign recruits that even though they are not in Palestine to advise Palestinians what to do, their work on the ground serves as an example." Charmaine Seitz, "ISM at the Crossroads," 60–1.

12 Ahmed, *Strange Encounters*; Said, *Orientalism*.
13 Seitz, "ISM at the Crossroads," 60–1.
14 As indicated in the previous chapter, a report on the ISM by Seitz finds similar dynamics operating whereby the concern is on keeping the activists comfortable (Seitz, "ISM at the Crossroads," 50–67).
15 hooks, "Sisterhood"; Thompson, "Tiffany, Friend of People of Color"; Mohanty, *Feminism without Borders*.
16 It is important to note that the inner conflicts explored here are consistent with existing literature on accompaniment-observer activism. See Mahoney and Eguren, *Unarmed Bodyguards*; Pollock, "Using and Disrupting"; Weber, *Visions of Solidarity*; Thompson, *A Promise and a Way of Life*. Also see literature on international development workers: Heron, *Desire for Development*.
17 It is noteworthy that most of the narratives presented here come from interviews with activists who had accumulated experiences either through lengthy stays, experiences in more than one geopolitical context, or through long-term (in some cases life-long) commitments to anti-violence activism. This suggests that activists who struggled the most with First World interventions (either their own or those of other activists) were those who had gained the most experience. Although it is not possible to draw definitive conclusions from this, it nevertheless suggests that activists are more likely to develop the sensibilities needed to understand or manage their positioning after participating in long-term projects.
18 Heron, "Gender and Exceptionality in North-South Interventions," 117–27.
19 It is important to note that although this criticism implies that other groups in the area do not collaborate with Palestinian groups, all of the groups discussed here do.
20 Frankenberg, *White Women, Race Matters*.
21 Frankenberg notes, for example, the white women's uses of euphemisms such as "the melting pot" (Frankenberg, *White Women, Race Matters*, 149) to suggest that such terms are easier and more comfortable to invoke.
22 Thompson, "Tiffany, Friend of People of Color."
23 Ibid., 9.

24 Exploring similar tensions between these approaches in the civil rights movement, Bob Blauner indicates that distinctions between the approaches are relational rather than absolute. See Blauner, "White Radicals, White Liberals, and White People."
25 Seitz makes a similar observation: "In times of crisis or campaign, internationals from the plethora of groups will work together, owning success and failures as one" (Seitz, "ISM at the Crossroads," 51).
26 See Foucault, "The Political Technology of Individuals"; Goldberg, *The Racial State*.
27 Thompson, "Tiffany, Friend of People of Color."
28 Heron, *Desire for Development*.
29 Ibid., 222.
30 Shalhoub-Kevorkian and Khsheiboun, "Palestinian Women's Voices Challenging Human Rights Activism."
31 They use the umbrella term "human rights activists" to refer to a number of different types of organizations.
32 Shalhoub-Kevorkian and Khsheiboun, "Palestinian Women's Voices," 359.
33 Ibid., 358.
34 Ibid., 360.
35 Ibid., 360.
36 See Incite! Women of Color Against Violence, *The Revolution Will Not Be Funded*.
37 Choudry, "Making a Killing."
38 Ibid., 19.
39 Ibid., 361. The important thing, according to Shalhoub-Kevorkian and Khsheiboun, is that these women's voices are drowned out. This parallels a dynamic During the 1990s "civil society" organizations and rhetoric mushroomed exponentially.
40 Three were conducted between March and May 2008 in Ramallah, and were conducted by Reem Attieh for the author. The forth was a telephone interview during the same time period. The interviews were audio taped and then transcribed. The first two were conducted in Arabic and then freely translated.
41 These perspectives are not comprehensive by any means, nor do they imply that there is a singular Palestinian perspective on these issues. Nevertheless they shed additional light on the power dynamics that develop in these contexts
42 ATG, "Palestine and Palestinians."

43 Sharoni is writing about the context of Palestine. Sharoni, "Compassionate Resistance."

CHAPTER SIX

1 Smith, "Split Affinities." Smith uses the notion of "split affinities" to show how, in cross-racial solidarity contexts, women activists often find themselves having to make a choice between gender and race.
2 Deutsch, "Feminist Criticism, Occupation and Sexual Harassment." One aspect of these debates centred on some Palestinian women's requests that the Israeli activists dress in a way that respects the values of the Palestinian residents of the neighbourhood. Some feminists argued that that such a request was against the free choices of women.
3 Deutsch, "Feminist Criticism, Occupation." It was in the specific neighborhood of Sheikh Jarrah where Israelis and Palestinians have been participating in a weekly demonstration against the evacuation of Palestinian families from their houses. The right-wing newspaper is called *Makor Rishon*.
4 Ibid.
5 Ibid.
6 Smith, "Split Affinities," 281.
7 Freeman, "Is Local."
8 Kirby, "Re: Mapping Subjectivity"; Mohanram, *Black Body*; Razack, *Looking White People in the Eye*.
9 Laware, "Circling the Missiles and Staining Them Red," 19. This site of protest which was started in 1981 was "one of the first and longest lasting" peace encampments and has been attributed to starting a women's peace movement.
10 Cranford, "'Aqui Estamos Y No Nos Vamos!'"
11 Sasson-Levy and Rapoport, "Body, Gender and Knowledge in Protest Movements."
12 Blee, "Introduction."
13 Sasson-Levy and Rapoport, "Body, Gender and Knowledge."
14 Dierenfield, *The Civil Rights Movement*.
15 Ibid., 104.
16 Thompson, *A Promise and a Way of Life*, 193–4.
17 Heron, *The Education of White Women as Development Workers*
18 For more on this, see Kotef and Amir, "(En)Gendering Checkpoints."

19 She was sixty-two years old at the time of the interview.
20 More details on this are in Chapter One.
21 Dierenfield, *The Civil Rights Movement*; Riches, *The Civil Rights Movement*.
22 For more on this see Thompson, *A Promise and a Way of Life*.
23 Razack, "A Violent Culture or Culturalized Violence?" 82, 100. In the example she explores, at the centre of the story of sexual violence in mainstream understandings of South Asian "culture" is the woman who is *more* victimized, the assailant who is *more* violent, and the culture that creates and maintains these conditions.
24 Frankenberg, *White Women, Race Matters*, 81. Frankenberg notes that other figures in this discursive family of the rape scenario include the white male saviour and, although problematically invisible, the black woman who has historically been a much more frequent target of assault by white men.
25 Davis, *Women, Race & Class*; Pinar, *The Gender of Racial Politics and Violence in America*.
26 Brownmiller, *Against Our Will*, 281.
27 Ibid., 279–80.
28 Ibid., 280.
29 Ibid., 279.
30 As cited in Pinar, *The Gender of Racial Politics and Violence in America*, 804. One person who made this critique is Angela Davis. While Pinar believes that Brownmiller overstated her case, he concedes that she is not entirely mistaken, agreeing that in revalorizing the bodies of black men, white liberals did sometimes occupy the other side of the same coin. Pinar further points out that neither Brownmiller nor Davis notices the buried homoerotic at work in the white male subjugation of the black man.
31 Hesford, "Reading Rape Stories," 200.
32 Eagleton, "Ethical Reading," 191.
33 Hesford, "Reading Rape Stories," 199.
34 See Jiwani, *Discourses of Denial*; Razack, "Violent Culture or Culturalized Violence?"; Crenshaw, "Demarginalizing the Intersection of Race and Class"; Bannerji, *The Dark Side of the Nation*; Davis, *Women, Race and Class*.
35 Brownmiller and more recently Pinar both point out that the charge of interracial sexual violence is so emotionally charged that it was commonly considered to be the "most terrible crime on earth" (Pinar, *The Gender of Racial Politics*, 65) and one that has long fascinated the public to

the extent that it has been characterized as a national obsession (Brownmiller, *Against Our Will*, 237).
36 Warshaw, *I Never Called It Rape*, 90–2. Most rapes are committed by someone the assailant knows and most go unreported.
37 Writing about such dilemmas, Devon Carbado agrees that although there is a justifiable concern about the ways men of certain communities of colour are represented as violent, we must question how such acts may perpetuate victimhood for men of colour. Moreover, Carbado is concerned that the silence that surrounds the violence can function as political apologia for black men. In his view, what is needed is a way to acknowledge that men of colour commit acts of sexual violence that does not deny that they are also victims of racism. Carbado, "Black Male Racial Victimhood."
38 Smith, "Native American Feminism, Sovereignty, and Social Change."
39 Built into such attitudes, Andrea Smith writes, is the idea that "maybe all this feminism business is just another extension of the same old racist, colonialist mentality" (Smith, "Native American Feminism," 117).
40 Smith, "Native American Feminism."
41 Sasson-Levy and Rapoport, "Body, Gender and Knowledge."
42 Smith, "Native American Feminism," 127.
43 Mehta and Bondi, "Embodied Discourse."
44 Ibid., 75.
45 Ibid., 74–5.
46 Mehta and Bondi, "Embodied Discourse," 79.
47 Razack, *Dark Threats and White Knights*.
48 Ibid., 90.
49 Mehta and Bondi, "Embodied Discourse."
50 The Combahee River Collective, "A Black Feminist Statement"; Blee, "Introduction"; Sasson-Levy and Rapoport, "Body, Gender and Knowledge."
51 Indu Vashist in personal communication with author.
52 http://hugoschwyzer.net/2010/10/14/keep-quiet-for-the-cause-on-sexual-abuse-in-progressive-movements/ and http://www.kersplebedeb.com/mystuff/feminist/activist_abuse.html http://www.owjn.org/owjn_2009/index.php?option=com_content&view=article&id=190&Itemid=107 and http://zapagringo.blogspot.com/2010/06/challenging-male-supremacy-project.html

53 http://www.transformativejustice.eu/wp-content/uploads/2010/02/Ways-Perpetrators-Avoid-Accountability.pdf.
54 Many of these are strategies that have been generated during the anti-globalisation movement in North America.
55 See http://phillysurvivorsupportcollective.wordpress.com/.

CHAPTER SEVEN

1 Cooper, *Colonialism in Question*, 233.
2 Allan, "The Politics of Witness," 275.
3 Sometimes this was done through identifying articles of clothing (vests or caps) or flags to signify that they were people from elsewhere.
4 This would be a reliance on what Alcoff refers to as "the visual registry of race." See Alcoff, "Towards a Phenomenology of Racial Embodiment," 267–83.
5 Dyer, *White*, 12.
6 CPT, 2007.
7 Ibid.
8 Brown, "Christian Peacemaker Teams," 14.
9 IPT, 2007. Their objections are also made on the grounds that the word "shield" connotes weaponry and militarism. The International Women's Peace Service (IWPS) has a similar stance based on a similar interpretation of the term, explicitly stating, "We will not allow ourselves to be used as a shield for violence from others" (IWPS, 2007). Their concern appears to be that they might unwittingly be used as human shields by the Palestinians.
10 Mahoney and Eguren, *Unarmed Bodyguards*.
11 Klein, "Moving through the Symbols."
12 Novak, "Accompaniment or Charity?".
13 Mills, "Racial Liberalism."
14 Ibid., 1381.
15 Goldberg, *Racist Culture*.
16 Ibid., 4.
17 Ibid., 9.
18 In tracing the historical lines of the discourse of racelessness, Barnor Hesse has shown that the changes in geopolitical relations that came about after World War II and mechanisms such as the Human Rights charter of the United Nations sought to render racial discrimination morally indefensible. This created a problem insofar as statements for-

mulated in race-thinking (equated with overtly racist regimes such as that of the Nazis) could no longer be uttered, thereby making it difficult to acknowledge the constituting effects of race. Characterizing this as a conceptual double-bind, Hesse argues that the casting of all forms of race-thinking as wrong, effectively and inevitably reaffirms liberalism. See Hesse, "Im/Plausible Deniability."

19 Mohanram, *Black Body*.
20 Ibid.
21 Ibid., 9–10.
22 Fanon, "The Fact of Blackness"; see also Mohanran, *Black Body*.
23 Dyer, 14.
24 Shohat, "Area Studies, Gender Studies"; Alexander and Mohanty, "Introduction"; Ahmed "Declarations of Whiteness; Hesford and Kozol, *Just Advocacy*; Grewal and Kaplan, "'Warrior Marks.'"
25 Frankenberg explains this phenomenon as a conflation between "ought" and "is." Frankenberg, *White Women, Race Matters*, 148.
26 For more on this see Boyd, D. (2004). "The Legacies of Liberalism and Oppressive Relations: Facing a Dilemma for the Subject of Moral Education."
27 Blauner, 1995; Sasson-Levy & Rapoport, 2003.
28 Goldberg, 217.
29 Brush, "Problematizing the Race Consciousness of Women of Color," 180.
30 Arendt, *Responsibility and Judgment*.
31 Bauman, *Society under Siege*.
32 Ibid., 205.
33 Ibid., 206.
34 Ibid., 205.
35 Ahmed, *Strange Encounters*.
36 Razack, *Dark Threats and White Knights*.
37 Goldberg, *Racist Culture*.
38 Ibid., 215. Here Goldberg is drawing from Kimberlé Crenshaw's critique of the limits of the Critical Studies project.
39 Ibid., 215–16.
40 de Jong, "Constructive Complicity Enacted?"
41 Bernice, "Coalition Politics."
42 Seitz, "ISM at the Crossroads," 64.
43 Choudry, "Global Justice? Contesting NGOization."
44 See Thompson, *A Promise and a Way of Life*, 54.
45 Ibid.

46 Although this dynamic did not necessarily come up for the activists I interviewed, the added peril that activists of colour face has been documented in other studies: Mahoney and Eguren, *Unarmed Bodyguards*; Weber, *Visions of Solidarity*.
47 Fanon, *The Wretched of the Earth*, 59.
48 Mignolo, "Who Speaks for the 'Human' in Human Rights?"; see also Cooper, *Colonialism in Question*.
49 Synott, "Peace Education as an Educational Paradigm"; Perkins, "Paradox of Peace"; Bar-Tal, "Philosophy of Peace Education"; Gur-Ze've, "Elusive Nature of Peace Education". In some earlier work, I reviewed these bodies of literature such as peace education (see Mahrouse, 2006) to show that within the majority of educational strategies put forward in them, the underlying assumption is that social injustice is caused by ignorance and therefore remedied through individual change.
50 Cooper, *Colonialism in Question*, 233.
51 Nelson, *Reckoning*.
52 See http://decolo.pasc.ca/
53 Ahmed, *Strange Encounters*, 167.
54 Ibid., 180.
55 Ibid., 164.
56 Ibid.

AFTERWORD

1 Rachel Corrie, *My Name Is Rachel Corrie*, 45.
2 Steven Flusty, "Portable Autonomous Zones.".
3 Ben-Simhon, "Occupation Tourism."
4 Freedman, "Palestine's Occupation Tourism."
5 Mor, "Jerusalem Reality Tours."
6 For discussion on mainstream understandings of privilege, see Thomas Nakayama and Robert Krizek. "Whiteness as a Strategic Rhetoric," in *Whiteness: The Communication of Social Identity*, eds. Thomas K. Nakayama and Judith N. Martin (Thousand Oaks: Sage Publications, 1999), 87–106.
7 See Klein, "Moving through the Symbols," and South End Press Collective, "Katrina, Race, and the State of the Nation."
8 *Le Devoir*, "Canadiens libérés en Chine: Une manifestante persévérante." *Le Devoir*, 10 August 2007. Accessed 5 September 2007, http://www.lede-

Notes to pages 158–61

voir.com/societe/justice/152985/canadiens-liberes-en-chine-une-manifestante-perseverante.
9 Kassam, "Passport, or Carte Blanche to Raise Hell?" *Toronto Star*, http://www.thestar.com/article/252118.
10 "Topic: 2 Canadian Activists Arrested in China." *Rabble*, accessed 6 September 2007, http://rabble.ca/babble/national-news/2-canadian-activists-arrested-china?page=1
11 Kaplan, "Questions of Travel," 62.
12 Fennell and Malloy, *Codes of Ethics in Tourism: Practice, Theory, Synthesis* (Toronto: Channel View Publications, 2007).
13 An earlier version of this argument was published in Mahrouse, "Feel Good Tourism."
14 McLaren, *Rethinking Tourism and Ecotravel*. 2nd ed. (Bloomfield, CT: Kumarian Press, 2003).
15 Ibid.
16 See Mahrouse, "Feel Good Tourism." I was curious about these trips offered by Global Exchange partly because they have received so much praise and are, arguably, some of the most politicized forms of tourism out there. For instance, they distribute materials to tourists before-hand to raise awareness about power imbalances; emphasize resilience and resourcefulness of local people, make use of locally-owned businesses, and one has to agree to abide by a basic code of conduct which states things like, "I will not take pictures without asking."
17 Sichel, "'I've Come to Help' Can Tourism and Altruism Mix?" Accessed 6 August 2013, http://briarpatchmagazine.com/articles/view/ive-come-to-help-can-tourism-and-altruism-mix/.
18 See Lilie Chouliaraki, *The Ironic Spectator*. See also Wan, "Can Feel-Good Activism Save the World?" (Think Africa Press, March 2013), accessed 6 August 2013, http://thinkafricapress.com/culture/interview-lilie-chouliaraki-can-feel-good-activism-save-world.
19 See Jo Littler, "I Feel Your Pain: Cosmopolitan Charity and the Public Fashioning of the Celebrity Soul." *Social Semiotics* 18, no. 2 (2008): 237–51.
20 See Choudry, "Global Justice?," 20.
21 http://www.metowe.com/about-us/our-story/ accessed on 4 January 2014.
22 Ibid.
23 Free the Children's founder is Craig Kielburger, a white Canadian man from Thornhill who first became known in 1995 at the age of twelve

when, as the story goes, he was searching for the comics in the newspaper one morning when he saw a headline about the death of a Pakistani child labourer, also twelve years old. He discovered that the boy, Iqbal Masih, was sold into slavery at the age of four, had escaped to speak out on children's rights, and was murdered as a result. Baffled at how a child his own age could be subjected to such cruel conditions, Kielburger convinced his parents to let him travel to Asia where on a very publicized trip, he met with high profile politicians as well as local activists and immediately became an international spokesperson on the issue of child labour.

24 For more on this see David Jefferess, "Global Citizenship and the Cultural Politics of Benevolence." *Critical Literacy: Theories and Practices* 2, no. 1 (2008): 27–36.

25 For an excellent discussion of volunteer tourism, see Wanda Vrasti, *Volunteer Tourism in the Global South: Giving Back in Neoliberal Times*.

26 In 2007, an online travel agency called responsibletravel.com which describes itself as the first business in the world to talk about responsible travel and tourism, offered 2,500 holidays from 270 tour operators.

27 I borrow the notion of "anti-conquest" from Pratt, *Imperial Eyes*.

28 See for example, The Alternative Tourism Group. http://www.atg.ps/

29 Steven Flusty, *Portable Autonomous Zones*, 197.

30 Ibid.

Bibliography

Abbott, Beth. "Project Accompaniment: A Canadian Response." *Refuge* 13, no 10 (1994): 26.
Abraham, Matthew. "Tracing the Discourses of Defiance: Remembering Edward W. Said Through the Resistance of the Palestinian Intifada." *Nebula* 2, no. 2 (2005): 21–32.
Adamson, Lyn. "Why Peace Teams Risk Their Lives." *Toronto Star*, 29 March 2006. Accessed 28 February 2011. http://www.npcanada.org/WhyPeaceTeamsRiskTheirLives.htm.
Ahmed, Sara. "Declarations of Whiteness: The Non-Performativity of Anti-Racism." *Borderlands E-journal* 3, no. 2 (2004): 1–15.
– *The Cultural Politics of Emotion*. New York: Routledge, 2004.
– *Strange Encounters: Embodied Others in Post-Coloniality*. Transformations. London; New York: Routledge, 2000.
Alcoff, Linda Martin. "Toward a Phenomenology of Racial Embodiment." In *Race*, edited by Robert Bernasconi, 267–83. Malden, MA, and Oxford: Blackwell Publishers, 2001.
– "What Should White People Do?" *Hypatia* 13, no. 3 (1998): 6–26.
Alexander, M. Jacqui, and Chandra Talpade Mohanty. "Introduction: Genealogies, Legacies, Movements." In *Feminist Genealogies, Colonial Legacies, Democratic Futures*, edited by M. Jacqui Alexander and Chandra Talpade Mohanty, xiii–xlii. New York and London: Routledge, 1997.
Alexander, M. Jacqui. "Imperial Desire/Sexual Utopias: White Gay Capital and Transnational Tourism." In *Talking Visions: Multicultural Feminism in a Transnational Age*, edited by Ella Shohat, 281–305. Cambridge, MA: MIT Press, 1998.

Allan, Diana K. "The Politics of Witness: Remembering and Forgetting 1948 in Shatila Camp." In *Nakba: Palestine, 1948, and the Claims of Memory*, edited by Ahmad H. Sa'di and Lila Abu-Lughod. New York: Columbia University Press, 2007.

Allan, Stuart, Prasun Sonwalkar, and Cynthia Carter. "Bearing Witness: Citizen Journalism and Human Rights Issues." *Globalisation, Societies and Education* 5, no. 3 (2007): 373–89.

Anderson, Benedict R. *Imagined Communities: Reflections on the Origin and Spread of Nationalism*. [2nd] rev. and extended ed. London and New York: Verso, 1991.

Anderson, Kathryn. *Weaving Relationships: Canada-Guatemala Solidarity. Comparative Ethics Series*. Waterloo, Ontario: Wilfrid Laurier University Press, 2003.

Andoni, Ghassan, Renad Qubbaj, George N. Rishmawi, and Tomas Saffold. "International Solidarity." In *Live from Palestine: International and Palestinian Direct Action against the Israeli Occupation*, edited by Nancy Stohlman and Laurieann Aladin, 62–6. Cambridge, MA: South End Press, 2003.

Arat-Koc, Sedef. "New Whiteness(es), Beyond the Colour Line? Assessing the Contradictions and Complexities of 'Whiteness' in the (Geo)Political Economy of Capitalist Globalism." In *States of Race: Critical Race Feminism for the 21st Century*, edited by Sherene Razack, Malinda Sharon Smith, and Sunera Thobani. Toronto: Between the Lines, 2010.

Arendt, Hannah. *On Revolution*. New York: Penguin, 1977.

– *Responsibility and Judgment*. New York: Schoken Books, 2003.

Ashcroft, Bill, Gareth Griffiths, and Helen Tiffin. *Key Concepts in Post-Colonial Studies*. London and New York: Routledge, 1998.

Asia to Gaza. "Asian People's Movement For Gaza." *AsiaToGaza.org*, 2011. Accessed 11 March 2011. http://www.asiatogaza.org/.

ATG. "Palestine and Palestinians: Guidebook." *Alternative Tourism Group*. Accessed 2005. http://www.atg.ps/index.php?lang=en&page=orderourguidebook.

Babson, Steve, Dave Riddle, and Dave Elsila. *The Color of Law: Ernie Goodman, Detroit, and the Struggle for Labor and Civil Rights*. Detroit: Wayne State University Press.

Bannerji, Himani. *The Dark Side of the Nation: Essays on Multiculturalism, Nationalism and Gender*. Toronto: Canadian Scholars' Press, 2000.

Barrows-Friedman, Nora. "During war there are no civilians." *Al Jazeera*

English online, 8 September 2010. Accessed 10 March 2011, http://english.aljazeera.net/indepth/opinion/2010/09/201098123618465366.html.
Bar-Tal, D. "Elusive Nature of Peace Education." In G. Salomon and B. Nevo, eds, *Peace Education: The Concepts, Principles, and Practices around the World*, pp. 27–36. Mahwah, NJ: Lawrence Erlbaum Associates, 2002.
Barth, Willy. "James Loney." *The Current*. Radio. Produced by John Chipman. Canada: CBC Radio, 2006.
Bauman, Zygmunt. Society Under Siege. Cambridge: Polity, 2002.
Beale, Andy. "Honouring Rachel Corrie, 10 Years On." Aljazeera 2013. Accessed December 23, 2013. http://www.aljazeera.com/indepth/features/2013/03/2013316131725108877.html
Behrens, Matthew. "Reflections from the Freedom Caravan and Camp Hope." The website for Homes Not Bombs. Accessed 10 March 2009. http://www.homesnotbombs.ca/caravandiary.htm.
– 2008. "A Great Hand of Solidarity: Jim Loney and Canada's Secret Trial Detainees." In *118 Days: Christian Peacemaker Teams Held Hostage in Iraq*, edited by Tricia Gates Brown, 162–70. Toronto: Christian Peacemaker Teams.
Ben-Simhon, Coby. "Occupation Tourism: A New Trend at West Bank Fence Protest." Haaretz.com, no. 14.01.10 (2010). Accessed 10 March 2011. http://www.haaretz.com/weekend/magazine/occupation-tourism-a-new-trend-at-west-bank-fence-protest-1.261458.
Berlant, Lauren. "Compassion (and Withholding)." In *Compassion: The Culture and Politics of an Emotion*, edited by Lauren Berlant, 1–13. New York and London: Routledge, 2004.
– "The Subject of True Feeling: Pain, Privacy, and Politics." In *Feminist Consequences: Theory for the New Century*, edited by Elisabeth Bronfen and Misha Kavka, 126–60. New York: Columbia University Press, 2001.
Bhabha, Homi K. "Of mimicry and man: The ambivalence of colonial discourse." In *Race Critical Theories*, edited by Philomena Essed and David T. Goldberg, 112–22. Malden, MA: Blackwell Publishers, 2002.
Bhalla, Nita. "Asian aid ship to Gaza fraught with challenges, say activists," Reuters, accessed 10 March 2011, http://in.reuters.com/article/2011/01/12/idINIndia-54098920110112?pageNumber=2.
Bhattacharyya, Gargi, John Gabriel, and Stephen Small. *Race and Power: Global Racism in the Twenty-First Century*. London & New York: Routledge, 2002.
Blauner, Bob. "White radicals, white liberals, and white people: Rebuild-

ing the anti-racist coalition." In *Racism and anti-racism in world perspective*, edited by Benjamin P. Bowser, 115–137. London: Sage Publications, 1995.

Blee, Kathleen. "Introduction: Women on the Left/Women on the Right." In *No Middle Ground: Women and Radical Resistance*, edited by Kathleen Blee, 1–18. New York and London: New York University Press, 1998.

Boyd, Dwight. "The Legacies of Liberalism and Oppressive Relations: Facing a Dilemma for the Subject of Moral Education." *Journal of Moral Education* 33 (2004):1, 3–22.

Brecher, Jeremy. "Globalization Today." In *Implicating Empire: Globalization and Resistance in the 21st Century World Order*, edited by Stanley Aronowitz and Heather Guatney, 199–210. New York: Basic Books, 2003.

Brown, Tricia Gates. "Christian Peacemaker Teams: An Introduction." In *Getting in the Way: Stories from Christian Peacemaker Teams*, edited by Tricia Gates Brown, 11–15. Waterloo, Ontario: Herald Press, 2005.

– ed. *118 Days: Christian Peacemaker Teams Held Hostage in Iraq*. Toronto: Christian Peacemaker Teams. 2008.

Brownmiller, Susan. *Against Our Will: Men, Women and Rape*. New York: Bantam Books, 1976. Reprint, Bantam edition.

Brush, P. "Problematizing the race consciousness of women of color." *Signs* 1 (2001): 171–98.

Burman, T. "Thanks, Mr. Loney. Just Don't Read The News." *CBC.ca*, 2006. Accessed 6 June 2008. http://www.cbc.ca/news/about/burman/20060327.html.

Butler, Judith. *Precarious Life: The Powers of Mourning and Violence*. London and New York: Verso, 2004.

– *The Psychic Life of Power: Theories in Subjection*. Stanford, California: Stanford University Press, 1997.

Campbell, Colin. "A Dedicated Presence in Iraq." Macleans.ca. Accessed 19 June 2009. http://www.macleans.ca/topstories/world/article.jsp?content=20060529_127768_127768 (page discontinued).

Canadian Press. "Statement by James Loney After Arrival Home." *CTV.ca*, 27 March 2006. Accessed 10 March 2011. http://www.ctv.ca/servlet/ArticleNews/story/CTVNews/20060327/loney_statement_060327/20060327/.

Carbado, Devon W. "Black Male Racial Victimhood." *Callaloo* 21, no. 2 (1998): 337–61.

Bibliography 203

CBC. "Catholic Conference Retracts Invitation to Former Iraq Hostage." CBC.ca, 26 October 2007. Accessed 28 February 2011, http://www.cbc.ca/news/canada/manitoba/catholic-conference-retracts-invitation-to-former-iraq-hostage-1.641784.

CBC. "Ex-Hostage Loney Arrives in Toronto, Seeks Privacy." CBC.ca, 27 March 2006. Accessed 28 February 2011. http://www.cbc.ca/canada/toronto/story/2006/03/27/to-loney20060327.html#skip300x250.

CBC. "'Great to Be Alive': Former Canadian Hostage." CBC.ca, 26 March 2006. Accessed 28 February 2011. http://www.cbc.ca/canada/story/2006/03/26/loney-home060326.html.

CBC. "Loney Says Camp Closing Because of His Homosexuality." CBC.ca, 20 June 2006. Accessed 28 February 2011. http://www.cbc.ca/news/canada/story/2006/06/20/loney-camp.html.

CBC. "Toronto's CanStage May Get Rachel Corrie Play." CBC.ca, 20 November 2006. Accessed 28 February 2011. http://www.cbc.ca/news/arts/theatre/story/2006/11/20/rachel-corrie.html.

CBC. "Two Canadians Held Hostage in Iraq: A Timeline." CBC.ca, 27 March 2006. Accessed 12 November 2006. http://www/cbc.ca/includes/printablestory.jsp (page discontinued).

Choudry, Aziz. "Global Justice? Contesting NGOization: Knowledge Politics and Containment in Antiglobalization Movements." In *Learning from the Ground Up: Global Perspectives on Social Movements and Knowledge Production*, edited by A. A. Choudry and Dip Kapoor, 17–34. New York: Palgrave Macmillan, 2010.

Choudry, Aziz. "Making a Killing: Military-Industrial Complex and Impacts on the Third World." *Toward Freedom*, 20 August 2008. Accessed 10 March 2011. http://www.towardfreedom.com/globalism/1386-making-a-killing-the-military-industrial-complex-and-impacts-on-the-third-world.

Chouliaraki, Lilie. *The Ironic Spectator: Solidarity in the Age of Post-Humanitarianism*. Cambridge: Polity Press, 2013.

Christian Peacekeeper Teams. 2007. Accessed 26 February 2007. http://www.cpt.org/archives/ws03.php.

– "About CPT." Accessed 15 March 2013. http://www.cpt.org/about_cpt.

– "About: Mission and Vision." Accessed 15 March 2013. http://www.cpt.org/about/mission.

– "CPT Statement, 23 March 2006: CPTers Missing in Baghdad Released."

2006. Accessed 23 March 2006. http://www.cpt.org/iraq/response/06-23-03statement.htm (page discontinued).
- "Dialogue." Signs of the Times 13, no. 1-2: (2003). Accessed 26 February 2007. http://www.cpt.org/archives/ws03.php.
- "Iraq: God is Great Despite the Bombs." 2007. Accessed 26 February 2007. http://www.cpt.org/archives/ws03.php
- "Our Work." Accessed 15 March 2013. http://www.cpt.org/work.
- "Why We Are Self-Publishing." In *118 Days: Christian Peacemaker Teams Held Hostage in Iraq*, edited by Tricia G. Brown, xiii. Toronto: Christian Peacemaker Teams, 2008.

Coleman, Daniel. *White Civility: The Literary Project of English Canada*. Toronto: University of Toronto Press, 2006.

Combahee River Collective. "A Black Feminist Statement." In *All the Women Are White, All the Blacks Are Men, But Some of Us Are Brave: Black Women's Studies*, edited by Gloria T. Hull, Patricia B. Scott, and Barbara Smith, 13–22. New York: The Feminist Press, 1982.

Cooper, Frederick. *Colonialism in Question: Theory, Knowledge, History*. Berkeley: University of California Press, 2005.

Corrie, Rachel, Alan Rickman, and Katharine Viner. *My Name Is Rachel Corrie: Taken from the Writings of Rachel Corrie*. 1st TCG ed. New York: Theatre Communications Group, 2006.

Corrie, Rachel. "Rachel's Reports." In *Live from Palestine: International and Palestinian Direct Action against the Israeli Occupation*, edited by Nancy Stohlman and Laurieann Aladin, 169–76. Cambridge, Massachusetts.: South End Press, 2003.
- "Rachel's War." *The Guardian*, 18 March 2003. Accessed 28 February 2011. http://www.guardian.co.uk/israel/Story/0,2763,916299,00.html.

Cranford, Cynthia. "'Aqui Estamos Y No Nos Vamos!': Justice for Janitors in Los Angeles and New Citizenship Claims." Paper presented at Migrantes Mexicanas en contextos transnacionales: Trabajo, familia y actividades politico-communitarias, Ajijic, Jalisco, Mexico, 22–24 March 2001.

Crang, Mike. "Picturing Practices: Research Through the Tourist Gaze." *Progress in Human Geography* 21, no. 3 (1997): 359–73.

Crenshaw, Kimberlé W. "Demarginalizing the intersection of race and class. A Black Feminist Critique of Antidiscrimination Doctrine, Feminist Theory, and Antiracist Politics." In *Critical Race Feminism: A Reader*, 2nd ed., edited by Adrien K. Wing, 23–33. New York: New York University Press, 2003.

CTV.ca News Staff. "Aid Group Blames U.S., U.K. For Iraq Abductions." *CTV News online*, 30 November 2005. Accessed 28 February 2011. http://www.ctv.ca/servlet/ArticleNews/story/CTVNews/20051129/aid_workers_051129/20051129?hub=TopStories.

CTV.ca. News Staff. "Former Hostage Offers Bail to Alleged Terrorist." *CTV News online*, 2 October 2006. Accessed 28 February 2011. http://toronto.ctv.ca/servlet/an/local/CTVNews/20061002/loney_bail_061002/20061002?hub=TorontoHome.

CTV.ca News Staff. "Loney Feels Terror Suspects Being Unfairly Judged." *CTV News online*, 7 June 2006. Accessed 28 February 2011. http://toronto.ctv.ca/servlet/an/local/CTVNews/20060607/loney_intvu_060607?hub=TorontoHome.

Davis, Angela Y. *Women, Race and Class*. New York: Vintage Books, 1983.

Davies, Bronwyn and Rom Harré. "Positioning: The Discursive Production of Selves." In *Discourse Theory and Practice: A Reader*, edited by Margaret Wetherell, Stephanie Taylor and Simeon J. Yates. Thousand Oaks: Sage Publications, 2001.

de Jong, Sara. "Constructive Complicity Enacted? The Reflections of Women NGO and IGO Workers on their Practices." *Journal of Intercultural Studies*. 30, no 4. (2009): 387–402.

Dearnaley, Mathew and Claire Trevett. "Auckland Man Held in Hostage." *New Zealand Herald*, 1 December 2005. Accessed 28 February 2011. http://www.nzherald.co.nz/section/print.cfm?c_id=1&objectid=10357895.

Deutsch, Yvonne. "Feminist Criticism, Occupation and Sexual Harassment." *AWID: Association for Women's Rights in Development*. Accessed March 6, 2011. http://www.awid.org/eng/Issues-and-Analysis/Issues-and-Analysis/Feminist-Criticism-Occupation-and-Sexual-Harassment.

Dierenfield, Bruce J. *The Civil Rights Movement*. Rev. ed. Harlow, England: Pearson, 2004.

Dornfeld, Barry. *Producing Public Television, Producing Public Culture*. Princeton, New Jersey: Princeton University Press, 1998.

Duggan, Lisa. "The New Homonormativity: The Sexual Politics of Neoliberalism." In *Materializing Democracy: Toward a Revitalized Cultural Politics*, edited by Russ Castronovo and Dana D. Nelson, 175–94. Durham, NC: Duke University Press, 2002.

Dyer, Richard. *White*. London and New York: Routledge, 1997.

Eagleton, Mary. "Ethical Reading: The Problem of Alice Walker's 'Advancing Luna – and Ida B. Wells' and J.M. Coetzee's Disgrace." *Feminist Theory* 2, no. 2 (2001): 189–203.

Ecumenical Accompaniment Program in Palestine and Israel. "About EAPPI: Overview." Accessed 19 June 2013. http://eappi.org/en/about/overview.html.

El-Haddad, Laila. "Israeli Activist Bridges Worlds." Aljazeera.net, 2 July 2005. Accessed 4 March 2011. http://english.aljazeera.net/archive/2005/07/2008491304576071.html.

Enders, David. *Baghdad Bulletin: Dispatches on the American Occupation.* Ann Arbor: University of Michigan Press, 2005.

Fanon, Frantz. "The Fact of Blackness." In *"Race," Culture and Difference*, edited by James Donald and Ali Rattansi, 220–40. London: The Open University, 1992.

– *The Wretched of the Earth* trans. C. Farrington. New York: Grove Weidenfeld, 1963.

Fassin, Didier. "La biopolitique n'est pas une politique de la vie" ("Biopolitics is not a politics of life"). *Sociologies et sociétés* 38, no. 2 (2006): 35–48.

– "Humanitarianism as a Politics of Life." *Public Culture* 19, no. 3 (2007): 499–520.

Fennell, David, and David Malloy. *Codes of Ethics in Tourism: Practice, Theory, Synthesis.* Toronto: Channel View Publications, 2007.

Flam, Helena, and Debra King. "Emotions and Social Movements," *Advances in Sociology.* London; New York: Routledge, 2005.

Flusty, Steven. "Portable Autonomous Zones: Tourism and the Travels of Dissent." In *Travels in Paradox: Remapping Tourism*, edited by Claudio Minca and Tim Oakes, 185–204. Lanham: Rowman and Littelfield, 2006.

Foucault, Michel. *The History of Sexuality, Volume 1: An Introduction.* Translated by Robert Hurley. New York: Vintage Books / Random House, 1980.

– "On the Genealogy of Ethics: An Overview of Work in Progress." In *The Foucault Reader*, edited by Paul Rabinow, 340–72. New York: Pantheon Books, 1984.

– "The Political Technology of Individuals." In *Michel Foucault: Power*, edited by James Faubion, 403–17. New York: The New Press, 1994.

– "Politics and Ethics: An Interview." In *The Foucault Reader*, edited by Paul Rabinow, 373–80. New York: Pantheon, 1984.

– "Society Must Be Defended:" *Lectures at the College De France, 1975–*

1976. Translated by David Macey. Edited by Arnold I. Davidson, Mauro Bertani, Alessandro Fontana and Francois Ewald. New York: Picador, 2003.
- "The Subject and Power." In *Michel Foucault: Beyond Structuralism and Hermeneutics*, edited by Hubert L. Dreyfus and Paul Rabinow, 208–26. Chicago: University of Chicago Press, 1982.

Foucault, Michel, and Colin Gordon. *Power/Knowledge: Selected Interviews and Other Writings, 1972–1977*, 1st American edition. New York: Pantheon Books, 1980.

Frankenberg, Ruth. "The Mirage of an Unmarked Whiteness." In *The Making and Unmaking of Whiteness*, edited by Birgit Brander Rasmussen, Eric Klinenberg, Irene J. Nexica and Matt Wray, 72–96. Durham and London: Duke University Press, 2001.
- *White Women, Race Matters: The Social Construction of Whiteness*. Minneapolis: University of Minnesota Press, 1993.

Freedman, Seth. "Palestine's Occupation Tourism: Palestinian Protesters Are Often Joined by International Tourists Who See Their Struggle as an Entertaining Spectacle." *Guardian.co.uk*, 20 January 2010. Accessed 12 March 2011. http://www.guardian.co.uk/commentisfree/2010/jan/20/palestine-israel-protest-tourism.

Freeman, Carla. "Is Local: Global as Feminine:Masculine? Rethinking the Gender of Globalization." *Signs* 26, no. 4 (2001): 1007–1037.

Gillis, Charlie. "Just Getting in the Way? Abductions in Iraq Have Given Christian Peacemakers a Higher Profile, but That's Not Helping Their Cause." Macleans.ca. Accessed 16 June 2006. http://www.macleans.ca/topstories/world/article.jsp?content=20051226_118754_118754

Gillmor, Dan. *We the Media: Grassroots Journalism by the People, for the People*. O'Reilley Media: Sebastopol, 2004.

Gilroy, Paul. "The End of Antiracism." In *"Race," Culture and Difference*, edited by James Donald and Ali Rattansi, 49–61. London: Sage Publications in association with the Open University, 1992.
- *Postcolonial Melancholia*. New York: Columbia University Press, 2005.

Goldberg, David Theo. "Killing Me Softly: Race, Civility, Violence." *Review of Education, Pedagogy, and Cultural Studies* 27, no. 4 (2005): 337–66.
- *The Racial State*. Oxford: Blackwell publishers, 2002.

- *Racist Culture: Philosophy and the Politics of Meaning.* Cambridge, Mass.: Blackwell, 1993.
Gregory, Derek. *The Colonial Present: Afghanistan, Palestine, Iraq.* Malden, MA: Blackwell publishing, 2004.
Grewal, Inderpal. "On the New Global Feminism and the Family of Nations: Dilemmas of Transnational Feminist Practice (Copy 1)." In *Talking Visions: Multicultural Feminism in a Transnational Age*, edited by Ella Shohat, 501–30. New York: New Museum of Contemporary Art / MIT Press, 1998.
Grewal, Inderpal, and Caren Kaplan. "Introduction: Transnational Feminists Practices and Questions of Postmodernity." In *Scattered Hegemonies: Postmodernity and Transnational Feminist Practices*, edited by Inderpal Grewal and Caren Kaplan, 1–33. Minnesota: University of Minnesota Press, 1994.
- "'Warrior Marks': Global Womanism's Neo-Colonial Discourse in a Multicultural Context." *Camera Obscura* 39 (1996): 4–33.
Gulliver, Tanya. "A Life-or-Death Closet: In Person, Christian Peacekeeper's Partner Back in the Picture." Xtra, 8 June 2006. Accessed 4 March 2011. http://www.xtra.ca/public/viewstory.aspx?AFF_TYPE =3&STORY_ID=1748&PUB_TEMPLATE_ID=2.
Gunter, Lorne. "The Tyrant's Best Friend." *National Post*, 27 March 2006. Accessed 4 March 2011. http://www.canada.com/nationalpost/news /editorialsletters/story.html?id=e0d757cb-a57a-4807-9b20- 2995486e2205.
Gur-Ze'ev, I. "Philosophy of Peace Education in a Postmodern Era." *Educational Theory* 51, no. 3 (2001): 315–36.
Hackett, Robert A. News and Dissent: The Press and the Politics of Peace in Canada. *Communication and Information Science.* Norwood, NJ: Ablex Pub. Corp., 1991.
Hackett, Robert A., and Richard Gruneau. *The Missing News: Filters and Blind Spots in Canada's Press.* Ottawa: Canadian Centre for Policy Alternatives; Toronto: Garamond, 2000.
Hage, Ghassan. *White Nation: Fantasies of White Supremacy in a Multicultural Society.* Sydney: Pluto Press, 1998.
- "'Comes a Time We Are All Enthusiasm': Understanding Palestinian Suicide Bombers in Times of Exighophobia." *Public Culture* 15, no. 1 (2003): 65–89.
Hall, Stuart. "New Ethnicities." In *"Race," Culture and Difference*, edited by

James Donald and Ali Rattansi, 252–59. London: Sage Publications in association with the Open University, 1992.
- "The West and the Rest: Discourse and Power." In *Modernity: An Introduction to Modern Societies*, edited by Stuart Hall et al., 185–227. Cambridge: Blackwell, 1996.

Hammad, Suheir. "On the Brink of War," *The Electronic Intifada*, accessed 10 March 2011. http://electronicintifida.net/v2/article1272.shtml.

Hammer, Joshua. "The Death of Rachel Corrie: Martyr, Idiot, Dedicated, Deluded. Why Did This American College Student Crushed by an Israeli Bulldozer Put Her Life on the Line?" *Mother Jones*, September/October 2003, 69–75 and 98–103.

Henriques, Julian, Wendy Hollway, Cathy Urwin, Couze Venn, and Valerie Walkerdine. "Introduction to Section 3: Theorizing Subjectivity." In *Changing the Subject: Psychology, Social Regulation and Subjectivity*, 203–26. London and New York: Routledge, 1998.

Herman, Edward S., and Robert W. McChesney. *The Global Media: The New Missionaries of Corporate Capitalism*. Delhi: Madyham Books, 1997.

Heron, Barbara. *Desire for Development: Whiteness, Gender, and the Helping Imperative*. Waterloo, ON: Wilfrid Laurier Press, 2007.
- "Gender and Exceptionality in North-South Interventions: Reflecting on Relations." *Journal of Gender Studies* 13, no. 2 (2004): 117–27.
- "Self-Reflection in Critical Social Work Practice: Subjectivity and the Possibilities of Resistance." *Reflective Practice* 6, no. 3 (2005): 341–51.

Hesford, Wendy S. "Reading Rape Stories: Material Rhetoric and the Trauma of Representation." *College English* 62, no. 2 (1999): 192–221.

Hesford, W.S., and W. Kozol, *Just Advocacy?: Women's human rights, transnational feminisms, and the politics of representation*. New Brunswick, NJ: Rutgers University Press, 2005.

Hesse, Barnor. "Im/Plausible deniability: Racism's conceptual double bind." *Social Identities*, 10, no. 1 (2004): 9–29.

Hochschild, Arlie Russell. *The Managed Heart: Commercialization of Human Feeling*. 20th anniversary ed. Berkeley: University of California Press, 2003.

Hogwarth, David. *Documentary Television in Canada: From National Public Service to Global Marketplace*. McGill-Queen's University Press, 2002.

Hollway, Wendy. "Gender Difference and the Production of Subjectivity." In *Changing the Subject: Psychology, Social Regulation and Subjectivity*, edited by Julian Henriques, Wendy Hollway, Cathy Urwin, Couze Venn and

Valerie Walkerdine, 227–63. New York and London: Routledge, 1998.

Hooker, Juliet. *Race and the Politics of Solidarity.* Oxford and New York: Oxford University Press, 2009.

hooks, bell. "Sisterhood: Political Solidarity Between Women." In *Dangerous Liaisons: Gender, Nation, and Postcolonial Perspectives,* edited by Ann McClintock, A. Mufti and Ella Shohat, 396–411. Minneapolis: University of Minnesota Press, 1997.

Hopgood, Stephen. *Keepers of the Flame: Understanding Amnesty International.* Ithaca and London: Cornell University Press, 2006.

Hunt, Dan. "Taken Twice." In *118 Days: Christian Peacemaker Teams Held Hostage in Iraq,* edited by Tricia G. Brown, 90–101. Toronto: Christian Peacemaker Teams, 2008.

Hurst, Lynda. "Activists' Action Poses Dilemma." *Toronto Star,* 25 March 2006. A23.

INCITE! Women of Color Against Violence. *The Revolution Will Not Be Funded: Beyond the Non-Profit Industrial Complex.* Cambridge, Mass.: South End Press, 2007.

International Solidarity Movement. "About ISM." Accessed March 2013. http://palsolidarity.org/about-ism/.

– "ISM Home." Accessed 15 March 2013. http://palsolidarity.org/.

– "Join the 2010 Olive Harvest Campaign." 29 August 2010. Accessed 11 March 2011. http://palsolidarity.org/2010/08/14103/.

– "Palestine: ISM update." Scoop, 15 April 2005. Accessed 4 March 2011. http://www.scoop.co.nz/stories/WO0504/S00243.html.

International Solidarity Movement Canada. "Principles." 2007. Accessed 28 March 2007. http://www.ismcanada.org/en/principles.shtml

International Women's Peace Service: Nonviolence in Action. "About IWPS." Accessed 15 March 2013. http://iwps.info/?page_id=62.

– "About IWPS: Nonviolence." Accessed 15 March 2013. http://iwps.info/?page_id=101.

International Women's Peace Service "Villages," accessed March 15, 2013, http://1wps.info/?page_id=910.

Iraq Peace Team. "Iraq Peace Team" 2007. Accessed 26 February 2007. From http://vitw.org/ipt/

Isin, Engin F. "Theorizing Acts of Citizenship." In *Acts of Citizenship,* edited by Engin F. Isin and Greg M. Nielsen, 15–43. London: Zed Books, 2008.

Bibliography 211

Jasper, James M. *The Art of Moral Protest: Culture, Biography, and Creativity in Social Movements*. Chicago, IL: University of Chicago Press, 1997.

Jean-Klein, Iris E. "Alternative Modernities, or Accountable Modernities? The Palestinian Movement(S) and Political (Audit) Tourism During the First Intifada." *Journal of Mediterranean Studies* 12, no. 1 (2002): 43–79.

Jefferess, David. "Global Citizenship and the Cultural Politics of Benevolence." *Critical Literacy: Theories and Practices* 2, no. 1 (2008): 27–36.

Jiwani, Yasmin. *Discourses of Denial: Mediations of Race, Gender and Violence*. Vancouver: UBC Press, 2006.

Johnson, Jimmy. "Film Review: Simone Bitton's investigative documentary, 'Rachel.'" *The Electronic Intifada*, 16 April 2010. Accessed 10 March 2011. http://electronicintifada.net/v2/article11214.shtml.

Kaplan, Caren. "'Beyond the Pale': Rearticulating U.S. Jewish Whiteness." In *Talking Visions: Multicultural Feminisms in a Transnational Age*, edited by Ella. Shohat, 451–84. New York: New Museum of Contemporary Art / MIT Press, 1998.

– *Questions of Travel: Postmodern Discourses of Displacement*. Durham, NC: Duke University Press, 1996.

– "The Politics of Location as Transnational Feminist Practice." In *Scattered Hegemonies: Postmodernity and Transnational Feminist Practices*, edited by Inderpal Grewal and Caren Kaplan, 137–52. Minnesota: University of Minnesota Press, 1994.

Kirby, Kathleen, M. "Re: Mapping Subjectivity: Cartographic Vision and the Limits of Politics." In *Body Space: Destabilizing Geographies of Gender and Sexuality*, edited by Nancy Duncan, 45–55. London and New York: Routledge, 1996.

Klein, Naomi. "On Rescuing Private Lynch and Forgetting Rachel Corrie: The Israeli Army Got Away with Murder – and Now All Activists Are at Risk." *The Guardian*, 22 May 2003. Accessed 4 March 2011. http://www.guardian.co.uk/israel/comment/0,10551,961025,00.html.

– "Moving through the Symbols." In *Globalize Liberation: How to Uproot the System and Build a Better World*, edited by David Solnit, 249–62. San Francisco: City Lights Books, 2004.

Kotef, Hagar, and Merav Amir. "(En)Gendering Checkpoints: Checkpoint Watch and the Repercussions of Intervention." *Signs: Journal of Women in Culture* 32, no. 4 (2007): 973–96.

Kozol, Wendy. "Domesticating NATO's War in Kosovo/A: (In)Visible Bodies and the Dilemma of Photojournalism (Copy 2)." *Meridians: Feminism, Race, Transnationalism* 4, no. 2 (2004): 1–38.

Krause, Hans-Ulrich. "About Protective Accompaniment." *Peace Brigades International*, accessed 5 August 2013. http://www.peacebrigades.org/sobre-pbi/about-protective-accompaniment/?L=1%3FL%3Do.

Kristal-Schroder, Carrie. "Free Hostages, Canadian Detainees Urge." *The Ottawa Citizen*, 4 December, 2005. Accessed 4 March 2011. http://www.canada.com/ottawacitizen/story.html?id=df44046d-afee-4ebd-b19e-131d807768ba&rfp=dta.

Kumar, Deepa. "War Propaganda and the (Ab)Uses of Women: Media Constructions of the Jessica Lynch Story." *Feminist Media Studies* 4, no. 3 (2004): 297–313.

Kymlicka, Will. "Being Canadian." *Government and opposition* 38, no. 3 (2003): 357–85.

Laware, Margaret L. "Circling the Missiles and Staining Them Red: Feminist Rhetorical Invention and Strategies of Resistance at the Women's Peace Camp at Greenham Common (Copy 2)." *NWSA Journal* 16, no. 3 (2004): 18–41.

Littler, Jo. "I Feel Your Pain: Cosmopolitan Charity and the Public Fashioning of the Celebrity Soul." *Social Semiotics* 18, no. 2 (2008): 237–51.

Loney, James. Interview. *The Current*, 6 June 2006. Canada: CBC Radio.

Lutz, Catherine, and Jane Collins. "The Photograph as an Intersection of Gazes: The Example of National Geographic." In *Visualizing Theory: Selected Essays from V.A.R. 1990-1994*, edited by Lucien Taylor, 363–84. New York and London: Routledge, 1994.

Mahoney, Liam, and Luis Enrique Eguren. *Unarmed Bodyguards: International Accompaniment for the Protection of Human Rights*. Hartford: Kumarian Press, 1997.

Mahrouse, Gada. "Celebrity Philanthropy and the Celebration of Care." *Celebrity Studies* 3, no. 1 (2012): 109–11.

– "Feel Good Tourism: The Ethical Option for Socially-Conscious Westerners." *ACME: An International E-Journal of Critical Geographies* 10, no. 3 (2011): 372–91.

– "Producing Peaceful Citizens through a Lesson on the FTAA Quebec Summit Protests." *Canadian Journal of Education* 29, no. 2 (2006): 436–53.

Maloney, Sean M. "Are We Really Just Peacekeepers? The Perception Versus the Reality of Canadian Military Involvement in the Iraq War."

Working paper series no. 2003-02, Institute for Research on Public Policy, Montreal, QC, 2003.

Marchildon, Gilles. "When Silence is Golden." *InQueeries*, 6 April 2006. Accessed 4 March 2011. http://www.egale.ca/index.asp?lang=E &menu=12&item=1314.

McLaren, Deborah. *Rethinking Tourism and Ecotravel*. Bloomfield, CT: Kumarian Press, 2003.

McNay, Lois. *Foucault and Feminism: Power, Gender and the Self*. Boston, MA: Northeastern University Press, 1993.

Mehta, Anna, and Liz Bondi. "Embodied Discourse: On Gender and Fear of Violence." *Gender, Place and Culture* 6, no. 1 (1999): 67–84.

Mignolo, Walter. "Who Speaks for the 'Human' In Human Rights." *Hispanic Issues On Line* (Fall): 7–24.

Miles, Robert. *Racism. Key Ideas*. London and New York: Routledge, 1989.

Mills, Charles. "Racial Liberalism." *PMLA* 123, no. 5 (2008): 1380–97.

Mohanram, Radhika. *Black Body: Women, Colonialism, and Space*. Minneapolis: University of Minnesota Press, 1999.

Mohanty, Chandra Talpade. *Feminism without Borders: Decolonizing Theory, Practicing Solidarity*. Durham: Duke University Press, 2003.

Mor, Rotem. "Jerusalem Reality Tours." http://www.jerusalemrealitytours.com/.

Morrison, Toni. *Playing in the Dark: Whiteness and the Literary Imagination*. 1st Vintage Books ed. New York: Vintage Books, 1993.

Mother Jones. "About Mother Jones." Accessed 6 May 2007. http://www.motherjones.com/about/index.html

Moynagh, Maureen Anne. *Political Tourism and Its Texts. Cultural Spaces*. Toronto: University of Toronto Press, 2008.

Mufti, Aamir, and Ella Shohat. Introduction to *Dangerous Liaisons: Gender, Nation and Postcolonial Perspectives*, edited by Anne McClintock, Aamir Mufti, and Ella Shohat, 1–12. Minneapolis: University of Minnesota Press, 1997.

Naber, Nadine. "Introduction: Arab Americans and U.S. Racial Formations." In *Race and Arab Americans Before and After 9/11: From Invisible Citizens to Visible Subjects*, edited by Jamal Amaney and Nadine Naber. Syracuse, NY: Syracuse University Press, 2008.

Nafziger, Tim and Simon Barrow. "Writing Peace Out of the Script." In *118 Days: Christian Peacemaker Teams Held Hostage in Iraq*, edited by Tricia G. Brown, 135–52. Toronto: Christian Peacemaker Teams, 2008.

Nakayama, Thomas and Robert Krizek. "Whiteness as a Strategic Rhetoric," in *Whiteness: The Communication of Social Identity*, edited by Thomas K. Nakayama and Judith N. Martin, 87–106. Thousand Oaks: Sage Publications, 1999.

Nepstad, Sharon Erickson. "Creating Transnational Solidarity: The Use of Narrative in the U.S.-Central America Peace Movement." In *Globalization and Resistance: Transnational Dimensions of Social Movements*, edited by Jackie Smith and Hank Johnston. New York & Oxford: Rowman & Littlefield Publishers, 2002.

Novak, Shirley. "Accompaniment or Charity?" *Doctor's for Global Health*, http://www.dghonline.org/nl12/charity_accompany.html.

Nyers, Peter. "In Solitary, In Solidarity: Detainees, Hostages, and Contesting the Anti-Policy of Detention." *European Journal of Cultural Studies* 11, no. 3 (2008): 333–49.

Olson, James Stuart. *Historical Dictionary of the 1960s*. Westport, CT; London: Greenwood Press, 1999.

OSN. "Oaxaca Solidarity Network – February '07 Humanitarian Delegation." The CASA Collective website, January 2007. Accessed March 11, 2011. http://www.casacollective.org/story/reposts/oaxaca-solidarity-network-february-07-humanitarian-delegation.

Osuri, Goldie, and Subhabrata Bobby Banerjee. "White Diasporas: September 11 and the Unbearable Whiteness of Being in Australia." *Social Semiotics* 14, no. 2 (2004): 151–71.

PASC. "Our Mission." Project Accompaniment Solidarity Colombia website. Accessed 13 March 2011. http://www.pasc.ca/spip.php?article59.

Peace Brigades International. "About PBI: Vision and Mission." Accessed 15 March 2013. http://www.peacebrigades.org/about-pbi/vision-and-mission/.

- "About Protective Accompaniment." Accessed 11 March 2013. http://www.peacebrigades.org/sobre-pbi/about-protective-accompaniment/?L=1%3FL%3Do.
- "How We Work." November 2001. Accessed 11 March 2013. http://www.peacebrigades.org/about-pbi/how-we-work/.
- "Title." 2007. Accessed March 10, 2011. http://www.peacebrigades.org/
- "What We Do." Accessed March 15, 2013. http://www.peacebrigades.org/country-groups/pbi-uk/what-we-do/international-protective-accompaniment/.

Pedelty, Mark. *War Stories: The Culture of Foreign Correspondents*. New York and London: Routledge, 1995.

Perkins, D. "Paradoxes of Peace and the Prospects of Peace Education." In G. Salomon and B. Nevo, eds, *Peace Education: The Concept, Principles, and Practices around the World*, pp. 37–53. Mahwah, NJ: Lawrence Erlbaum Associates, 2002.

Pinar, William. *The Gender of Racial Politics and Violence in America: Lynching, Prison Rape, & the Crisis of Masculinity*. New York: Peter Lang, 2001.

Pollock, Mica. "Using and Disrupting: US Youth and Palestinians Wielding 'International Privilege' To End the Israeli-Palestinian Conflict Nonviolently." Working Paper, *Centre for public leadership, Harvard University*, 2005. Pratt, Geraldine, and Philippines-Canada Task Force on Human Rights. "International Accompaniment and Witnessing State Violence in the Philippines." *Antipode* 40, no. 5 (2008): 761–79.

Pratt, Geraldine and Phillipines-Canada Task Force on Human Rights. "International Accompaniment and Witnessing State Violence in the Phillipines." *Antipode* 40, no. 5 (2008): 751–9.

Pratt, Mary Louise. "Fieldwork in Common Places." In *Writing Culture: The Poetics and Politics of Ethnography*, edited by James Clifford and G.E. Marcus. Cambridge: University of Cambridge Press, 1986.

– *Imperial Eyes: Travel Writing and Transculturation*. London and New York: Routledge, 1992.

Pratt, Minnie Bruce. "Identity: Skin, Blood, Heart." In *Yours in Struggle: Three Feminist Perspectives on Anti-Semitism and Racism*, edited by Elly Bulkin, Minnie Bruce Pratt, and Barbara Smith, 11–63. New York: Long Haul Press, 1984.

Pritchard, Doug, and Carol Rose. "Unless a Grain of Wheat Falls: A View from the CPT Crisis Team." In *118 Days: Christian Peacemaker Teams Held Hostage in Iraq*, edited by Tricia G. Brown, 1–14. Toronto: Christian Peacemaker Teams, 2008.

Puar, Jasbir K. "Mapping U.S. Homonormativities." *Gender, Place and Culture* 13, no. 1 (2006): 67–88.

Razack, Sherene. *Casting Out: The Eviction of Muslims from Western Law and Politics*. Toronto: University of Toronto Press, 2008.

– "Stealing the Pain of Others: Reflections on Canadian Humanitarian Responses." *The Review of Education, Pedagogy, and Cultural Studies* 29, no. 4 (2007): 375–94.

– *Dark Threats and White Knights: The Somalia Affair, Peacekeeping, and the New Imperialism*. Toronto: University of Toronto Press, 2004.

– "A Violent Culture or Culturalized Violence? Feminist Narratives of

Sexual Violence Against South Asian Women." *Studies in Practical Philosophy* 3, no. 1 (2003): 80–103.
- *Looking White People in the Eye: Gender, Race, and Culture in Courtrooms and Classrooms*. Toronto: University of Toronto Press, 1998.

Reagon, Bernice J. "Coalition Politics: Turning the Century." In *Home Girls: A Black Feminist Anthology*, edited by Barbara Smith. New York: Kitchen Table, Women of Color Press, 1983.

Riches, William T. Martin. *The Civil Rights Movement: Struggle and Resistance*. 2nd ed. New York: Palgrave Macmillan, 2004.

Roman, Leslie. "Conditions, Contexts, and Controversies of Truth-Making: Rigoberta Menchú and the Perils of Everyday Witnessing and Testimonial Work." *Qualitative Studies in Education* 16, no. 3 (2003): 275–86.
- "Denying (White) Racial Privilege: Redemption Discourses and the Uses of Fantasy." In *Off White: Readings on Race, Power, and Society*, edited by Michelle Fine, Lois Weis, Linda C. Powell and L. Mun Wong, 270–82. New York and London: Routledge, 1997.

Ross, Thomas. "Whiteness after 9/11." *Journal of Law and Policy* 18 (2005): 223–43.

Said, Edward. "The Meaning of Rachel Corrie." In *Peace under Fire: Israel/Palestine and the International Solidarity Movement*, edited by Josie Sandercock, Radhika Sainath, Marissa McLaughlin, Hussein Khalili, Nicholas Blincoe, Huwaida Arraf, and Ghassan Andoni, ix–xxii. London & New York: Verso, 2004.
- *Covering Islam: How the Media and the Experts Determine How We See the Rest of the World*. Rev. ed. New York: Vintage Books, 1997.
- *Peace and Its Discontents: Essays on Palestine in the Middle East Peace Process*. New York: Vintage Books, 1996.
- *The Question of Palestine*. Vintage Trade Paperback, 1992.
- *Orientalism*. London: Routledge, 1978.

Said, Edward and Christopher Hitchens. *Blaming the Victims: Spurious Scholarship and the Palestinian Question*. London and New York: Verso, 1988.

Sandercock, Josie, Radhika Sainath, Marissa McLaughlin, Hussein Khalili, Nicholas Blincoe, Huwaida Arraf, and Ghassan Andoni, eds. *Peace under Fire: Israel/Palestine and the International Solidarity Movement*. London and New York: Verso, 2004.

Sasson-Levy, Orna, and Tamar Rapoport. "Body, Gender and Knowledge in Protest Movements: The Israeli Case." *Gender & Society* 17, no. 3 (2003): 379–403.
Schueller, Malini Johar. *Locating Race: Global Sites of Post-Colonial Citizenship*. Albany: SUNY Press, 2009.
Scrivener, Leslie. "Getting into Harm's Way: Critics Say Group Should Stay out of War Zone, but CPT Insists It Belongs in Baghdad." *The Toronto Star online*, 26 March 2006. Accessed 4 November 2006. http://www.thestar.com/NASApp/cs/ContentServer?pagename=thestar/LayoutArticle_PrintFriendlyandc=Articleandcid=1143327032642 andcall_pageid=970599119419 (page discontinued).
Seitz, Charmaine. "ISM at the Crossroads: The Evolution of the International Solidarity Network." *Journal of Palestine Studies* 32, no. 4 (2003): 50–67.
Shalhoub-Kevorkian, Nadera, and Sana Khsheiboun. "Palestinian Women's Voices Challenging Human Rights Activism." *Women's Studies International Forum* 32 (2009): 354–62.
Sharoni, Simona. "Compassionate Resistance: A Personal/Political Journey to Israel/Palestine." *International Feminist Journal of Politics* 8, no. 2 (2006): 288–99.
Sharp, Gene. "The Techniques on Nonviolent Action." In *A Peace Reader: Essential Readings on War, Justice, Non-Violence and World Order*, edited by Joseph J. Fahey and Richard Armstrong, 223-29. New York: Paulist Press, 1992.
Shephard, Michelle. "Horror, Prayers Follow Ultimatum." *Toronto Star*, 3 December 2005, A1.
- "Muslim Groups Call for Release of Canadians." *Toronto Star*, 6 December 2005, A10.
- "You're a Target, Father Told Loney." *Toronto Star*, 1 December 2005, A12.
Shohat, Ella. "Area Studies, Gender Studies, and the Cartographies of Knowledge." *Social Text* 20, no. 3 (2002): 67–78.
- Introduction. In *Talking Visions: Multicultural Feminism in Transnational Age*, edited by E. Shohat. New York, NY, Cambridge MA: New Museum of Contemporary Art, MIT Press, 1998.
Sichel, Benjamin. "'I've Come to Help': Can Tourism and Altruism Mix?" *Briarpatch Magazine* Accessed 6 August 2013. http://briarpatchmagazine.com/articles/view/ive-come-tohelp-can-tourism-and-altruism-mix/.

Slotkin, Richard. *Regeneration Through Violence: The Mythology of the American Frontier, 1600-1860.* 1st Harper Perennial ed. New York, NY: Harper Perennial, 1996.
Smith, Andrea. "Native American Feminism, Sovereignty, and Social Change." *Feminist Studies* 31, no. 1 (2005): 116–32.
Smith, Valerie. "Split Affinities: The Case of Interracial Rape." In *Conflicts in Feminism*, edited by Marianne Hirsch and Evelyn Fox Keller, 271–287. New York and London: Routledge, 1990.
Sontag, Susan. "The Power of Principle." *The Guardian*, 26 April 2003. Accessed 8 May 2007. http://www.jfjfp.org/BackgroundW/sontag_yeshgvul.htm (page discontinued).
– *Regarding the Pain of Others.* New York: Farrar, Strauss and Giroux, 2003.
South End Press Collective. "Katrina, Race, and the State of the Nation." February 2007, Accessed 5 August 2013. eds. *South End Press Collective.* http://www.southendpress.org/2006/items/87670
Spelman, Elizabeth V. *Fruits of Sorrow: Framing Our Attention to Suffering.* Boston: Beacon Press, 1997.
Spivak, Gayatri. "Can the Subaltern Speak?" In *Marxism and the Interpretation of Culture*, edited by Cary Nelson and Lawrence Grossberg, 271–313. University of Illinois Press, 1988.
Stasiulis, Daiva K. and Nira Yuval-Davis. *Unsettling Settler Societies: Articulations of Gender, Race, Ethnicity and Class.* London: Sage, 1995.
Stillman, Sarah. "'The Missing White Girl Syndrome': Disappeared Women and Media Activism." *Gender & Development* 15, no. 3 (2007): 491–502.
Stohlman, Nancy and Laurieann Aladin, eds. *Live from Palestine: International and Palestinian Direct Action against the Israeli Occupation.* Cambridge, Mass.: South End Press, 2003.
Stoper, Emily. *The Student Nonviolent Coordinating Committee: The Growth of Radicalism in a Civil Rights Organization.* New York: Carlson Publishing, 1989.
Sturma, Michael. "Aliens and Indians: A Comparison of Abduction and Captivity Narratives." *Journal of Popular Culture* 36, no. 2 (2002): 318–34.
Synott, J. "Peace Education as an Educational Paradigm: Review of a Changing Field Using an Old Measure." *Journal of Peace Education* 2, no. 1 (2004): 3–16.

Taylor, John. "Problems in Photojournalism: Realism, the Nature of News and the Humanitarian Narrative." *Journalism Studies* 1, no. 1 (2000): 129–43.

Thobani, Sunera. *Exalted Subjects: Studies in the Making of Race and Nation in Canada*. Toronto: University of Toronto Press, 2007.

Thomas, Deborah A. and Kamari Maxine Clarke. "Introduction: Globalization and the Transformations of Race." In *Globalization and Race: Transformations in the Cultural Production of Blackness*, edited by Kamari Maxine Clarke and Deborah A. Thomas. Durham, NC: Duke University Press, 2006.Thompson, Audrey. "Tiffany, Friend of People of Color: White Investments in Antiracism." *Qualitative Studies in Education* 16, no. 1 (2003): 7–29.

Thompson, Becky. *A Promise and a Way of Life*. Minneapolis: University of Minnesota Press, 2001.

– "El Testigo Verdadero Libra Las Almas: The Central American Peace Movement and Anti-Racism." In *Disrupting White Supremacy from Within: White People on What We Need to Do*, edited by Jennifer Harvey, Karin Case, A. and Robin Hawley Gorsline, 163–87. Cleveland: The Pilgrim Press, 2004.

Tilley, Elspeth and John Cokely. "Deconstructing the Discourse of Citizen Journalism: Who Says What and Why It Matters." *Pacific Journalism Review* 14, no. 1(2008): 94–114.

Tobias, Saul. "Foucault on Freedom and Capabilities." *Theory, Culture & Society* 22, no. 4 (2005): 65–85.

Vrasti, Wanda. *Volunteer Tourism in the Global South: Giving Back in Neoliberal Times*. London: Routledge, 2012.

Waked, Ali. "Ramallah Presents: Rachel Corrie Restaurant," *YNEt News .com*, accessed 3 January 2014. http://www.ynetnews.com/articles /0,7340,L-3973994,00.html.

Wall, Melissa. "Blogging Gulf War II." *Journalism Studies* 7, no. 1 (2006): 111–26.

Wan, James. "Can Feel-Good Activism Save the World?" Think Africa Press, March 2013. Accessed 6 August 2013. http://thinkafricapress.com /culture/interview-liliechouliaràki-can-feel-good-activism-save-world.

Ware, Vron and Les Back, eds. *Out of Whiteness: Color, Politics, and Culture*. Chicago: University of Chicago Press, 2002.

Warshaw, Robin. *I Never Called It Rape: The Ms. Report on Recognizing,*

Fighting and Surviving Date and Acquaintance Rape. New York: Harper and Row, 1988.

Weber, Clare. *Visions of Solidarity: Us Peace Activists in Nicaragua from War to Women's Activism and Globalization*. New York and Toronto: Lexington Books, 2006.

Weber, Terry. "Peace Group Says No to Violence in Hostage Talks." *GlobeandMail.com*. Accessed 5 December 2005. http://www.theglobeandmail.com/servlet/story/RTGAM.20051129.whostag1129/BNStory/National/.

Weedon, Chris. "Principles of Poststructuralism." In *Feminist Practice and Poststructuralist Theory*, 12–41. Oxford and Cambridge, MA: Blackwell, 1997.

– *Feminism, Theory, and the Politics of Difference*. Malden, MA: Blackwell Publishers, 1999.

Wiegman, Robyn. "Whiteness Studies and the Paradox of Particularity." *Boundary 2* 26, no. 3 (1999): 115–150.

Woodward, Kathleen. "Calculating Compassion." In *Compassion: The Culture and Politics of an Emotion*, edited by Lauren Berlant, 59–86. London and New York: Routledge, 2004.

Yang, Goubin. "Emotions and Movements." In *The Blackwell Encyclopedia of Sociology*, edited by George Ritzer, 1389–92. Oxford: Blackwell Publishing, 2007.

Yuval-Davis, Nira. "Intersectionality, Citizenship and Contemporary Politics of Belonging." *Critical Review of International Social and Political Philosophy* 10, no. 4 (2007): 561–74.

Zinn, Howard, ed. *The Power of Nonviolence: Writings by Advocates of Peace*. Boston: Beacon Press, 2002.

Zulaika, Joseba. "The Anthropologist as Terrorist." In *Violence in War and Peace: An Anthology*, edited by Nancy Scheper-Hughes and Phillipe Bourgois. Malden and Oxford: Blackwell Publishing, 2004.

Index

Aboriginal, 10, 69, 70
Abu Ghraib, 69, 179
accountability: community, 136;
  for Corrie's death, 34–6, 43;
  global, 29; governmental, 7;
  legal, 32; political, 26
acts of citizenship, 58, 61, 62
advocacy, 12–13, 38, 57, 93, 116,
  159
Afghanistan, 52, 55
Ahmed, Sara, 17, 42, 71–2, 77, 147,
  153
Alcoff, Linda Martin, 6, 96
allegiances, 7, 43
allies and allied, 7, 120, 129, 133,
  153
Alternative Tourism Group, 115
altruism and altruistic, 110, 159
ambivalent and ambivalence, 41,
  43, 55, 94–5, 101, 104–5, 109,
  116, 188
ambulance, 6, 22, 82, 100
anti-globalization, 149
anti-imperialist, 149
anti-racism, and anti-racist, 93, 109,
116, 145; commitments to, 120;
  movements, 146
anti-war, 12, 40, 54, 67–9, 74–5, 173
apartheid, 9, 10, 173
Arab, 7, 18, 35, 37, 70, 86, 175, 182
Arat-Koç, Sedef, 14, 18
Arendt, Hannah, 80, 89–90, 147
arrogance, 8, 158
asymmetrical, 16–17, 23, 33, 73,
  112
authority, 8, 50, 70, 78–9, 146; displays of, 72; positions of, 109

Baghdad, 7, 45–9, 69
Bauman, Zygmunt, 91, 147
belonging, 50, 55, 57, 135
Berlant, Lauren, 25, 43, 90
binary and binaries, 19–20, 44, 53,
  73, 119
biopolitics, 15, 49, 180
biopower, 15
Bitton, Simone, 41–2
black, 127–31, 143, 148, 150;
  activists, 27–8, 31; blackness,
  120, 130, 132

Black Panther, 28
Black Power, 28, 145, 173
British, 29, 32, 45–6, 52, 61; British Broadcasting Corporation (BBC), 51
bulldozer, 25, 31, 35, 38–40, 42, 176–7, 208
Burman, Tony, 51–2
Butler, Judith, 30, 31, 86
Bystanders, 91, 147

camera(s), 65–6, 79, 81–2, 84, 156
campaign and campaigning, 21, 38, 47, 60, 161; Freedom Summer, 27–8, 31, 126–9; Olive Harvest, 3
Canadian, 17, 51–61, 88–9, 108–9; 150, 152; identity, 48; lives, 12; media, 21, 63–7, 76; officials, 158; passport, 6, 94, 158
Canadian Broadcasting Corporation (CBC), 51–2, 55, 67–8, 75–6; *The Current*, 52, 60
Capital Xtra, 56, 57
capitalism, 149, 152, 159
captivity, 46, 54–6, 60, 138, 151
Catholic, 13, 58
celebrity, 39, 161
Central America, 6, 65, 81, 83, 166, 188, 213, 218
Central American Peace Movement, 6
Chaney, James, 27–8
charity, 102, 161
checkpoint(s), 6, 29–30, 121, 137, 174–5
Chiapas, 10, 155, 159, 163
Christian and Christianity, 10, 19, 45, 48, 53–5, 107, 143, 167, 180–1
Christian Peacemaker Team, 7, 10, 13, 21, 45–47, 49–53, 54–62, 69, 93, 95–6, 102, 107, 138–40, 168, 179, 180–1, 183
citizen and citizenship, 4–7, 14, 18–19, 21–2, 32–4, 47–9, 52, 57, 59–62, 72, 74, 159–60; journalist and journalism, 63–4, 67, 70–7, 184
civil: rights, 27–8, 120, 127–8, 131, 136, 145, 147, 150, 173, 190; disobedience, 6, 96; society, 11, 37, 60, 112, 184, 190
class and classism, 11, 13–14, 17–18, 47, 122, 157; middle class, 3, 17, 32, 159
Cold War, 14, 52
collaboration, 95, 105
Colombia, 10–1; Project Accompaniment and Solidarity Colombia, 3, 152–3
colonial and colonialism, 16–17, 19, 24, 34, 55–6, 69, 105, 123, 133, 143, 152, 154, 166, 171, 188, 193. *See also* neo-colonial
colour, 5–6, 14, 18, 123; people of, 48, 57, 130–1, 134–6, 150, 152–3, 162, 167, 183, 196
compassion, 31, 34, 36, 70, 88–91, 130; appeals for, 22; and coldness, 25, 43; politics of, 86
conflict zone, 3, 10–11, 31, 49, 63, 71, 112, 145, 155, 158, 160
conquest, 16, 162
controversial, 7–8, 21, 47, 75, 156
Cooper, Frederick, 137, 152

corporeal, 20, 123, 143. *See also* embodiment
Corrie, Rachel, 3, 7–8, 20–1, 25–6, 30–44, 50–1, 139–40, 175–8; Craig, 37, 41; Cindy, 41
Coy, Alice, 41–2
cross-racial, 28, 120, 129, 130–1, 148; solidarity, 150

Davies, Bronwyn, 72–3
death, Rachel Corrie's, 7, 20–1, 25–6, 31–9, 41–4, 51, 86
decolonial and decolonizing, 5, 23, 137, 142, 146, 151–4
dependency, 100, 102–3
depoliticization, 24, 155, 158
development, 17, 101, 107, 145, 160–1
dialectic, 15, 169, 180
diary, 68, 183
diaspora, 18, 162
Dierenfield, Bruce, 120
dilemma, 22, 63, 69, 80, 82–3, 85, 92, 118, 153, 193
direct action, 9, 29, 39, 93, 117, 140, 155, 174, 188
disenfranchised, 31, 153
dissent, 33, 35, 39, 120, 174, 181
Doctors for Global Health, 140
dogmatic, 14, 34
Dyer, Richard, 19, 26, 48, 72

Eagleton, Mary, 130–1
East Jerusalem, 117, 156, 173
economy, economic, and economies, 9, 12, 14–15, 115, 156, 159, 163
Ecumenical Accompaniment Program in the Palestine and Israel, 12–13, 93, 107, 168
El Salvador, 6, 11
embody and embodiment, 4, 15–17, 20, 47, 71, 85, 118–19, 130, 134, 137, 139, 142–4, 157; embodying whiteness, 10, 22–3; gendered, 119, 127, 135; of international rights, 11. *See also* corporeal
emergency, 3, 11, 13
encounter, 5, 8, 14, 16–17, 19, 23, 55, 63, 153–4
entitlement, 8, 81, 162
ethic(s) and ethical, 5, 73, 80–1, 102, 131–2, 146, 157, 160; actors, 106; 109; dilemmas, 22, 85, 91–2; 147; struggle, 95, 104, 116; travel, 159–61
euphemism, 144
Europe, 10, 29, 40
exclusionary, 14, 71, 145

faith, Christian, 45; faith-based, 10, 19, 93, 96, 107, 167
family, 40–1, 48, 64, 84, 87–8, 113–14, 125; concern, 119; members, 32, 56, 60–1, 70, 103, 165
Fanon, Frantz, 16, 143, 151
Fassin, Didier, 15, 48, 49, 50, 72
fear, 30, 56, 98–9, 104, 128, 130, 134, 148, 178
femininities, 34
feminist, 13, 16, 76–7, 117–19, 130, 133–4; activists, 31; movements, 148, 152–3, 191; postcolonial theory, 22, 143–4
financial, 96, 98, 101–2

Flusty, Stephen, 155, 163
foreign and foreigner, 5–6, 8, 14, 121, 123–6, 139; activists, 96, 110, 113; 139; Canadian policy, 51, 109; foreign-assisted, 29; lands, 158; US policy, 34; war correspondents, 75
Foucault, Michel, 15–16, 49, 80
Fox, Tom, 45–6, 56
Frankenberg, Ruth, 93, 106, 116
Free the Children, 161
freedom, 9, 14, 21, 56, 59–60, 68, 75, 143, 151; discourses, 51; freedom fighter, 35, 66
Freedom Summer, 27–8, 31–2, 126, 128–9
fund and funding, 13, 51, 101–2, 161

gay, 21, 47, 55–8, 182
Gaza, 6, 30, 33, 35–7, 166, 177
gaze, 22, 80–1, 92; patronizing, 111; voyeuristic, 83–4, 86, 88
gender and gendered, 11, 13, 17, 20, 23–4, 26, 31–2, 34–5, 47, 87, 117–22, 126–7, 129–30, 132–6, 152; norms, 39; privileges, 140, 157
Geneva Convention, 30, 33
geographies, 6, 17
geopolitical: activity, 9–10, 18, 63; contexts, 5, 7, 26, 32, 46, 49, 76, 124; locations, 16; political processes, 14
Gilroy, Paul, 33–4
global, 9–12, 14–15, 17, 29–30, 32–3, 92, 96, 110–11, 119, 152, 158–60; capitalism, 152; citizenship, 72, 160; conditions, 147, 149; conflicts, 70; hegemony, 26, 80, 145–6; racial hierarchy, 6, 46; situation, 86; suffering, 89
global North/South, 146, 159–60
globalization: conditions, 160; militarism and war, 39; movements, 61; neoliberal, 14. *See also* antiglobalization
Goldberg, David Theo, 47, 142–3, 145, 147
grassroots, 6, 11, 74, 159
Gregory, Derek, 32–3
grief, 26, 30–2, 36, 38, 50, 86–8
Guatemala, 5–6, 9, 11, 94, 101, 109; accompaniment work in, 99; solidarity activism in, 121
Guatemala Network Coordinating Committee, 13

Hamas, 47, 59
Hammad, Suheir, 25–6, 38
Hebron, 82. *See also* accompaniment; West Bank
hegemony and hegemonic, 21–2, 26, 74–5, 80, 88, 91–2, 103, 120, 142–3, 145–6, 148; reproduced, 52–3
hero, heroism, 20, 34, 36–9, 41, 43–4, 89, 92
Heron, Barbara, 17, 105, 110, 121
hetero-: normative, 87–8; patriarchy, 32; sexism, 122; sexuality, 58
Hezbollah, 47, 59
hierarchy, hierarchies, 6, 46, 59, 91; of gender/race, 121–2; of grief, 30–1, 36, 38, 50, 86
hijab, 35

history, histories, and historicize, 14, 16–18, 19, 51, 113, 115, 130–1, 133, 143, 152–4, 162; personal, 86; subaltern, 137
homo, homosexuality, homophobic, 56–8
human rights, 3, 7, 8–12, 30, 81, 110–12; observer, 140; solidarity groups, 69
human shield, 4, 40, 138–41, 144
humanitarian, 3, 48–50, 52, 59–62, 72, 89, 101; cargo ship, 37
Hunt, Dan, 55–8
Hurndall, Tom, 32, 34

identity, 17–19, 32, 48, 150; activist, 74; Canadian, 48, 51–2, 109; constructed, 26; Israeli, 29; national, 47, 76, 94, 108; Palestinian, 37; political, 92; religious, 14; sexual, 57
ideology, and ideological, 24, 28, 36, 107, 114, 142, 145, 149
imagined communities, 17, 76
immunity, 5, 7
imperialism and imperialist, 16, 24–5, 51, 53–4, 77, 116, 149, 152; history of, 152; US, 38. *See also* anti-imperialist
independent, 11, 68, 73, 75; media, 11, 22, 35, 63, 73, 158
India, 5, 160, 162
indigenous, 69, 159
Indonesia, 7, 9, 11, 94–5, 122
information systems, 91
innocence and innocent, 38, 52, 59, 63, 74, 86–7, 150

intentionality, 105, 109
interlock and interlocking, 13–14, 16, 21, 23, 26, 87, 118, 120, 122, 132, 127, 152
internal, 6, 19, 28, 49, 53
international(s), 3–6, 8–12, 33, 57, 100, 138–140, 152–3; community, 46; development, 17, 107, 160–1; euphemism, 144; media, 9, 45–6, 72; participation, 30; presence, 26, 157; pressure, 30, 45; solidarity activists, 29, 94–5, 97–8, 122, 148. *See also* International Solidarity Movement; International Women's Peace Service; Peace Brigades International
International Solidarity Movement, 3, 6–7, 9–10, 13, 20, 25, 28–32, 37, 40–1, 51, 93, 95, 102, 107–8, 113; leaders, 121; members of, 25, 34–5, 97, 139
International Women's Peace Service, 11, 13, 93, 107, 168, 194
interracial, 27–8, 128, 167, 192
intervention, 10, 50, 96–7, 158
Intifada, 29, 40, 87
Iraq(i), 7–10, 12, 21, 45–6, 48–52, 54, 58, 60–1, 66–70, 73–6, 94–6, 102, 105, 123, 138–9; American invasion of, 25; custody, 34; travel to, 63
Iraq Peace Team, 12–13, 67, 94, 105, 139
Isin, Engin, 61–2
Israel(i), 9–10, 19, 29–33, 37–41, 96–8, 103, 107–8, 114, 120, 122–3, 156, 160; authorities, 101;

bulldozer, 25, 35; demolition practices, 110; feminists, 117–18

Jerusalem, 40, 117
Jew and Jewish, 19, 120, 122
Johar Schueller, Malini, 34
journalist and journalism: 4, 33, 65, 67–9, 71, 138; alternative or independent, 72–5; Canadian, 51; foreign, 96; photo-, 83, 85, 87; right-wing, 117; Wall Street, 31

Kember, Norman, 45; 50
kidnap, kidnapped, and kidnapping, 7–8, 21, 45–62, 138
King, Martin Luther, 41
Klein, Naomi, 34
knowledge production, 68, 74
Kozol, Wendy, 79, 85–7, 90
Ku Klux Klan, 28, 128
Kumar, Deepa, 34

language, 4, 10, 18, 52, 99, 106, 144; co-opted, 161; military language, 139–40
law: international violations, 9, 33, 38. *See also* legal
legacy and legacies, 16–17, 37, 104, 130
legal, 32–3; citizenship status, 47, 48, 61–2
legitimacy, 14, 20–1, 23, 28, 134
lesbian, 56–7
LGBT, 56
liberal and liberalism, 14, 23–4, 55–6, 106–7, 130, 134, 137, 142–6, 151

lobby and lobbying, 13, 57
local(s), 5, 9, 10–12, 17, 63–6, 72, 76, 81, 95–6, 101–6, 121, 123–6, 159; civilians, 49, 72; as feminine, 119; groups, 102, 105; insurgents, 34; leadership, 116; local/global binary, 119; organizations, 113; residents, 27
Loney, James, 21, 45, 48, 50–8, 60–1, 150
Lutz, Catherine, 79
Lynch, Jessica, 34

mandate, 9–11, 13, 49, 52, 68, 75, 93, 107, 132, 157; non-violence, 28
Manichean, 34
martyr, 35, 40
masculine, masculinist, and masculinity, 23, 39, 87, 119, 129, 134–5
media, 8–9, 11, 21–2, 28
Medicins Sans Frontiers, 48
Me to We, 161
Mexico and Mexican, 3, 5–6, 9, 10–11, 13, 94, 159, 163
middle class, 3, 32, 159
Middle East, 9, 18, 56, 70, 122
Mignolo, Walter, 151
militant, 28, 35, 59
military, militarism, and militarized, 9, 12, 15, 20–1, 25, 29–31, 33, 38–9, 51–2, 54–5, 96, 139; conditions of occupation, 112; negotiate with, 121; operation, 30, 46; spokespersons, 41; threatened by, 6; US forces, 69; US invasion, 46; violence, 70, 94
mission, 6, 9–10, 12, 48, 55

Mississippi, 27–8, 127–8
mixed-race, 18
mobility, 14, 16, 18, 138, 162; curtailment of, 30; relative, 70; resources, 146; restricted, 111
modes: of being, 62; of recognition, 53; of speech, 77
Mohanty, Chandra Talpade, 16, 20
money, 10, 101–2, 113
Montreal, 3, 40
moral, morality, 8, 12, 17, 53–4, 89, 90–2, 95, 97, 141, 161; commitments, 34, 73; imperative, 152; implications of photography, 22; pulling rank, 123; responsibility, 80, 147; support, 11
Mother Jones, 35
mourning, 21, 31, 86
Muslim, 21, 53–4, 57–60, 74, 86, 107, 123–4; media depictions, 70
mythology, 57, 74

nation, national, and nationalism, 7, 13–14, 16–17, 34–5; 49, 51–3, 55, 57, 75–6, 108–9, 152; consciousness, 89; identity, 47, 94, 108–9; imagination, 89; -making process, 21; patriotic, 26
Native, 132–3, 158
NATO, 52
Nazareth, 40
Nelson, Diane, 152
neo-colonial, 163. *See also* colonial
neoliberal, 14, 160–1
neutral, neutrality, 38, 63, 65, 72, 78–9, 89; 150; in journalism, 69
New Zealand(er), 5, 48, 56

newsworthy, 68, 72
Nicaragua and Nicaraguan, 6, 9, 11, 94, 160
non-governmental organization, 10–11, 24, 112, 159–61
North American, 5, 10, 67, 86
North-South, 163
Nyers, Peter, 59, 60

Oaxaca Solidarity Network, 3–4
occupation, 10, 12, 61, 76, 100, 114, 117; anti-occupation, 29, 107, 118, 136; Israeli, 9, 29–30, 37–8, 97; military, 33, 112; living under, 99; of Palestine, 37, 38, 120, 155; tourism, 156
Occupied Territories (Palestinian), 22, 33, 81, 87, 115, 148, 185
Olive Harvest Campaign, 3
Olympia, Washington, 25, 35, 37
oppressive- ion, 10, 40, 61, 65, 118, 136, 158; racial, 130; system of, 132; violence and, 79, 94, 147–8
Orientalism, -ist, 50, 55, 57, 151; racism, 34; representations of, 21
outrage, 7, 27, 37, 61

Palestine, -ian, 7–12, 19, 21–3, 25–44, 63–6, 81–2, 86–8, 92–3, 95–9, 102–3, 105, 107, 110–15, 117, 120–3, 148, 160; checkpoints, 121; communities, 3; community leaders, 155; curfews, 82; farmers, 100; movement, 120, 136, 155–7; paramedics, 84–5; suicide bombers, 139; urgency, 133
paradigm, 24, 55, 77, 133, 142, 144, 151

paradox and paradoxical, 23–4, 26, 43, 76–7, 92, 115, 142–4, 146
passport, 6–8, 65, 94, 150, 157–8
patriarchy, 117–18, 121–2; hetero-, 32; struggles against, 133
patriotic and patriotism, 7, 26, 51
patronizing, 35, 111
Peace Brigades International, 3, 10, 94, 95, 139–40
Pearl, Daniel, 31
pedagogical, pedagogies, 23–4, 43, 88, 151
Pedelty, Mark, 75, 86
performative, 42
peril(s), 20, 23, 157
photo: -graphy and graphic: 35, 39, 79–81, 83–92, 111, 156; journalist, 85; journalism, 83
physical, physicality, and physically, 90, 119, 121, 141; accompaniment, 13, 97; aggression, 129; attributes, 17; crossing of borders, 16; intervening, 30; present in war zones, 63; safety, 135; security, 126; traits, 138; violence, 57; vulnerability, 30
polarization, 19
Pollock, Mica, 6
post-9/11, 9, 20, 26, 30
pragmatism, 24, 127, 147–9
Pratt, Mary Louise, 16, 55, 77
Project Accompaniment, 3, 12, 93–4
protection, 5, 7–8, 10–11, 23, 46, 63, 96, 99, 104, 126, 140–2, 150; Geneva Convention, 30; institutional, 49; international bodies, 139; lend, 135; 100, 109, 146; sexuality, 120; social and political, 49; to Palestinians, 26, 29; women's bodies, 31, 122
psychic, 20
psychoanalytic, 30
Puar, Jasbir, 57
public relations, 27

Ramallah, 37, 40, 64
rape, 117–18, 122, 126–132
Rapoport, Tamar, 120
rational, 72, 80, 108, 134
Razack, Sherene, 89, 129, 135, 147
reality tours, 156, 159–60
reciprocity, 58–60, 162
reconciliation, 158
relational, -ity, 14, 17, 20, 36, 72, 91
religion, 4, 11, 18–19
reporting, 9, 21, 22, 46, 63–4, 66, 71–2, 76, 78
representation, 38, 69 71, 75–6; CPT kidnapping, 47, 50, 51, 52, 53, Loney's sexuality, 55, 56, 57; photography, 85; Rachel Corrie, 20, 26, 35, 40, 43
representational, practices 22, 64, 70–1, 77, 80, 92
resist and resistance, 15, 44, 71, 76, 96, 97, 101, 104, 120, 153; nonviolent, 9, 11; Palestinian, 9, 21, 36, 38; strategies, 62; alternative, 148
Rickman, Alan, 40–1
right-wing, 117–18
righteous, 59, 68, 110, 145, 160
rights, 33–4, 114, 140, 151–2; activist interventions, 110–12; civil rights, movement, 27–8, 120, 127–8, 131, 136, 145, 147;

150; gay, 57; human rights, 3, 7–12; international, 11; violations, 30, 69, 81
risk, 4, 6, 18, 43, 45–6, 54, 56, 64, 66, 91, 110, 140, 148; in antiracism, 109; personal, 50–1
Rwanda, 89, 160

Said, Edward, 19, 37–8, 71, 73
same-sex, 57. *See also* gay; LGBT
savior, arrogant, model, 92, 95, 98; -ism, 21
Schwerner, Mickey, 27–8
Security Certificates, 59–60
sexism, 23, 118-19, 120, 122, 127, 132, 133, 135, 150
sexual harassment, 117–18, 126
sexual violence, 23, 118, 129–31, 132–6, 150; definition, 122; white women, 123
sexuality, 11, 13, 21, 47, 55–7; between black men and white women, 120, 122; heterosexuality, 58
Shalhoub-Kevorkian, Nadera, 110, 112–13
Sharoni, Simona, 115
Shohat, Ella, 16, 35, 50, 76
skin, 5–6, 65, 138
slavery, 143
Smith, Andrea, 132–3
Smith, Valerie, 118
social justice, 5, 21, 24–6, 35, 38–40, 65, 71, 77, 90, 104, 118–19, 142, 151, 153, 155, 175–8, 160–1
social movements, 28, 112, 119–20, 136, 142, 149, 152, 158–9, 161
social responsibility, 22, 24

social systems, 157
socio-political, 30, 102
Sontag, Susan, 79, 83
Singh Sooden, Harmeet, 45, 48
spatiality, 16; spatial, 119, 128–9
spectatorship, 22, 80, 85
Spelman, Elizabeth, 90
Spivak, Gyatri, 148
split affinities, 117–18
Sri Lanka and Sri Lankans 5, 11
Student Non-Violent Coordinating Committee, 127–8
subaltern, 137
subvert and subversive, 21, 40, 58–9, 62, 76, 80, 86, 119, 151, 157
suffer and suffering, 12, 22, 37, 41, 59, 79–80, 86, 89–91, 94, 112, 146; Iraqi people, 61
suicide bombers, 35, 139
superhero, 41. *See also* hero
symbol, 12, 36–9, 41; symbolic, 7, 12, 20, 38–9, 81, 119, 137, 139, 146
systems, 4, 10, 13, 38, 43, 47, 53, 132–5, 143, 149, 157

Taylor, John, 83
Thompson, Audrey, 106, 109
Thompson, Becky, 6, 27, 120
tolerance, 56–7
tourism and tourist, 24, 82, 115, 155–63
transgender, 56–7
treason and treasonous, 25, 34–5

United Church of Canada, 13
United Kingdom, 4, 29, 59, 61
United Nations, 125

United States, 4–7, 29, 31–4, 52–3, 61, 108, 122, 159; Arabs in, 18; imperialism, 38; Marine Corps, 56; military invasion, 45
universal, 17

vacation, 115, 156
values, 51, 53, 55, 95, 151
victim(s), 15, 31–2, 38, 45, 86, 87, 97, 138–9; of distress, 132; Palestinian or Israeli, 40; of rape, 129–30; role of, 91
Viner, Katherine, 40–1
violatable, 134. *See also* vulnerable
voice, 9, 22, 63, 69, 74, 76–7
Voices in the Wilderness, 12
volunteer and volunteerism, 3–8, 11, 28, 29, 32, 75, 94, 157, 159–2
voyeurism, 22, 74, 85; voyeuristic gaze, 83–4, 88; voyeuristic privilege, 86
vulnerable, 7, 12, 46, 85–6, 119, 122, 124, 129, 130, 134, *See also* violatable

Ware, Vron, 79, 92
wealth, 14, 101–2
Weber, Clare, 6
well-meaning, 16, 22, 81, 105, 116, 146
West Bank, 11–12, 30; 32–3, 82, 108, 123
whiteness, 4, 7, 8, 13–14, 17–21, 25–6, 31, 36; 42–3; 46–8, 91, 142, 150; deployment of, 138; discursive, 72; position of dominance, 106; relationship of, 53; reproduction of, 64, 95; as status, 98; symbolic markers of, 137; systems, 118
Witness for Peace, 6
witness-observers, 4
Women in Black, 120
women of colour, 131, 153
World Council of Churches, 12

YouTube, 156

Zapatista, 155, 159, 163